Industrialism

Our Commitment to Impermanence

Christopher O. Clugston

BookLocker

Trenton, Georgia

ISBN: 978-1-958889-65-7

Published by BookLocker.com, Inc., Trenton, Georgia.

Printed on acid-free paper.

The characters and events in this book are fictitious. Any similarity to real persons, living or dead, is coincidental and not intended by the author.

BookLocker.com, Inc.
2023

First Edition

Library of Congress Cataloguing in Publication Data
Clugston, Christopher O.
Industrialism: Our Commitment to Impermanence by Christopher O. Clugston
Library of Congress Control Number: 2023907310

Summer,

I hope I'm wrong; but I fear I'm not...

Vovo

Preface

I first stumbled upon NNRs (nonrenewable natural resources) – fossil fuels, metals, and non-metallic minerals – in 2006, while researching our unsustainable economic behavior. I had no idea that our ecological behavior is unsustainable as well.

I had never stopped to consider that:

- NNRs enable our industrial existence,
- NNRs are finite and non-replenishing, and
- NNR supplies will inevitably become insufficient to enable our industrial existence.

As I conducted additional research into NNRs, I discovered that several other analysts also understood that our NNR utilization behavior is unsustainable. Interestingly, however, nearly every one of them believed that if we would simply "use NNRs more responsibly" – conserve, recycle, reuse, substitute – Earth's vast NNR reserves would enable relatively comfortable industrial lifestyles for us and our posterity for the indefinite future.

NNR utilization was not the problem; "irresponsible" NNR utilization was the problem.

My First Revelation In 2007, it occurred to me that "responsible" NNR utilization – however defined – is an oxymoron. All NNR utilization is "irresponsible" – in the sense that it is unsustainable. Persistent NNR utilization – especially NNR utilization on an industrial scale – will inevitably render globally available, economically viable NNR supplies insufficient to perpetuate our industrial existence.

So I initiated my first major research project on the subject of NNR scarcity, to determine when "inevitably" might occur.

During my research, I discovered that price trends associated with most of the 90+ NNRs that enable our industrial existence had increased significantly during the first decade of the 21st century. Because increasing NNR price trends indicate increasing NNR scarcity, most NNRs were "scarce" during that period – in the run up to the Great Recession.

My Second Revelation By the time I was finishing my research in 2010, it occurred to me that global NNR scarcity had caused the Great Recession of 2008/9. Historically unprecedented fossil fuel, metal, and nonmetallic mineral price increases between 2000 and 2008 had crashed the global economy in 2008.

I spent 2011 incorporating this ecological reality into my research findings – and my research project became a book, *Scarcity – Humanity's Final Chapter?*

By 2012, I had gained a better understanding of NNR scarcity dynamics. I knew that a major NNR scarcity episode had occurred during the 1970s, and that its adverse effects – severe and protracted economic recessions – were comparable to the effects imposed by the most recent NNR scarcity episode.

I also knew that significantly increasing NNR price trends caused by the 1970s NNR scarcity episode had prompted the global mining industry to aggressively search for new economically viable NNR deposits, in order to resolve the NNR scarcity situation.

In the process, the mining industry discovered and targeted previously untapped NNR frontiers – and 25 years of relatively robust global human prosperity ensued.

I expected the same scenario to occur following the Great Recession. The global mining industry would discover and target new NNR frontiers, global NNR scarcity would be resolved, the global economy would recover from the Great Recession, and several decades of relatively robust global human prosperity would ensue – until the next major NNR scarcity episode.

By the mid-teens, however, it was obvious that something was wrong. Each time industrial humanity attempted to recover from the Great Recession, NNR demand increased, NNR prices increased, and the nascent economic recovery stalled.

My Third Revelation In 2016, it finally dawned on me – **"inevitably" is NOW!** The global economy will NEVER recover from the Great Recession, because remaining globally available, economically viable NNRs are insufficient to enable a recovery.

Since the inception of our industrial era during the mid-18th century, we have persistently and increasingly depleted Earth's once abundant NNR reserves – to levels at which they are insufficient to enable a recovery from the Great Recession, much less to perpetuate our industrialized way of life for the foreseeable future.

I wrote ***Blip – Humanity's 300 year self-terminating experiment with industrialism*** to explain this phenomenon and assess its implications for industrial humanity. The message in ***Blip*** is straightforward:

> As humankind evolved from hunter-gathers, to agriculturalists, to industrialists, we became increasingly ingenious – and "less sustainable". Ironically, in our industrial incarnation, we extraordinarily ingenious, NNR-dependent *Homo sapiens* have become terminally unsustainable – we irreversibly undermine our existence, in the process of existing!

In this book, ***Industrialism – Our Commitment to Impermanence***, which focuses specifically on our industrial era, I follow the irrefutable evidence to the inescapable conclusion. I make the case that human industrialism will collapse – completely and permanently – by the year 2050.

Chris Clugston
April, 2023

Our Commitment to Impermanence

Author's Note: The following section provides an overview of my case for the complete and permanent collapse of human industrialism by the year 2050. The remainder of the book provides supporting details and evidence.

> **The point of this talk is simply that reliance on non-renewable natural resources (NNRs), which enabled us to do more things than we did before we began that reliance, has made us vulnerable.** *Such reliance is a commitment to impermanence.*[1] **(Catton)**

For approximately three million years, our hunter-gatherer ancestors subsisted on renewable natural resources (RNRs) – water, soil, and naturally-occurring plants and animals; their hunter-gatherer way of life was sustainable.

During the next 12 thousand years, our agrarian ancestors added human-modified renewable Earth resources (ERs) – domesticated and cultivated plants and animals – to the mix; their agrarian way of life was "quasi-sustainable".

During the past 250 years, our industrial existence has been enabled by our ever-increasing utilization of finite and non-replenishing nonrenewable natural resources (NNRs) – fossil fuels, metals, and nonmetallic minerals. Our industrialized way of life is terminally unsustainable – it is inevitably and irreversibly self-eradicating.

A Question of Perspective

> We must now see that people are indeed different from other creatures, but not *all together* different. Our cultural type of inheritance is tremendously significant; it evolves in response to differently operating selection pressures than those that change genotypic distributions. It was, however, a gross exaggeration to suppose that culture exempted us from the principles of ecology.[2] (Catton)

To properly understand human industrialism and its evolution, human existence must be viewed from the Nature-centered ecological perspective, rather than from the human-centered anthropocentric perspective.

The Anthropocentric Perspective

Almost without exception, people who are alive today view reality from the anthropocentric perspective, which perceives and interprets human existence in terms of human cultural circumstances – i.e., prevailing political, economic, and societal conditions.

Viewed from the anthropocentric perspective, our industrial existence occurs within the context of our cultural environment:

- **Human ingenuity** – human resourcefulness, technological innovations, efficiency improvements, and productivity enhancements – enables...
- **Human prosperity** – human economic output and material living standards – which governs...
- **Human cultural** – political, economic, and societal – **circumstances**.

Figure P-1: Humanity's Operating Environment (Anthropocentric Perspective)

Accordingly, our previously inconceivable industrial prosperity and cultural circumstances are products of our unparalleled ingenuity. So long as we continue to apply human ingenuity toward improving human prosperity, industrialism will flourish.

The critical limitation associated with the anthropocentric perspective is its failure to consider the fundamental role played by our natural environment in enabling and governing human existence.

The Ecological Perspective

Viewed from the ecological perspective, humankind numbers among the billions of biotic (living) and abiotic (nonliving) entities that interact and evolve through various biological, geological, chemical, and physical processes and phenomena, and that, in combination, comprise and govern existence on Earth.

From the ecological perspective, industrial human existence occurs within the context of our natural environment – the broader ecological context within which our cultural environment exists.

Accordingly, the primary enablers of our industrialized way of life – and of all life on Earth – are Earth resources:

- **Renewable Natural Resources (RNRs)** – water, soil, and naturally-occurring biota (plant and animal life), and
- **Nonrenewable Natural Resources (NNRs)** – fossil fuels, metals, and nonmetallic minerals.

Figure P-2: Humanity's Operating Environment (Ecological Perspective)

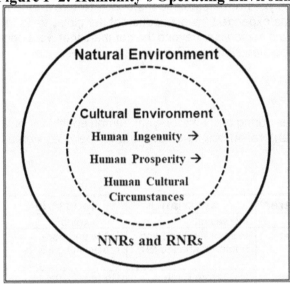

From the ecological perspective, our previously inconceivable industrial prosperity and cultural circumstances are enabled by our persistent and increasing depletion of Earth's finite and non-replenishing NNR reserves. All infrastructure, machines, products, energy, and services that define and perpetuate our industrial existence are NNR-based or NNR-derived.

And because the NNR depletion function follows a single-pulse – one-up and one-down – cycle, our NNR-enabled industrial era will follow a single-pulse cycle as well.

Figure P-3: Industrial Era Cyclicality

NNR Depletion Cycle

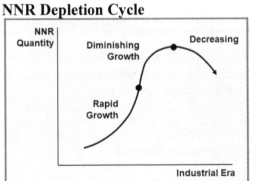

Human Industrialism Cycle

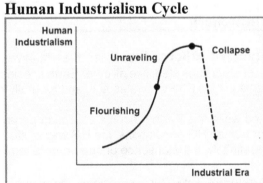

Industrialism, therefore, is a self-terminating human subsistence strategy in which finite and non-replenishing fossil fuels, metals, and nonmetallic minerals are converted into the infrastructure, machines, products, energy, and services that afford humanity's extraordinary – but temporary – industrialized way of life.

The Paradox of Human Industrialism

All life needs and uses natural resources. Man alone has changed natural distributions and productivities, and by doing so systematically, has shaped the form of controlled living we call civilization. He has managed to combat climatic extremes and to increase vastly the Earth's yield of palatable foods above Nature's random growth. As a consequence, he has expanded his occupation of the globe to its farthest reaches and proliferated *Homo sapiens* far beyond the numbers that were once in stable balance with an unmanipulated Nature.[3] (Skinner)

The Human Epoch

As we have become increasingly ingenious during our 3-million-year human epoch, we have become increasingly over-exploitive of Earth resources, and have thereby become increasingly prosperous – and "less sustainable".

Table P-1: The Human Epoch

Human Attributes	Hunter-Gatherer	Agrarian	Industrial
Human Ingenuity	Limited	Increasing	Extraordinary
Earth Resource Mix	Naturally-occurring and naturally-replenishing RNRs	Human-modified and human-managed ERs	Finite and non-replenishing NNRs
Human/Earth Interaction	Passive inhabitants	Deliberate Earth resource managers	Chronic Earth resource overexploiters
Human Population	Few million	Hundreds of millions	Several billion
Human Prosperity	Subsistence level for all	Subsistence level for the vast majority	Far beyond subsistence level for most
Human/Earth Relationship	Sustainable	Quasi-sustainable	Terminally unsustainable

Hunter-Gatherer Era Given their relatively limited ingenuity, our hunter-gatherer (HG) ancestors subsisted, like all other Earth species, exclusively on naturally-occurring, naturally-replenishing RNRs – water, soil, and naturally-occurring plants and animals.

And while this Earth resource utilization behavior afforded only subsistence-level existence for human HG populations, the HG way of life was sustainable – i.e., it would have persisted indefinitely in the absence of one or more terminally disruptive changes.

Agrarian Era Our increasingly ingenious agrarian ancestors deliberately modified naturally-occurring plant and animal species and habitats – primarily through domestication, selective breeding, cultivation, fertilization, irrigation, and weed and pest control – and thereby improved human prosperity. This Earth resource utilization behavior produced greatly expanded subsistence level agrarian populations, while simultaneously producing prosperity beyond subsistence level for small groups of elites.

Because it was enabled for the most part by human-modified – not naturally-occurring – Earth resources, pre-industrial agrarianism was "quasi-sustainable". That is, absent continuous management of human-modified species and habitats, humanity's pre-industrial agrarian way of life would have collapsed.

Industrial Era We extraordinarily ingenious industrial *Homo sapiens* are unique among Earth species, past and present, because our existence is enabled by finite and non-replenishing NNRs. And while this Earth resource utilization behavior has afforded previously inconceivable prosperity for billions of human beings, both human industrialism and the Earth resource utilization behavior by which it is enabled are terminally unsustainable.

That is, persistent NNR reserve depletion – especially depletion on an industrial scale – will inevitably render globally available, economically viable NNR supplies insufficient to perpetuate our industrial existence.

Human Prosperity Improvement

In stark contrast to the almost nonexistent prosperity improvement achieved during our HG era, and the negligible prosperity improvement achieved during our agrarian era, prosperity improvement during our NNR-enabled industrial era has been nothing short of spectacular.

Pre-Industrial Human Prosperity

Figure P-4: Pre-Industrial Human Prosperity

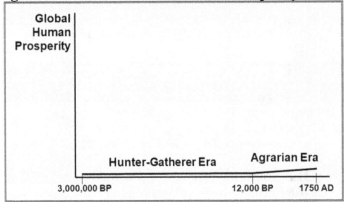

Pre-industrial hunter-gatherer and agrarian subsistence strategies, which were enabled by naturally-occurring Earth resources (HG) and human-modified Earth resources (agrarian), afforded only subsistence level existence for most of humankind.

Humanity's hunter-gatherer era spanned approximately three million years – over 120,000 human generations – from 3,000,000 BP (before present) to 12,000 BP.

During this period, the global human population probably never exceeded 5 million; annual global economic output, as defined by global gross domestic product (GDP), likely never exceeded $500 million; and the average HG era human material living standard, as proxied by global per capita GDP, remained below $100 per annum.[4]

Humanity's pre-industrial agrarian era spanned approximately 12,000 years – over 500 human generations – from 12,000 BP to 1750 AD.

By 1750, the global human population had reached approximately 720 million; annual global economic output, as defined by global gross domestic product (GDP), approximated $129 billion; and the average human material living standard, as proxied by global per capita GDP, had yet to reach $200 per annum.[5]

Industrial Era Human Prosperity

Figure P-5: Industrial Era Human Prosperity

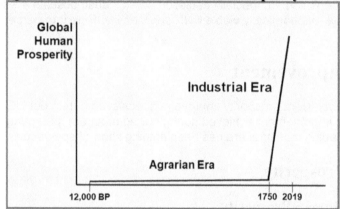

It was not until 18th century Great Britain established a cultural environment that encouraged British industrialists to fully exploit their extraordinarily favorable natural environment – i.e., to utilize NNRs on an industrial scale – that human prosperity improved significantly, and then meteorically.

Humanity's industrial era has spanned less than 300 years to date – approximately 10 human generations – from 1750 to present (2019). During this relatively brief period:[6]

- The global human population has increased by a factor of ten – from approximately 720 million to 7.7 billion;
- Annual global economic output, as defined by global gross domestic product (GDP), has increased by an astounding 393 times – from $129 billion to $50,685 billion; and
- The average human material living standard, as proxied by global per capita GDP, has increased by an extraordinary 37 times – from $178 per annum to $6,606 per annum.

The Enablers of Industrial Era Human Prosperity Our extraordinary industrial era prosperity has been enabled by our extraordinary NNR utilization during the period. (See Table P-2)

Between 1750 and 2019, the annual global extraction and production quantities associated with these indispensable NNRs increased spectacularly – coal and salt by over 1,000 times, copper, zinc, and sulfur by over 2,000 times, iron ore by over 9,000 times, and cement by nearly 25,000 times!

The sheer magnitude of human NNR extraction/production during 2019 was extraordinary as well.

Table P-2: Industrial Era Global NNR Extraction/Production Quantities 1750 and 2019

NNR	Metric Tonnes		Increase (Xs)
	1750	2019	1750-2019
Coal	7,000,000	7,921,000,000	1,132
Copper	10,000	20,400,000	2,040
Iron Ore	260,000	2,450,000,000	9,423
Lead	15,000	4,720,000	315
Zinc	5,000	12,700,000	2,540
Tin	4,500	296,000	66
Cement	165,000	4,100,000,000	24,848
Salt	220,000	283,000,000	1,286
Sulfur	27,500	80,000,000	2,909

Nearly 2.5 billion metric tonnes of newly mined iron ore, over 4 billion metric tonnes of newly produced cement, and nearly 8 billion metric tonnes of newly mined coal – over 2,000 pounds of coal for every man, woman, and child on planet Earth!

Sources: USGS, US EIA, and other.[7]

Notably, these extraordinary increases in global NNR extraction/production occurred despite ever-increasing NNR recycling, reuse, conservation, and substitution, and despite an ever-expanding array of productivity-increasing innovations and efficiency improvements intended to minimize our NNR utilization.

The indisputable fact remains,

> Strong [NNR] demand growth comes mainly from millions of aspiring individuals in emerging economies striving for a better material standard of living. Even with dramatic increases in recycling, an overall increase in newly mined materials is required to support the emergence of individuals, communities and countries from stagnation and poverty.[8] (ICMM)

Our NNR requirements will therefore increase unabated in the future, as nearly 2 billion industrialized humans attempt to remain industrialized, 4+ billion industrializing humans attempt to completely industrialize, and 2+ billion pre-industrial humans attempt to industrialize.

According a 2016 UN analysis,

> Assuming that the world will implement similar systems of production and systems of provision for major services – housing, mobility, food, energy and water supply – nine billion people will require 180 billion tonnes of materials by 2050, almost three times today's [2010] amounts.[9]

The Consequences of Industrial Era Human Prosperity No other species on Earth, past or present, has managed to live beyond subsistence level, much less to achieve the extraordinary prosperity enjoyed by industrial humanity, because no other species has possessed the ingenuity required to exploit NNRs on an industrial scale.

Only since the advent of industrialism have enormous real wealth surpluses been created by applying human ingenuity to fossil fuels, metals, and nonmetallic minerals. Consequently, only during our industrial era have billions of people been able to live, rather than simply exist.

Paradoxically, however, because industrial human prosperity, and human industrialism more broadly, are enabled by finite and non-replenishing NNRs, we uniquely ingenious industrial *Homo sapiens* have been irreversibly undermining our existence for the past 250 years.

The Demise of Human Industrialism

As one of the millions of species that inhabit planet Earth, *Homo sapiens* is subject to the same ecological laws of Nature that govern all other species. With respect to our industrial existence and to the Earth resource utilization behavior by which it is enabled, one natural law is paramount: **"Net Depletion" of Earth Resource Reserves is Unsustainable**.

That is, the rate at which an Earth resource reserve is depleted must not exceed the rate at which the reserve is replenished. Persistent "net depletion" will inevitably render the Earth resource reserve insufficient to support dependent species populations.

Given that all NNR depletion constitutes "net depletion", persistent human NNR depletion – especially depletion on an industrial scale – will inevitably render Earth's NNR reserves insufficient to support our NNR-dependent species. Unfortunately for humankind, "inevitably" is "now".

Trend Reversals

During the mid-20th century, the fundamental trends that govern the evolution of our industrial era – relative global NNR scarcity and global human prosperity improvement – transitioned permanently from favorable to unfavorable.

Global NNR Scarcity As illustrated by the Global NNR Scarcity Index – an indicator of aggregate relative global NNR scarcity between 1900 and 2019 – the secular (long term) global NNR scarcity trend transitioned permanently during the mid-20th century from "relative NNR abundance" to "increasing NNR scarcity". (See Figure P-6)

1 Between 1900 and 1944, the Global NNR Scarcity Index (dashed line) decreased by 33%, from 152 to 102, indicating relative global NNR abundance during the 44-year period.

2 In 1944, the Global NNR Scarcity Index reached its minimum of 102, indicating a permanent transition from relative global NNR abundance to increasing global NNR scarcity.

3 Between 1944 and 2019, the Global NNR Scarcity Index increased by an extraordinary 150%, from 102 to 248, indicating increasingly pervasive global NNR scarcity during the most recent 75-year period.

Figure P-6: Global NNR Scarcity Index 1900-2019

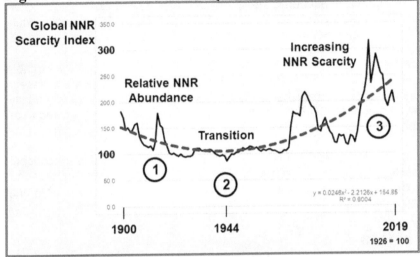

Global NNR Scarcity Index Trendline = Dashed Line.
Composite NNR Price Curve = Solid Line.
Sources: USGS, BP Statistical Review, US EIA, and other.[10]

Global Human Prosperity The transition from relative global NNR abundance to increasingly pervasive global NNR scarcity during the mid-20th century caused a simultaneous, permanent transition from rapidly improving global human prosperity to faltering global human prosperity.

Figure P-7: Industrial Era Global Human Prosperity Improvement
Economic Output (GDP)   Material Living Standard (pc GDP)

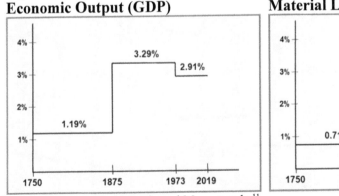

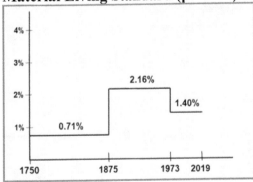

Sources: Delong, World Bank, and Macrotrends.[11]

- Between 1750 and 1875, global human prosperity improved rapidly by pre-industrial standards. Global GDP (economic output) increased by 1.19% compounded annually, while global pc GDP (the average material living standard) increased by 0.71% compounded annually.

- Between 1875 and 1973, global human prosperity improved extraordinarily – despite WW1, the 1918-1919 global flu pandemic, the Great Depression, and WW2. Global GDP (economic output) increased by an unprecedented 3.29% compounded annually, while global pc GDP (the average material living standard) increased by an equally unprecedented 2.16% compounded annually.
- Between 1973 and 2019, global human prosperity faltered – despite the remarkable industrialization initiatives launched by China and other Eastern nations. The increase in global GDP (economic output) diminished considerably to 2.91% compounded annually, while the increase in global pc GDP (the average material living standard) slowed to an anemic 1.40% compounded annually.

In the process of applying our unparalleled ingenuity toward achieving previously inconceivable prosperity, we extracted Earth's high quality, low cost, and low priced NNRs. What remains are Earth's low quality, high cost, and high priced NNRs – which can enable only faltering global human prosperity.

Trend Acceleration

The unfavorable trends that emerged during the mid/late 20th century – increasingly pervasive global NNR scarcity and faltering global human prosperity – accelerated during the first two decades of the 21st century.

Accelerating Global NNR Scarcity NNR prices increased to historically unprecedented levels during the first two decades of the new millennium, indicating accelerating global NNR scarcity during the period.

Figure P-8: Composite NNR Price Curve 1900-2019

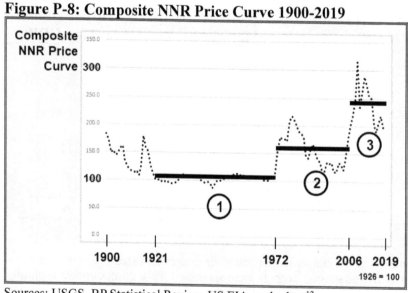

Sources: USGS, BP Statistical Review, US EIA, and other.[12]

1 During the latter years of our Old Normal, between 1921 and 1972, which were characterized by relative global NNR abundance (Nature's Stimulus), the Composite NNR Price Curve averaged a historically low 103.

2 During the pre-Great Recession years of our New Normal, between 1973 and 2006, which were characterized by increasingly pervasive global NNR scarcity (Nature's Squeeze), the Composite NNR Price Curve averaged 159, which exceeded by 54% the historically low level of 103 that existed between 1921 and 1972.

3 From the Great Recession forward, between 2007 and 2019, which was characterized by accelerating global NNR scarcity (Nature's Squeeze tightened), the Composite NNR Price Curve averaged 242, which exceeded by 52% the 159 level that existed between 1973 and 2006 – and exceeded by 135% the historically low level of 103 that existed between 1921 and 1972.

By the dawn of the 21st century, most NNR deposits that had been discovered during our industrial era were extensively depleted, and major previously untapped global NNR frontiers no longer existed. Accelerating global NNR scarcity – as indicated by inordinately high and rapidly increasing NNR price levels – was the inescapable consequence.

Rapidly Faltering Global Human Prosperity Accelerating global NNR scarcity constrained human prosperity improvement during the first two decades of the new millennium, to rates that were substantially lower than those that were achieved prior to the Great Recession, and significantly lower than those that were achieved during the mid-20th century.

Figure P-9: Global Human Prosperity Improvement 1945-2019

Economic Output (GDP)   **Material Living Standard (pc GDP)**

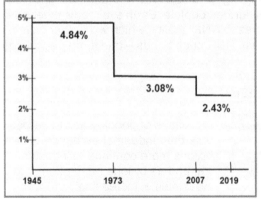

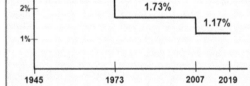

Sources: Delong, World Bank, and Macrotrends.[13]

- During the post-WW2 rebuilding period and the culmination of our Old Normal, between 1945 and 1973, global GDP (economic output) increased at an unprecedented 4.84% compounded annually, while the global pc GDP (the average material living standard) increased at an equally unprecedented 3.04% compounded annually.
- During the pre-Great Recession years of our New Normal, between 1973 and 2007, the compound annual growth rate in global GDP (economic output) decreased substantially, from 4.84% to 3.08%, while the compound annual growth rate in pc GDP (the average material living standard) decreased substantially as well, from 3.04% to 1.73%.
- During the Great Recession and post-recession "non-recovery", between 2007 and 2019, the compound annual growth rate in global GDP (economic output) further decreased from 3.08% to a lackluster 2.43%, while the compound annual growth rate in global pc GDP (the average material living standard) further decreased from 1.73% to a meager 1.17% – despite historically unprecedented global fiscal and monetary "stimulus" employed during the period.

The notion that global human prosperity will ever again improve at rates comparable to those that were achieved during the mid-20th century is geologically impossible. The high quality/low cost NNRs that enabled such prosperity improvement have long since been extracted.

It is unsurprising, therefore, that a post-GR "recovery" has failed to materialize. Rather, human industrialism and industrial humanity have been devolving toward collapse.

Devolution to Collapse

Going forward, as Nature's Squeeze tightens relentlessly and remorselessly, and global human prosperity peaks and enters terminal decline, industrial humanity will crack and human industrialism will collapse.

Nature's Squeeze Will Tighten In attempting to address our enormous and ever-increasing global NNR requirements, we will further deplete Earth's already extensively depleted NNR reserves – which will further decrease NNR quality, which will further increase NNR exploitation costs, which will further increase NNR price trends – and further accelerate global NNR scarcity.

Figure P-10: Nature's Squeeze Will Tighten

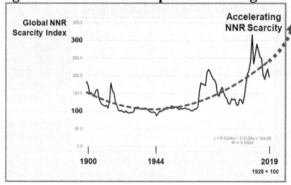

As billions of people seek to perpetuate their industrial existence, as billions more continue to industrialize, and as billions more attempt to industrialize, increasingly unfavorable global NNR demand/supply dynamics will engender increasingly severe and protracted resource wars.

Extensively depleted and irreparably damaged global NNR reserves will ultimately become permanently unproductive.

Industrial Humanity Will Crack Continuously increasing NNR price trends caused by accelerating global NNR scarcity will further suppress global NNR demand and utilization, which will further diminish global human prosperity improvement.

Figure P-11: Industrial Humanity Will Crack

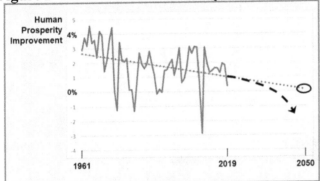

Extrapolating the linear trend-line (dotted line) derived from the 1961-2019 global pc GDP growth curve (solid line) indicates 0% global pc GDP growth – "peak human prosperity" – by the middle of the 21st century.

Sources: World Bank and Macrotrends through 2019.[14]

It is almost certain, however, that accelerating global NNR scarcity will cause faltering global human prosperity to accelerate as well, thereby "bending" the declining trajectory of the human prosperity improvement trendline from "downward linear" (dotted line) to "downward accelerating" (dashed line).

As global human prosperity plummets, social cohesion will be displaced by social entropy, and Earth's human population will be ravaged by war, starvation, pestilence, and disease. Self-preservation will become the primary human objective, as the veneer of civilization completely disappears.

Human Industrialism Will Collapse As extensively depleted and irreparably damaged Earth resource reserves become permanently unproductive, all industrialized nations – irrespective of their political ideologies, economic systems, and societal orientations – will collapse, completely and permanently, taking the aid-dependent, non-industrialized nations with them.

Human industrialism and industrial humanity will cease to exist – almost certainly by the year 2050. (See Figure P-12)

Under the best-case post-collapse scenario, a few million *Homo sapiens* will eke out a subsistence level existence by scavenging among the remnants of Earth's once-abundant resources. Under the worst-case scenario, our species will go extinct.

We Are Exceptional… It is certainly not the case that our quest for universal prosperity through global industrialism – and the unsustainable Earth resource utilization behavior by which our quest is enabled – are inherently evil.

Figure P-12: Human Industrialism Will Collapse

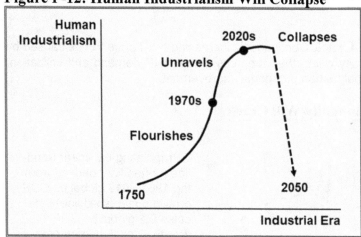

We *Homo sapiens* have simply behaved like any species that is introduced into a habitat in which it can succeed. We succeeded – and thrived – because we could.

We have employed our unparalleled ingenuity – our resourcefulness, technological innovations, efficiency improvements, and productivity enhancements – during the past three centuries to dramatically improve our prosperity, through our ever-increasing utilization of Earth's finite and non-replenishing NNRs.

But NOT "Exemptional"… It is the case, however, that despite our possibly justifiable naïveté as we ascended to industrial exceptionalism, and despite the fact that our predicament is an unintended consequence of our understandable efforts to continuously improve our prosperity, neither our NNR utilization behavior nor our industrialized way of life is sustainable.

Humanity's fate was sealed during the 18th century, at the inception of our industrial era. The NNR genie had been released from the bottle and could not be put back. We remained ignorant of our inevitable fate during the 19th and 20th centuries, by misconstruing our windfall of temporary NNR abundance as permanent NNR sufficiency. We are now paying the price for our ignorance.

We will soon discover that while we industrial *Homo sapiens* are indeed exceptional, we are not "exemptional" – having somehow transcended the ecological laws of Nature that apply to all "lesser species". Rather, we are the extraordinarily fortunate beneficiaries of a one-time, rapidly-depleting, natural legacy; and we are the unwitting and tragic victims of our own ingenuity.

Accordingly, there is no "solution" to our geologically-based predicament – that is, a scenario that will culminate in a favorable outcome for humankind. There is only a "resolution" – complete and permanent global societal collapse.

NNR-enabled industrialism is humanity's commitment to impermanence.

Contents

Introduction

Industrialism consists of two parts and nine chapters.

Part One: Human Industrialism presents a conceptual overview of human industrialism from the ecological perspective – focusing on industrialism's enablers and outcomes.

Chapter 1: NNRs discusses NNRs (nonrenewable natural resources) – fossil fuels, metals, and non-metallic minerals – which are the primary enablers of human industrialism.

Chapter 2: NNR Scarcity explains the mechanics of NNR scarcity, and how relative global NNR scarcity governs the evolution of human industrialism.

Chapter 3: Industrial Productivity examines human ingenuity – as manifested by industrial productivity – which is the secondary enabler of human industrialism.

Chapter 4: Human Prosperity analyzes human prosperity – economic output and human material living standards – which is the desired outcome of human industrialism.

Part Two: Industrial Era Evolution explores the evolving relationships between industrialism's enablers and outcomes during our 300-year industrial era.

Chapter 5: Industrialism1 – Industrialism Emerges describes the evolving relationships between industrialism's enablers and outcomes from 1750 to 1875.

Chapter 6: Industrialism2 – Industrialism Proliferates describes the evolving relationships between industrialism's enablers and outcomes from 1875 to 1973.

Chapter 7: Industrialism3 – Industrialism Unravels describes the evolving relationships between industrialism's enablers and outcomes from 1973 to 2019.

Chapter 8: Nature's Squeeze Tightens focuses on the evolving relationships between industrialism's enablers and outcomes during the first two decades of the 21st century.

Chapter 9: Humanity Will Crack – and Industrialism Will Collapse! makes the case for the complete and permanent collapse of human industrialism by the year 2050.

Part One:
Human Industrialism

Without minerals, industrial society and modern technology would be inconceivable.[1] (Diederen)

Industrialism is a human subsistence strategy in which human sustenance is obtained primarily from mechanized agricultural production and factory-based manufacturing. Humanity's desired outcome in pursuing an industrialized way of life is improved prosperity.

Industrial human prosperity (industrial success) is enabled primarily by NNRs (Nature) and secondarily by industrial productivity (human ingenuity).

NNRs (Nature) + Industrial Productivity (Human Ingenuity) → **Human Prosperity (Industrial Success)**

Chapter 1:
NNRs

Our civilization is dependent on minerals. Few people living in the United States and other developed nations pass through a single day without using raw or manufactured materials that have been made from, processed by, fertilized with, or in some other way affected by minerals or mineral products. Without a steady supply of minerals our civilization could not survive.[1] (USGS)

NNRs (nonrenewable natural resources) are the finite and non-replenishing fossil fuels, metals, and nonmetallic minerals that enable our industrialized way of life – the way of life that most of us who are alive today consider "normal".

NNR Attributes

Since no second crop may be expected, rich diverse mineral deposits are a nation's most valuable but ephemeral material possession – its quick assets.[2] (Lovering)

NNR Definition An NNR is an Earth resource – a component of Earth's planetary ecosystem – that exists as a consequence of one or more naturally-occurring biological, geological, chemical, or physical processes. NNRs do not replenish on a time scale that is relevant from the perspective of "human time", in the event that they replenish at all.

That is, finite and non-replenishing NNR reserves deplete irreversibly and permanently.

NNR Classification Of the thousands of Earth's naturally-occurring geologic materials, approximately 90 are of sufficient industrial value to be considered NNRs – 3 are fossil fuels, 48 are metals, and the remainder are classified as nonmetallic minerals.

- **Fossil Fuels** are carbon-based energy sources – coal, natural gas, and oil – which provided approximately 84% of the world's primary energy during 2019.[3]
- **Metals** are elements and alloys that are ideally suited to structural, electrical conductivity, and thermal (heat) conductivity applications. Examples include aluminum, chromium, copper, iron, lead, manganese, nickel, tin, and zinc.
- **Nonmetallic Minerals** are geologic materials that have commercial value in industrial and construction applications, and that are not classified as either fossil fuels or metals. Examples include cement, clays, crushed stone, gypsum, phosphate rock, potash, salt, and sulfur.

NNR Roles NNRs enable our industrialized way of life – they serve as the primary raw material inputs to our industrial economies, and have thereby enabled continuously improving prosperity for increasing segments of Earth's ever-expanding human population.

Figure 1-1: NNRs – the Building Blocks of Industrial Society

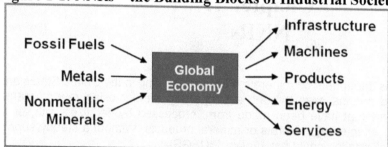

"Mineral resources have become essential ingredients for life – building blocks of society."[4] (Skinner)

Specifically, NNRs play three essential roles in enabling our industrialized way of life:

- NNRs enable the design, development, production, provisioning, and support of the infrastructure, machines, products, energy, and services that define and perpetuate our industrial existence – and that could not exist in the absence of NNRs. Examples include highway systems, communication networks, electric power grids, renewable energy converters, skyscrapers, houses, cars, airplanes, computers, gasoline stations, and nuclear power plants.
- NNRs enable humankind to exploit renewable natural resources (RNRs) – water, soil, plants, and animals – in ways and at levels that support Earth's industrial human population and material living standards. Examples include water storage, treatment, and distribution systems, and food production, processing, and distribution systems, which would support only an infinitesimal fraction of Earth's current human population in the absence of NNRs.
- NNRs enable the creation of enormous real wealth surpluses, which enable large segments of the global human population to live far beyond subsistence level, and thereby differentiate industrialized human societies from pre-industrial hunter-gatherer and agrarian societies.

"Thus, minerals will retain their dominant role as the basis for products used by society and, therefore, as the basis for world manufacturing and agriculture."[5] (USGS)

NNR Applications "If fossil fuels are the proverbial lifeblood of the global economy, then minerals are certainly its bone marrow."[6] (Diederen)

Generic NNR applications (uses) include primary energy sources, structural metals, metal alloys, high technology metals, construction materials, industrial materials, and fertilizers. Nearly all NNRs, especially those that are most critical to human industrialism, address multiple applications.

For example, petroleum (oil and natural gas) serves as the feedstock for thousands of products that are indispensable to our modern industrial existence, including fertilizers, plastics, pharmaceuticals, paints, insecticides, herbicides, pesticides, and synthetic fabrics.[7]

The following tables contain application profiles pertaining to the Core-20 NNRs – a diverse mix of 20 widely-deployed NNRs that are indispensable to the perpetuation of our industrialized way of life.

Table 1-1: Fossil Fuels Applications

Fossil Fuel	Fossil Fuels Applications
Coal	Major global source of industrial energy and electricity generation; provided 27% of global primary energy in 2019.
Natural Gas	Major source of industrial energy, electricity generation, and home heating and cooking; provided 24% of global primary energy in 2019.
Oil*	World's leading source of transportation energy; provided 33% of global primary energy in 2019.

Source: BP *Includes conventional crude oil, natural gas liquids, oil sands, and shale oil.[8]

Table 1-2: Metals Applications

Metal	Metals Applications
Aluminum	Transportation, packaging, building, and electrical; the most widely used non-ferrous metal in the world.
Chromium	Stainless steel alloy; electroplating; anodizing; pigment; dye; wood preservative; catalyst; and superalloy (jet engines & gas turbines).
Copper	Thermal conductor, electrical conductor, building material, metal alloy (brass & bronze), super-conductor, antibacterial, and fertilizer micronutrient.
Iron Ore	Primary feedstock for pig iron, which is used to make steel, the most widely used metal in the world.
Lead	Automotive batteries (starting-lights-ignition), ammunition, solder, pewter, alloy, and radiation shielding.
Manganese	Aluminum, iron & (stainless) steel alloy; gasoline additive; pigment; batteries; and fertilizer micronutrient.
Nickel	Batteries (rechargeable), steel alloy (stainless steel & cast iron), non-ferrous alloy and superalloy, catalyst, plating, magnets (wind turbines), and alkaline fuel cells.
Tin	Alloy (bronze, pewter, solder), metal coating, food packaging, window glass, superconducting magnets, LCD monitors, and circuit boards.
Zinc	Galvanizing, die casting, batteries, alloy (brass), dietary supplement, fertilizer micronutrient, and consumer products (deodorant & shampoo).

Source: USGS.[9]

Table 1-3: Nonmetallic Minerals Applications

Nonmetallic Mineral	Nonmetallic Minerals Applications
Cement	Ubiquitous building material; binder in mortar & concrete.
Clays	Tile; ceramics; pottery; bricks; pipes (drainage, sewer); paper; rubber; fiberglass; oil/gas well drilling mud; refractory agent; and sealant.
Gypsum	Wallboard and plaster, (Portland) cement, and soil conditioner.
Phosphate Rock	NPK (nitrogen, phosphorous, potassium) fertilizer component, macronutrient, animal feed supplement, and industrial chemicals.

Table 1-3: Nonmetallic Minerals Applications (continued)

Potash	NPK (nitrogen, phosphorous & potassium) fertilizer component, macronutrient, soap, glass, ceramics, chemical dyes, medicines, synthetic rubber, and explosives.
Salt	Food seasoning; food preservation; highway deicing; chemical industry feedstock (chlorine & caustic soda); and water treatment.
Stone (Crushed)	Macadam road construction; cement manufacture; riprap; railroad track ballast; filter stone; and soil conditioner.
Sulphur	Sulfuric acid feedstock, fertilizer macronutrient, fertilizer production (phosphate extraction), rubber (car tires), black gunpowder, insecticide, and fungicide.

Source: USGS.[10]

A complete list of the NNRs analyzed in *Industrialism*, and their respective major applications, can be found in Appendix A.

NNR Criticality "Critical" connotes importance. And while some NNRs are certainly more important than others, every NNR plays at least one vital role for which it is optimally suited – or we would not use it. NNR criticality is therefore a relative concept – a function of the degree to which an NNR is vital to the perpetuation of our industrialized way of life.

Oil, which addresses over 4,000 industrial applications, including motor fuels, heating oil, fertilizers, pharmaceuticals, plastics, textiles, and pesticides, is arguably the most critical NNR known to industrial humanity. However, a niche NNR such as the rare earth mineral neodymium addresses critical applications involving miniature magnets, which are indispensable to the communications, "renewable energy", and electric vehicle industries.

> It would be misleading to dwell on energy alone. The use of all natural resources is inter-twined. Oil is of little use unless we have engines built of iron, copper, lead, zinc, and other metals. Farm lands will only yield maximum crops if they are tilled by tractors and plows and fertilized with compounds of phosphorous, nitrogen, and potassium.[11] (Skinner)

Consequently, while the relative criticality among individual NNRs can be debated, NNRs in the aggregate are certainly the critical enablers of our industrialized way of life – and of the extraordinary prosperity derived from it. NNRs comprise approximately 95% of the raw material inputs to the US economy each year.[12]

The tightly-coupled causal relationship between NNR utilization and human prosperity is illustrated by America's industrial evolution. (See Figure 1-2)

Between the years 1800 and 2019, annual US NNR utilization increased by over 2000 times – from an estimated 3.18 million tons to 6.64 billion tons. As a result of this spectacular increase in NNR utilization, annual US GDP (economic output) increased by an equally spectacular 2200 times – from an estimated $8.4 billion to $19.1 trillion.

Figure 1-2: US NNR Utilization and Economic Output (GDP) 1800 to 2019

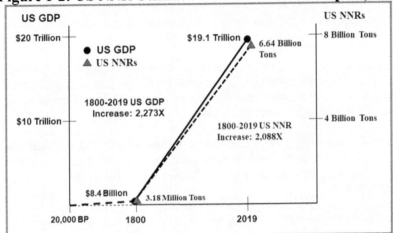

Thus, the correlation between the increase in US NNR utilization (economic input) and the increase in US GDP (economic output) – a proxy for human prosperity – was nearly one-to-one (unity) during the past 220 years.

Sources: Minerals Education Coalition, USGS, and Measuring Worth (2012 USD).[13]

The causal relationship between US NNR utilization and US economic output was well understood by the 1950s,

> The U.S. output in extractive sectors increased markedly from the Civil War to 1957. The increase in agriculture, following Engel's law, was slower than the increase in real gross national product (GNP). Minerals output, on the other hand, increased roughly as fast as real GNP.[14] (Smith)

Not surprisingly, the causal relationship between NNR utilization and human prosperity exists at the global level as well. A 2016 United Nations study found that global NNR utilization had increased from approximately 15.5 billion metric tonnes in 1970 to 51 billion metric tonnes in 2010 – a 229% increase.[15] During the same 40-year period, the UN estimated that inflation adjusted global GDP (economic output) had increased from $15.6 trillion to $52.7 trillion – a 238% increase.[16]

Again, the correlation between human NNR utilization and human prosperity improvement, as proxied by global economic (GDP) growth, was approximately one-to-one.

NNR Dynamics

> In contrast [to trees and fish], oil, metals, and coal are not renewable; they don't reproduce, sprout, or have sex to produce baby oil droplets or coal nuggets.[17] (Diamond)

NNR Origins According to prevailing theory, approximately 98% of the visible universe consists of hydrogen (73%) and helium (25%), which were formed (in addition to traces of lithium and beryllium) approximately 13.8 billion years ago, within the first three minutes of the Big Bang.

The other 86 naturally-occurring chemical elements, which comprise the remaining 2% of the mass of the visible universe, were synthesized in stars (iron and lighter) and during supernovae explosions (heavier than iron), a billion or more years later, as the overall temperature of the universe cooled.[18]

As planets in our solar system began to form approximately 4.6 billion years ago, chemical elements that were once part of stars coalesced to become Earth, generally in the form of multi-element molecules and mineral compounds. Put succinctly by British astronomer Sir Martin Rees, "We are literally the ashes of long dead stars."[19]

From these original elements and from elements comprising meteorites that subsequently struck Earth since its formation, all fossil fuels, metals, and nonmetallic minerals formed under circumstances that required rare or unique combinations of biological, geological, chemical, and physical processes.

The essential point is that absent the highly unlikely and almost certainly devastating eventuality of additional major meteorite strikes, there will be no new NNRs arriving on planet Earth during humanity's industrial era.

NNR Occurrence NNRs are widely distributed globally, and generally exist in great quantities within Earth's continental crust and oceanic crust. However, NNR deposits – highly concentrated NNR occurrences of economic value – are generally quite rare and are unevenly distributed throughout the world.

> The aggregate area underlain by mineral deposits of economic importance is only an insignificant fraction of 1 percent of the earth's surface, and the geographic position of the individual deposits is fixed by some accident of geology.[20] (Lovering)

Vast quantities of nearly all NNRs exist within Earth's undifferentiated continental crust, the granitic outer rocky shell that comprises approximately 40% of Earth's total crust, and that ranges in thickness from approximately 15 miles (25 km) to 40 miles (70 km).[21] NNR concentrations in Earth's continental crust range from 27% for silicon, to 60 parts per million for copper, to 0.3 parts per billion for indium.[22]

Earth's basaltic oceanic crust, which is formed as cooling lava spreads from oceanic ridges at tectonic plate boundaries, is thinner (4-6 miles thick), denser, younger, and of different chemical composition than Earth's continental crust.[23] The NNR mix comprising Earth's oceanic crust is less diverse – consisting primarily of minerals rich in calcium, magnesium, iron, and silicon – and is certainly less accessible to human exploitation.[24]

Because the mass of Earth's crust is enormous – on the order of 28 quintillion metric tons[25] – even NNRs exhibiting very small occurrences on a percentage basis exist in extremely large quantities within Earth's entire undifferentiated crust. However, these randomly distributed NNR occurrences are insufficiently concentrated to be of economic value.

NNR concentrations that are of economic value exist in NNR deposits classified by the USGS as reserves. An NNR reserve is "(t)hat part of the reserve base which could be economically extracted or produced at the time of determination."[26] (USGS)

To put NNR occurrence into perspective, if the total quantity of NNRs in Earth's continental crust (~20 quintillion metric tonnes) was represented by an area the size of Disneyland (approximately 60 American football fields), the economically viable NNR reserves would approximate the size of a human fingernail.[27]

NNR Quality Economically valuable NNR occurrences – NNR deposits – vary in terms of their relative value, or quality. Specific factors that determine NNR deposit quality are size, accessibility, grade, and purity. High quality (and low cost) NNRs typically occur in large, easily accessible deposits of high grade and purity – and are typically exploited early in an NNR depletion cycle.

NNR Depletion "Compounding the problem is the fact that in the United States and worldwide, the most easily recovered, higher grade mineral and energy mineral deposits are used first. Thus there is increased demand each year against resources which are declining in quality and cost more to obtain."[28] (Youngquist)

Depletion is the process of drawing down a natural resource reserve through extraction. NNR depletion commences with the initially extracted quantity of a fossil fuel, metal, or nonmetallic mineral, and culminates with the finally extracted quantity (but not the extraction of the final quantity!) of that NNR.

The NNR depletion cycle[29] is an irreversible, one-time process, which typically proceeds from high quality, low complexity, low cost NNR extraction, to low quality, high complexity, high cost NNR extraction.

Figure 1-3: NNR Depletion Cycle

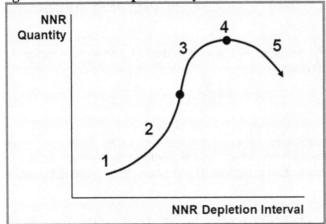

The NNR depletion cycle, which is depicted graphically by a "slanting-S" shaped curve, is imposed by the geologic laws of Nature, which govern the occurrence of NNRs in Earth's crust, and by the economic law of diminishing returns, which governs economic viability pertaining to NNR exploitation.

1 Given the limited scope and scale of NNR exploitation activities during the **early phase** of a global NNR depletion cycle, the high quality NNR deposits have typically yet to be discovered and targeted. Annual NNR quantities extracted from then-available, relatively low quality/high cost NNR deposits are therefore extremely modest.

2 During the **acceleration phase**, as the scope and scale of NNR exploitation activities expand rapidly into previously untapped frontiers, NNR quality increases continuously – the largest, most accessible NNR deposits of the highest grade and purity are discovered and targeted. Annually extracted NNR quantities accelerate – increase at increasing rates.

3 During the **deceleration phase**, the scope and scale of NNR exploitation activities slow, as few previously untapped NNR frontiers remain to be exploited. NNR quality decreases continuously, as high quality NNR deposits become extensively depleted, and smaller, less accessible NNR deposits of lower grade and purity are targeted. Annually extracted NNR quantities decelerate – increase at decreasing rates.

4 At the **peak** of a global NNR depletion cycle, the scope and scale of global NNR exploitation activities stagnate, as previously untapped NNR frontiers no longer exist. NNR quality further decreases, as even the smaller, less accessible NNR deposits of lower grade and purity become extensively depleted. The annually extracted NNR quantity reaches its maximum.

5 During the **decline phase**, the scope and scale of NNR exploitation activities contract, as targeted NNR deposits become "exhausted" – i.e., unmined NNRs become subeconomic. NNR quality decreases rapidly, as only the least accessible NNR deposits of the lowest grade and purity remain. Annually extracted NNR quantities decrease continuously and permanently.

NNR depletion reconciles NNR geology and NNR economics in the sense that the depletion cycle determines which NNRs will ultimately be exploited and which NNRs are destined to remain in the ground.

"The economic cycle is the discovery, development, and then decline and exhaustion of the one-time crop which is minerals."[30] (Youngquist)

NNR Exploitation

> Unlike most other natural resources, minerals are not renewable. They are formed in the earth's crust by infinitesimally slow natural geologic processes acting for thousands or millions of years. Once removed and used, they cannot be grown again.[31] (USGS)

Exploitation "Exploit", as it pertains to NNRs, means "to use". NNR exploitation refers to the processes by which NNRs are made useful to humankind. Specifically:

- Exploration, extraction, and refinement are the processes by which raw material NNRs are discovered, removed from the Earth, and improved – the processes by which NNRs are made useful as NNR-based economic inputs.
- Construction, manufacturing, generation, and provisioning exemplify the processes by which refined NNRs are converted into infrastructure, machines, products, energy, and

services – the processes by which NNRs are made useful as NNR-derived economic outputs.

NNR exploration, extraction, and refinement entail enormous investments in physical capital (infrastructure and machines) and human capital (labor and management); enormous expenditures of financial capital (currency); long lead times; complex and dangerous facilities, equipment, and processes; ever-increasing risk and costs; and extensive public relations.

Figure 1-4: Global Industrial Mosaic

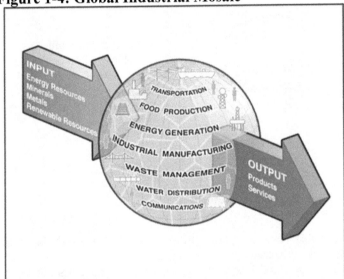

Processes such as construction, manufacturing, generation, and provisioning occur within our incomprehensibly complex global industrial mosaic, which consists of billions of independently operating yet interdependent human and non-human entities.

Our industrial mosaic must function continuously at the local, national, and global levels in order to produce the infrastructure, machines, products, energy, and services that comprise industrial humanity's societal support systems – which include water storage/distribution, food production/distribution, energy generation/distribution, industrial production/distribution, NNR exploitation, sanitation, healthcare, governance, education, transportation, communications, and law enforcement.

Impairments or failures within our global industrial mosaic can disrupt, temporarily or permanently, the availability of NNR-based and NNR-derived societal essentials – clean water, food, energy, infrastructure, products, and services – to broad segments of our global population.

NNR Economic Viability "Materials make a significant impact on human society only in proportion to how economical they are to obtain and then fashion into something useful."[32] (Sass)

Economically viable NNRs are profitable to "produce" and affordable to "procure". That is:

- The production – discovery, extraction, and refinement – of raw material NNRs is economically beneficial (profitable) to NNR suppliers.
- The procurement – acquisition and provisioning – of refined NNRs for conversion into infrastructure, machines, products, energy, and services is economically beneficial (affordable) to NNR users.

Figure 1-5: Economically Viable NNR Supply Cycle

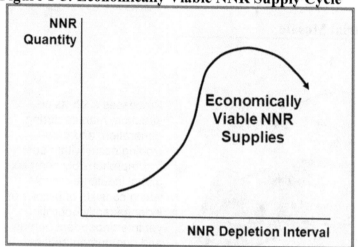

As is the case with the NNR depletion cycle, the economically viable NNR supply cycle is depicted graphically by a "slanting-S" shaped curve.

Note that while the economically viable NNR supply cycle is similar to the NNR depletion cycle – both are depicted graphically by "slanting-S" shaped curves – the two cycles are typically dissimilar in terms of NNR quantities. Economically viable NNR supplies consist of recycled and otherwise reused NNRs in addition to newly mined NNRs, while NNR depletion considers only newly mined NNRs.

NNR Overexploitation While Earth resource requirements vary among species, all species, including *Homo sapiens*, exploit (use) Earth resources – i.e., they deplete natural resource reserves and degrade natural habitats – in the process of living.

Accordingly, all species, including *Homo sapiens*, are subject to a common natural law: Earth resource overexploitation – i.e., depleting a natural resource reserve at a rate that exceeds the rate at which it is replenished, or degrading a natural habitat at a rate that exceeds the rate at which it is regenerated – is unsustainable ecological behavior.

Nature's immutable law regarding Earth resource overexploitation is based upon biological, geological, chemical, and physical processes and phenomena that cannot be evaded. This ecological reality is especially problematic for humankind, given that our industrial existence is enabled by non-replenishing Earth resources – NNRs.

"It [the UN's material footprint indicator] indicates that the level of development and well-being in wealthy industrial countries has been achieved largely through highly resource-intensive patterns of consumption and production, which are not sustainable..."[33] (UNEP)

Chapter 2:
NNR Scarcity

Long run [NNR] shortages ... produce rising trends in real prices over many decades, rather than sharp surges for a few months or years. As a result, they pose, at least potentially, a much more serious threat to the well being of the human race.[1] (Tilton, J. et al.)

NNR scarcity is the inevitable consequence of human industrialism; it is also the inevitable undoing of human industrialism.

The NNR Tree[2] – a Metaphor for NNR Scarcity

The process of depleting an NNR reserve is very similar to that of harvesting fruit from a tree.

Figure 2-1: The NNR Tree

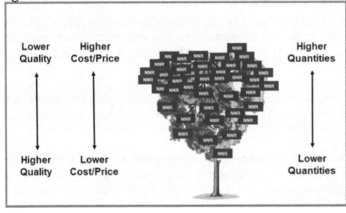

The low hanging fruit – the fruit closest to the ground, which is most easily picked – is typically harvested early on. The high hanging fruit – the fruit further up the tree, which is increasingly difficult (and costly) to pick – is typically harvested after the low hanging fruit has been harvested.

With respect to depleting – "harvesting" – Earth's NNR reserves, the high quality NNRs (the low hanging fruit) – from large, easily accessible deposits of the highest grade and purity – are typically extracted early in the NNR depletion cycle. Such NNRs are the least complicated and least costly to exploit.

As the high quality NNRs become extensively depleted, it becomes necessary to extract lower quality NNRs (the higher hanging fruit) – from smaller, less accessible deposits of lower grade and purity. Such NNRs are increasingly complicated and increasingly costly to exploit.

It is this gradual transition from high quality/low cost NNRs to lower quality/higher cost NNRs – within the context of industrial humanity's enormous and ever-increasing NNR require-ments – that causes increasingly pervasive NNR scarcity.

NNR Scarcity Concepts

Question: "If industrial development means depletion of resources and eventual dependence on others, what happens when every country has cashed its quick assets?"

Answer: "The world is finite in size, so the worldwide pattern must also come to an end. Although we may debate when the end will be reached, it is already apparent that, for many resources, an end to rich, quick assets will arrive during the century ahead [21st] – not only for the United States but for the world as a whole."[3] (Skinner)

Scarce In a general sense, "scarce" means "insufficient" or "not enough".

Scarcity A condition of scarcity exists when the requirement for an item of perceived value exceeds the available supply of the item at a specified place and time. Note, however, that "scarce" is not synonymous with "critical". Scarcity assesses relative availability, while criticality assesses relative importance. For example, while atmospheric oxygen is critical to human existence, it is generally not scarce – so far.

Economic Scarcity A condition of economic scarcity exists when the requirement for an item of perceived value – e.g., water, food, or a consumer good – exceeds the freely available supply. Obtaining (producing or procuring) an economically scarce item therefore entails acquisition costs.

At the most fundamental level, acquisition costs involve human capital, physical capital, and natural capital – some combination of which must be expended to produce or provision an economically scarce item.

In order to facilitate transactions involving economically scarce items, all acquisition costs are typically expressed in terms of a commonly accepted unit of account – i.e., a currency, such as the US dollar or the Japanese yen.

A currency is a commonly accepted medium of exchange, which facilitates transactions involving products and services of various types – e.g., a ton of copper, a milling machine, and a human machine operator – and aggregates constituent acquisition costs into the total cost (and price) of an economically scarce item.

Price serves as an effective mechanism for quantifying the perceived value of an economically scarce item, and for comparing relative values of economically scarce items over time and with respect to each other.

Relative NNR Scarcity Given that industrial humanity's NNR requirements always exceed Earth's freely available supplies, all NNRs are inherently and perpetually scarce in economic terms. NNR scarcity is therefore a relative concept – as is the case with NNR criticality and NNR quality.

Figure 2-2: Relative NNR Scarcity

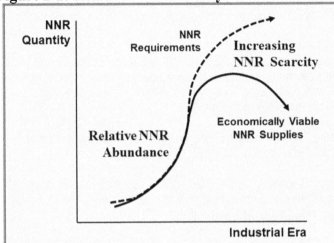

Of interest to industrial humanity, therefore, is relative NNR scarcity – NNR scarcity status at a specified time or during a specified time period. Relative NNR scarcity can be understood conceptually – and depicted graphically – as the evolving relationship between industrial humanity's NNR requirements and Earth's economically viable NNR supplies.

Industrial humanity's NNR requirements are NNR inputs to the global industrial economy that produce rapidly improving (desired) human prosperity. Earth's economically viable NNR supplies are actual NNR inputs to the global industrial economy that produce actual (attainable) human prosperity.

NNR Lifecycle The evolving relationship between industrial humanity's ever-increasing NNR requirements and Earth's initially-rapidly-increasing, but inevitably diminishing, economically viable NNR supplies is depicted graphically by the NNR lifecycle.

Figure 2-3: NNR Lifecycle

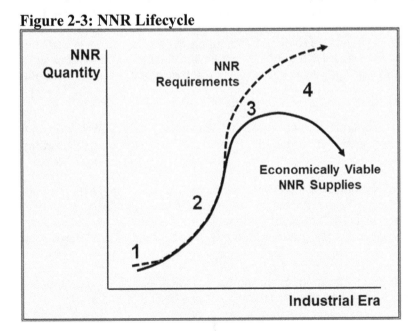

1 As an NNR is initially exploited on an industrial scale, newly emerging users addressing newly emerging uses generate rapidly-increasing, albeit relatively modest, requirements for the newly exploited NNR.

Given that Earth's large, easily accessible NNR deposits of high grade and purity have typically yet to be discovered, NNR deposits available to address humanity's initial requirements are of relatively low quality and high complexity, and therefore entail high production costs – a scenario that initially constrains NNR supplies.

Prices pertaining to these low quality, highly complex, and costly NNRs also remain high – a scenario that initially suppresses NNR demand.

As a result of these initially unfavorable NNR demand/supply dynamics, initially available, economically viable NNR supplies fail to completely address humanity's initial NNR requirements – an interval of **initial global NNR scarcity** ensues.

2 As NNR uses and users continue to increase rapidly, industrial humanity's annual NNR requirements increase at increasing rates (accelerate).

In order to address these rapidly increasing NNR requirements, human NNR exploitation expands into previously untapped, high-potential – high quality, low complexity, and low cost – NNR frontiers. NNR quality increases continuously and NNR production costs decrease continuously – as Earth's largest, most accessible NNR deposits of the highest grade and purity are exploited – a scenario that stimulates NNR supplies.

As the complexity and costs associated with exploiting Earth's high-quality NNRs decrease over time, NNR price trends decrease as well – a scenario that stimulates NNR demand.

As a result of these increasingly favorable NNR demand/supply dynamics, rapidly increasing, globally available, economically viable NNR supplies remain sufficient to address humanity's rapidly increasing NNR requirements – a secular trend of **relative global NNR abundance** ensues.

3 As NNR uses and users continue to increase, albeit inevitably more slowly, industrial humanity's annual NNR requirements continue to increase, but at decreasing rates (decelerate).

Human NNR exploitation expansion slows as well, as fewer high-potential NNR frontiers remain to be targeted. NNR quality decreases and NNR production complexity and costs increase, as Earth's highest quality NNR deposits become extensively depleted, and smaller, less accessible NNR deposits of lower grade and purity are targeted – a scenario that constrains NNR supplies.

As the complexity and costs associated with exploiting Earth's lower-quality NNRs increase, NNR price trends increase as well – a scenario that suppresses NNR demand.

As a result of these increasingly unfavorable NNR demand/supply dynamics, diminishing globally available, economically viable NNR supplies fail increasingly to address humanity's more rapidly increasing NNR requirements – a permanent trend of **increasing global NNR scarcity** ensues.

4 As NNR uses and users further increase, albeit even more slowly, industrial humanity's annual NNR requirements continue to increase more slowly as well.

Human NNR exploitation stagnates and inevitably contracts, as previously untapped global NNR frontiers no longer exist. NNR quality decreases rapidly and NNR production complexity and costs increase rapidly, as Earth's smaller, less accessible NNR deposits of lower grade and purity also become extensively depleted – a scenario that severely constrains NNR supplies.

As the complexity and costs associated with exploiting Earth's lowest-quality NNRs increase rapidly, NNR price trends increase rapidly as well – a scenario that severely suppresses NNR demand.

As a result of these terminally unfavorable NNR demand/supply dynamics, rapidly diminishing (and inevitably contracting) globally available, economically viable NNR supplies fail catastrophically to address humanity's persistently increasing NNR requirements – **accelerating (and inevitably terminal) global NNR scarcity** ensues.

Gaps The ever-widening gap between humanity's enormous and ever-increasing NNR requirements and Earth's inevitably-decreasing economically viable NNR supplies – the NNR gap – causes a comparable ever-widening gap between the level of "desired" human prosperity and "attainable" human prosperity – the human prosperity gap.

Figure 2-4: Widening Gaps

NNR Gap   **Human Prosperity Gap**

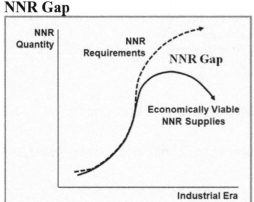
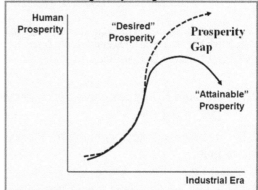

NNR Scarcity Indicators

In the absence of a capacity for the positive contributors to productivity [human ingenuity] to outweigh the negative effects of depletion [continuously decreasing NNR quality], then costs of mineral production must rise and so, eventually, must prices.[4] (Humphreys)

While the primary indicator of relative NNR scarcity at the sub-global (local, national, and regional) level is NNR import reliance – i.e., greater import reliance indicates greater NNR scarcity – the primary indicator of relative NNR scarcity at the global level is the secular NNR price trend – i.e., the trajectory of the trendline derived from the long term NNR price curve.

A decreasing secular NNR price trend indicates relative global NNR abundance, while an increasing secular NNR price trend indicates increasing global NNR scarcity. Per the USGS, "...a rising long-term price for a commodity indicates increasing scarcity of supply relative to demand. This is what we should expect with minerals as depletion progresses."[5]

Figure 2-5: Global NNR Scarcity Cycle

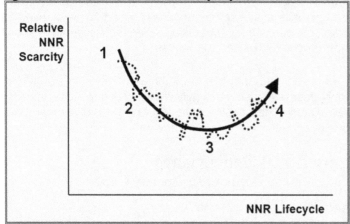

As depicted graphically by the global NNR scarcity cycle, relative global NNR scarcity is indicated by the trajectory of the trend-line (solid line) derived from the long term NNR price curve (dotted line).[6]

NNR Price Curve Trendline (and Global NNR Scarcity Cycle) = Solid Line.
NNR Price Curve = Dotted Line.

1 The elevated NNR price curve trendline indicates **initial global NNR scarcity**.

2 The decreasing trajectory of the NNR price curve trendline indicates **relative global NNR abundance**.

3 The reversing trajectory of the NNR price curve trendline indicates the **permanent transition** from relative global NNR abundance to increasing global NNR scarcity.

4 The increasing trajectory of the NNR price curve trendline indicates **permanently increasing global NNR scarcity**.

NNR Scarcity Effects

The story [of American industrialism] has been a spectacular one, and our material well-being is proof of the bounty won from the ground. But the record tells us too that [US] production of some metals is now [1979] declining and production of others grows less rapidly than our needs.

As a result, we are becoming more and more an importing country, less and less a producer and exporter of minerals. The pattern is familiar because it is one seen in the history of essentially all industrial countries – as their mining districts become depleted, foreign sources have to fill their needs.[7] (Skinner)

When a nation's NNR requirements permanently exceed its domestic NNR supplies, the nation can mitigate the adverse effects associated with increasingly pervasive domestic NNR scarcity by importing NNRs from foreign sources.

When the world's NNR requirements permanently exceed globally available, economically viable supplies, foreign NNR imports are not an option – there is only one Earth. NNR price trends inevitably increase, as NNR suppliers are forced to target lower quality/higher cost NNR deposits in their attempt to address industrial humanity's ever-increasing requirements.

Accordingly, increasingly pervasive global NNR scarcity increases the prices of EVERYTHING – NNRs, NNR-based economic inputs, and NNR-derived infrastructure, machines, products, energy, and services. The inescapable effects of increasingly pervasive global NNR scarcity for NNR-dependent industrial humanity are therefore catastrophic.

Chapter 3:
Industrial Productivity

Mineral commodities are extracted from nonrenewable resources, which has raised concerns about their long-term availability. Many believe that, as society exploits its favorable existing mineral deposits and is forced to then exploit poorer quality deposits that are more remote and more difficult to process, the real costs and prices of essential mineral commodities will rise. This could threaten the living standards of future generations and make sustainable development more difficult or impossible. Mineral depletion tends to push up the real prices of mineral commodities over time. However, innovations and new technologies tend to mitigate this upward pressure by making it easier to find new deposits, enabling the exploitation of entirely new types of deposits, and reducing the costs of mining and processing mineral commodities. With innovations and new technologies more abundant resources can be substituted for less abundant resources. In the long run the availability of mineral commodities will depend on the outcome of a race between the cost-increasing effects of depletion and the cost-reducing effects of new technologies and other innovations.[1] (National Research Council)

Industrial Productivity Significance Humanity's only recourse against increasingly pervasive global NNR scarcity is human ingenuity – human resourcefulness, technological innovations, efficiency improvements, and productivity enhancements – which, within the context of human industrialism, is manifested by industrial productivity.

Through industrial productivity, industrial humanity seeks to optimize the effectiveness with which economic inputs are converted into economic outputs – and thereby to mitigate the impact of NNR scarcity. Specifically, industrial productivity entails:

- Constraining inevitably increasing NNR production (exploration, extraction, and refinement) costs, through the development of productivity-increasing NNR mining tools and techniques; and
- Offsetting inevitably increasing NNR price trends, through the development and deployment of broadly-applicable, productivity-increasing innovations and efficiency improvements.

Industrial Productivity Evolution The origin of human productivity dates to the appearance of genus *Homo* approximately 3 million years ago. From the first stone tools – e.g., hammers, cutters, scrapers, and grinders – to simple machines – the wheel and axle, wedge, lever, pulley, inclined plane, and screw – to complex machines – e.g., scissors, wheelbarrow, and bicycle – increasing total output per unit of human input has been a primary (albeit initially unstated) human objective.

With the advent of human industrialism, human productivity evolved into industrial productivity, which has become increasingly concerned with optimizing the effectiveness with which industrial capital inputs – human capital, physical capital, and natural capital – are converted into product and service outputs within mass production economies.

This scenario has led to extraordinary industrial productivity growth and resultant extraordinary human prosperity improvement during our industrial era, through the development and deployment of highly-impactful, productivity-increasing innovations and efficiency improvements.

Industrial Productivity Attributes

Productivity (as measured by output per unit of single input or total inputs), and its growth, is well recognized by essentially all economists as the key variable to long-run improvement in income and (un)employment.[2] (Calcagnini, G. et al.)

As the secondary enabler of human industrialism, industrial productivity has empowered humankind to exploit finite and non-replenishing NNRs – persistently and increasingly – on an industrial scale, and thereby to dramatically improve prosperity for increasing segments of Earth's ever-expanding human population.

Industrial Productivity Definition Industrial productivity is defined as the effectiveness with which economic inputs are converted into economic outputs.

Industrial productivity is measured by the ratio of an economic output quantity to one or more economic input quantities – output per unit of input – during a specified time period. If, for example, the total industrial capital deployed within a factory produces 32 widgets during an 8-hour workday, the factory's productivity is 4 units per hour.

Industrial Productivity Role Industrial productivity derives its significance from the fact that total economic output is determined by two factors:

1. The mix and quantities of economic inputs – primarily NNRs, and
2. The effectiveness with which economic inputs are converted into economic outputs – infrastructure, machines, products, energy, and services – through the deployment of:
    - Industrial capital – i.e., human capital (labor and management), physical capital (infrastructure and machines), and natural capital (Earth resources), and
    - Industrial processes – e.g., construction, manufacturing, generation, and provisioning.

Thus, the role of industrial productivity is to maximize economic output – by optimizing industrial capital deployment and industrial process efficiency – and thereby maximize human prosperity.

Industrial Productivity Sources Industrial productivity is derived from:

- Innovations, through which the industrial state-of-the-art is advanced by newly developed productivity-increasing tools and techniques, and

- Efficiency improvements, through which the industrial state-of-the-art is advanced by enhancements to existing productivity-increasing tools and techniques.

Industrial Productivity Effectiveness In *Industrialism*, industrial productivity is analyzed and evaluated in at two levels:

- Overall industrial productivity, which considers productivity-increasing innovations and efficiency improvements that are broadly applicable across multiple industrial sectors, and
- Mining sector productivity, which considers the subset of productivity-increasing innovations and efficiency improvements that are relevant specifically to the mining sector – i.e., NNR exploration, extraction, and refining.

In both cases, industrial productivity analyses involve:

- Single factor productivity – i.e., labor productivity and capital productivity – which relates a single economic output to a single economic input – e.g., the number of widgets produced per worker, or the number of widgets produced per machine, and
- Multifactor productivity, which relates a single economic output to multiple economic inputs – e.g.; the number of widgets produced by an entire factory, or the number of widgets produced by an entire national economy.

"Multifactor productivity (MFP) reflects the overall efficiency with which labour and capital inputs are used together in the production process. Changes in MFP reflect the effects of changes in management practices, brand names, organizational change, general knowledge, network effects, spillovers from production factors, adjustment costs, economies of scale, the effects of imperfect competition and measurement errors."[3] (OECD)

Industrial Productivity Dynamics

> Productivity change is the key factor of long-run economic growth and development. This is well recognized since the first growth accountants (Abramovitz, 1956; Solow, 1957) and by economic historians (e.g., Mokyr, 2005).[4] (Krüger)

Industrial Productivity Growth Definition Industrial productivity growth is defined as the change over time (positive or negative) in the effectiveness with which economic inputs are converted into economic outputs.

Industrial productivity growth is measured by the change over time in the ratio of economic output to economic input – initial output per unit of input, versus subsequent output per unit of input.

If, for example, the industrial capital deployed within a factory produces 4 widgets during period 1, and 8 widgets during period 2, productivity growth between the two periods is 100% (4 widgets to 8 widgets).

Maximizing industrial productivity growth – i.e., maximizing the effectiveness with which industrial humanity converts economic inputs into economic outputs over time – is therefore achieved by:

- Maximizing the quantity and quality (impactfulness) with respect to newly-developed, productivity-increasing innovations and efficiency improvements, and
- Optimizing existing industrial capital deployment and industrial process efficiency.

Industrial Productivity Growth Cycle The evolution of industrial productivity during humanity's industrial era is depicted graphically by a "slanting-S" shaped curve.

Figure 3-1: Industrial Productivity Growth Cycle

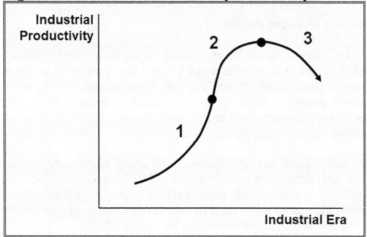

1 During the early phase of humanity's industrial era, industrial productivity growth is governed by relative global NNR abundance, which is characterized by:

- Many newly-available NNR "building blocks" with which to develop productivity-increasing innovations and efficiency improvements, and
- Decreasing NNR price trends, which reduce over time the costs associated with developing and deploying productivity-increasing innovations and efficiency improvements.

This reinforcing "geological tailwind" – which encourages the development and deployment of an expanding array of productivity-increasing innovations and efficiency improvements – fosters **rapid industrial productivity growth** during the period.

2 During the intermediate phase of humanity's industrial era, industrial productivity growth is governed by increasingly pervasive global NNR scarcity, which is characterized by:

- Few newly-available NNR "building blocks" with which to develop productivity-increasing innovations and efficiency improvements, and
- Increasing NNR price trends, which increase over time the costs associated with developing and deploying productivity-increasing innovations and efficiency improvements.

This increasingly-debilitating "geological headwind" – which discourages the development and deployment of productivity-increasing innovations and efficiency improvements – causes **diminishing industrial productivity growth** during the period.

3 During the latter phase of humanity's industrial era, industrial productivity growth is governed by terminal global NNR scarcity, which is characterized by:

- No newly-available NNR "building blocks" with which to develop productivity-increasing innovations and efficiency improvements, and
- Rapidly increasing NNR price trends, which rapidly increase over time the costs associated with developing and deploying productivity-increasing innovations and efficiency improvements.

This inevitably devastating "geological headwind" – which precludes the development and deployment of productivity-increasing innovations and efficiency improvements – causes **negative industrial productivity growth** (permanently decreasing industrial productivity) during the period.

Increasingly pervasive global NNR scarcity inevitably causes decreasing industrial productivity – i.e., Nature inevitably overwhelms human ingenuity.

> Technology cannot make something out of nothing. Some Earth resources must be used to provide the necessities of life, and many more resources are needed to achieve a good standard of living.[5] (Youngquist)

Industrial Productivity Growth Indicator The industrial productivity growth rate – the primary indicator of industrial productivity growth – is defined as the compound annual growth rate (CAGR) associated with industrial productivity – labor productivity, capital productivity, or multifactor productivity – between two specified periods of time.

If, for example, industrial productivity was 10 units (10 units of output per unit of input) in 1950, and 15 units in 1955, the rate of industrial productivity growth between 1950 and 1955 was 8.45% compounded annually.

The industrial productivity growth rate achieved during a specified time period can be compared with growth rates achieved during prior periods, in order to analyze industrial productivity growth trends – and thereby assess the evolving contribution of industrial productivity toward human prosperity improvement.

Chapter 4:
Human Prosperity

The discussion about the relationship of material use and human development has shown, not surprisingly, that the most developed nations have the highest level of per capita resources available to support their long, healthy, and affluent lives.[1] (UNEP)

Prosperity is the primary driver – the desired outcome – of human industrialism. Humanity's desire to live beyond subsistence level through an industrialized way of life has, in fact, become a reality for billions of people during our industrial era.

Industrial human prosperity is enabled primarily by Nature (NNRs) and secondarily by human ingenuity (industrial productivity) – forces that are initially reinforcing, then opposing, and finally terminally-opposing.

Human Prosperity Attributes

At the beginning of the Industrial era, huge new markets and a multiplication of inventions caused a rapid rise in logistic curves depicting the demand for metals and the prosperity of manufacturing nations.[2] (Lovering)

Industrial human prosperity is derived from surplus real wealth – wealth exceeding that which is required to provide basic human subsistence. Industrial human prosperity has far exceeded basic subsistence – a unique development in human history, and in the history of the world.

Human Prosperity Definition Prosperity refers to an individual's or population's state of material wellbeing,[3] which ranges from "basic subsistence" to "gluttonous". Human prosperity is measured by "total economic output" at the population level, and by "the average material living standard" at the individual level.

Human Prosperity Derivation Viewed from the ecological perspective, human prosperity is derived from real wealth, which is created through the exploitation of Earth resources. Specifically, real wealth is created by human exploitation of renewable and nonrenewable Earth resources that exist on the ground, in the ground, under the ground, and in the water:

- Naturally-occurring, cultivated, and domesticated terrestrial plant and animal species,
- Naturally-occurring and cultivated aquatic plant and animal species, and
- Naturally-occurring fossil fuels, metals, and nonmetallic minerals.

These Earth resources are extracted and/or processed to improve human material wellbeing.

The primary enablers of our extraordinary industrial prosperity are economically viable NNRs, with which humankind has created sufficient surplus real wealth to provide extraordinary material living standards for Earth's ever-expanding human population.

NNR-derived surplus real wealth is arguably the most profound benefit afforded by human industrialism. In addition to enabling extant industrialized human populations to enjoy previously inconceivable material living standards, NNR-derived surplus real wealth provides the basis for future real wealth creation – through investment – thereby providing a prosperity legacy for future generations.

Human Prosperity Dynamics

> Continued production from any mineral deposit is accompanied by increasing costs per ton. ... As the costs rise, the competition with other deposits more favorably located or more cheaply worked becomes increasing bitter. Profits diminish, wages are cut, and the living standards of all concerned suffer accordingly.[4] (Lovering)

The evolution of industrial era human prosperity is governed by the availability of surplus real wealth, which is governed by the evolving relationship between relative global NNR scarcity and industrial productivity growth.

Human Prosperity Cycle As is the case with the NNR depletion cycle, the economically viable NNR supply cycle, and the industrial productivity growth cycle, the industrial human prosperity cycle is depicted graphically by a "slanting-S" shaped curve.

Figure 4-1: Human Prosperity Cycle

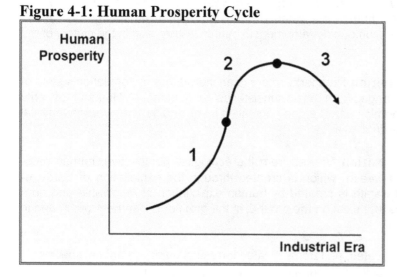

1 During the early phase of humanity's industrial era, increasingly favorable enabling trends – relative global NNR abundance and rapid industrial productivity growth – stimulate surplus real wealth creation to levels that produce **rapidly improving human prosperity**, and rapidly improving human cultural circumstances.

2 During the intermediate phase of humanity's industrial era, increasingly unfavorable inhibiting trends – increasingly pervasive global NNR scarcity and diminishing industrial productivity growth – suppress real wealth creation to levels that produce **faltering human prosperity**, and deteriorating human cultural circumstances.

3 During the latter phase of humanity's industrial era, terminally unfavorable inhibiting trends – terminal global NNR scarcity and negative industrial productivity growth (permanently decreasing industrial productivity) – further suppress real wealth creation to levels that produce **permanently declining human prosperity**, and disintegrating cultural circumstances.

Human Prosperity Indicators The following quantitative measures of human prosperity and human prosperity improvement are universally employed, owing to the availability of relatively reliable, long-term national and global data in each case.

Gross Domestic Product (GDP) measures the market value of total economic output – i.e., all goods and services – produced by a human population during a specified time period. Because it includes service sector economic output, GDP is a proxy for "total value" created by a national economy or by the global economy.

Per capita Gross Domestic Product (pc GDP) measures the market value of economic output produced per person, on average, during a specified time period. Per capita GDP is a proxy for "the average material living standard" experienced by members of a human population.

Industrial Production (IP) measures the market value of total output produced by an economy's industrial sector – mining, manufacturing, utilities, and construction – during a specified time period. Because industrial sector economic output consists of infrastructure, machines, products, and energy, IP is a proxy for "total real wealth" created by a national economy or by the global economy.

Part Two:
Industrial Era Evolution

But the geologic framework of the Earth developed over eons of time, with its varied resources distributed unevenly over the globe, established the environment which we are inevitably destined to accept. Human history, the present, and the human future have been, are, and will be subject to geology.[1] (Youngquist)

Nobody fired a starting gun or flipped a switch during the mid-18th century to signal the commencement of our industrial era – and there has been no roadmap for planning and charting its evolution. Both the origin of human industrialism and its eventual global proliferation were unplanned occurrences.

Industrialism has evolved spontaneously during the past three centuries – from local "pockets" within nations, to nations, to multi-nation regions, to global – through the interaction of billions of independently operating human and non-human entities.

A uniquely favorable global natural environment, featuring enormous quantities of economically viable NNRs, has enabled the establishment of our increasingly favorable national cultural environments, which have encouraged our ever-increasing exploitation of those NNRs – thereby enabling our extraordinary industrial era prosperity.

Industrial Development Dynamics

Throughout the Industrial Era, parallel conditions and events have been repeated in various countries so often that a definite pattern seems discernable. The curves representing the statistical history of many phases of our industrial activity have a remarkably similar form. **The typical shape of such a change-with-time curve is that of a slanting attenuated S. This seems to be the general pattern of the Industrial Era.**[2] **(emphasis mine)** (Lovering)

Figure P2-1: The "Slanting-S" Shaped Curve

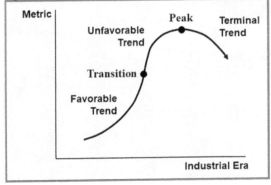

As Lovering correctly observed, "the general pattern of the Industrial Era" – the common evolutionary cycle that governs all aspects of industrial development – can be depicted graphically by a "slanting-S" shaped "change-with-time" curve.

- **Favorable Trend** – the metric increases at an increasing rate over time (accelerates).
- **Transition** – the trend shifts from favorable to unfavorable (inflection point).
- **Unfavorable Trend** – the metric increases at a decreasing rate over time (decelerates).
- **Peak** – the trend shifts from increasing to decreasing (inflection point).
- **Terminal Trend** – the metric decreases continuously over time.

As discussed in Part One of the book, the evolutionary cycles that govern the enablers of human industrialism – NNRs and industrial productivity – are depicted graphically by "slanting-S" shaped curves.

Figure P2-2: Industrialism Enablers

NNR Depletion Cycle

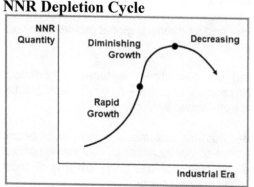

Industrial Productivity Growth Cycle

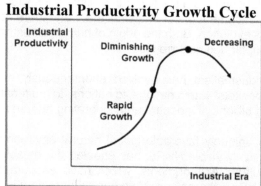

Unsurprisingly, the evolutionary cycles that govern the outcomes of human industrialism – human prosperity and human cultural (political, economic, and societal) circumstances – are depicted graphically by "slanting-S" shaped curves as well.

Figure P2-3: Industrialism Outcomes

Human Prosperity Cycle

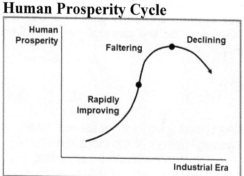

Human Cultural Circumstances Cycle

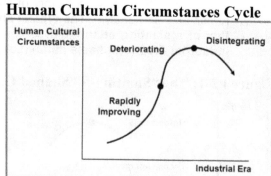

34

Industrial Development Cycle

> The countries within whose boundaries such mineral treasures lie possess temporarily an asset that gives them a great commercial advantage over their less fortunate trade rivals. As long as the minerals can be dug up and profitably converted into fabricated goods, trade booms, and the lucky owners become increasingly wealthy.[3] (Lovering)

As originally documented by Hewett and subsequently refined by Lovering, industrial development evolves through five stages – as depicted by an interrelated set of "slanting-S" shaped change-with-time curves.

Figure P2-4: Industrial Development Cycle (Change-with-Time Curves)

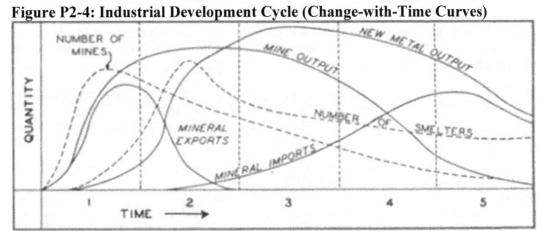

Sources: Lovering adapted from Hewett.[4]

Per Lovering:[5]

Stage 1 – Mine Development: exploration, discovery of new districts, boom towns, many small mines working; first recognition of large deposits and development of large mines; rapidly increasing production of metal.

Stage 2 – Smelter Development: few new discoveries; small mines becoming exhausted; increasing output from large mines; many smelters competing for the ore.

Stage 3 – Industrial Development: decreasing costs, increasing standard of living; rapid accumulation of wealth; expanding internal and external markets; approaching zenith of commercial power.

Stage 4 – Rapid Depletion of Cheap Domestic Raw Materials: ever-increasing costs of mining and of materials produced; more and more energy is required to get the same amount of raw material. The stage is set for a bitter struggle with competing sources of raw materials; some foreign markets are lost; some foreign goods invade the home market. Usually some auxiliary raw materials first appear (agricultural products and minerals).

Later, competing manufactured goods of foreign make begin to usurp the home markets unless temporarily blocked by tariffs.

Stage 5 – Decreasing Internal and External Markets: Increasing dependence on foreign sources of raw materials brings increasing costs to manufacturers. This period is characterized by a decreasing standard of living with its accompanying social problems and political unrest; tariffs, subsidies, cartels, and other artificial expedients are used in the effort to maintain a competitive price in the domestic and world market. This is a period of decreasing commercial power. It is a time when military pressure may be used to strangle competition or to seize control of new sources of raw materials. A drive is generally made to acquire cheap foreign sources of raw materials when the domestic sources become low. Commercial control is first established, but political control may follow later. Commercial control of foreign sources of supply keeps the profits within the home country, helps to maintain purchasing power, and assures a supply that will be as cheap as can be obtained. Control of foreign sources also gives the owner an obvious advantage in dealing with competing nations that also need the raw material in question. The pursuit of this advantage has frequently led to international friction.

The critical difference between industrial development at the sub-global level and the global level is the availability of imported NNRs at the sub-global level. While imported NNRs provide a "safety valve" for NNR-deficient industrial nations, no such "safety valve" exists at the global level.

Industrial Era Chronology

> The machine age has created wealth through the extraction of raw materials from the ground [NNRs] and has multiplied this wealth through the skillful fabrication of raw material [human ingenuity] into the multitude articles demanded by our Industrial era. (Lovering)

Industrial Era Intervals

While the evolution of our industrial era contains few "hard starts" and "hard stops", several significant intervals – three increasingly expansive industrial revolutions interspersed with four increasingly severe NNR scarcity episodes[7] – are discernable.

Figure P2-5: Industrial Era Intervals

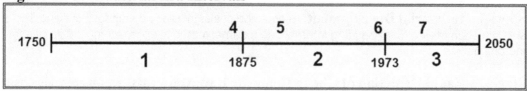

1 During **Industrialism1**, which spanned from 1750 to 1875, several Western European nations launched pioneering industrialization initiatives, other Western nations subsequently followed, and Great Britain attained global industrial supremacy.

2 During **Industrialism2**, which spanned from 1875 to 1973, most of the West became industrialized, and the US displaced Great Britain with respect to global industrial supremacy.

3 During **Industrialism3**, which has spanned from 1973 forward, the industrializing East has emerged, the industrialized West has deteriorated, and industrialism globally has unraveled toward collapse.

4 During **Scarcity1**, which occurred between the mid/late 1860s and the early/mid 1870s, Great Britain's NNR reserves became extensively depleted, and permanent British (national) NNR scarcity ensued.

5 During **Scarcity2**, which occurred between 1914 and 1916, Europe's NNR reserves became extensively depleted, and permanent European (regional) NNR scarcity ensued.

6 During **Scarcity3**, which occurred between 1969 and 1980, Western (especially American) NNR reserves became extensively depleted, and permanent Western (super-regional) NNR scarcity ensued.

7 During **Scarcity4**, which occurred between 1999 and 2008, global NNR reserves became extensively depleted, and permanent global NNR scarcity ensued.

Industrial Era Periods

Figure P2-5: Industrial Era Periods

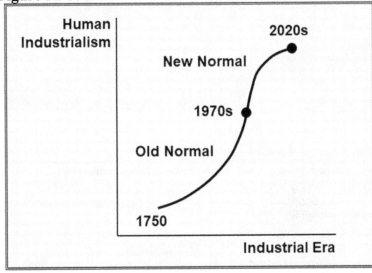

At the broadest level, our industrial era is comprised of two sharply contrasting periods – our Old Normal and our New Normal.

Our Old Normal

The Industrial Revolution also gave rise to a "Great Specialization", with stark North-South patterns of specialization characterizing international trade flows (Robertson 1938; Lewis 1978). The new technologies gave Britain, France, Germany, the United States (US) and eventually other countries in Western Europe and North America a powerful potential comparative advantage in manufacturing relative to the economies of the European periphery, Africa, Latin America, the Middle East, and even Asia, which in the middle of the eighteenth century accounted for the lion's share of world industrial output (Bairoch 1982).[8] (NBER)

Figure P2-6: Old Normal Operating Environment

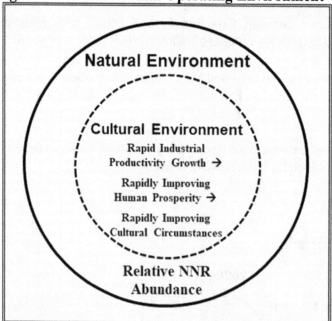

Our Old Normal, which spanned from the mid-18th century to the 1970s, was characterized by an extra-ordinarily favorable global natural environment and increasingly favorable cultural environments within industrializing nations.

Owing to uniquely favorable "enabling" trends that prevailed during our Old Normal, industrialism flourished during the period.

Table P2-1: Enabling Old Normal Trends

- **Relative Global NNR Abundance (Nature's Stimulus)** – characterized by increasing NNR quality, decreasing NNR exploitation costs, and decreasing NNR price trends, which stimulated economically viable NNR supplies sufficiently to address humanity's rapidly increasing NNR requirements.
- **Rapid Industrial Productivity Growth** – characterized by an increasingly-reinforcing "geological tailwind" – relative global NNR abundance – which encouraged the development and deployment of an expanding array of productivity-increasing innovations and efficiency improvements.

Table P2-1: Enabling Old Normal Trends (continued)

- **Rapidly Improving Global Human Prosperity** – characterized by accelerating global economic growth and rapidly improving human material living standards, which engendered rapidly improving human cultural circumstances.
- **Rapidly Improving Human Cultural Circumstances** – characterized by increasingly favorable political, economic, and societal conditions, which fostered rapid industrial development.
- **Constructive Human Responses** – characterized by increasing optimism and innovation, which reinforced rapidly improving human cultural circumstances and facilitated rapid industrial development.

Regrettably, the uniquely favorable enabling trends that defined our Old Normal were transient – and nonreplicable. More regrettably, given industrial humanity's anthropocentric perspective, these transient trends were misperceived as "normal" – and "sustainable".

Our New Normal

In the past half century, resurgent Asian countries have demonstrated that an important degree of catch–up is feasible. Nevertheless world economic growth has slowed substantially since 1973, and the Asian advance has been offset by stagnation or retrogression elsewhere.[9] (Maddison)

Figure P2-7: New Normal Operating Environment

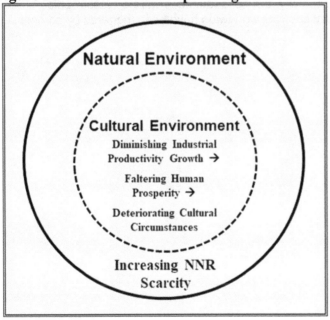

Our New Normal, which has spanned from the 1970s forward, is characterized by an increasingly unfavorable global natural environment and an increasingly unfavorable global cultural environment.

The favorable "enabling" trends that prevailed during our Old Normal have been displaced by increasingly unfavorable "inhibiting" trends during our New Normal; industrialism has unraveled during the period.

Table P2-2: Inhibiting New Normal Trends

- **Increasingly Pervasive Global NNR Scarcity (Nature's Squeeze)** – characterized by continuously decreasing NNR quality, increasing NNR exploitation costs, and increasing NNR price trends, which have constrained economically viable NNR supplies to levels at which they have failed increasingly to address humanity's rapidly increasing NNR requirements.
- **Diminishing Industrial Productivity Growth** – characterized by an increasingly-debilitating "geological headwind" – increasingly pervasive global NNR scarcity – which has discouraged the development and deployment of productivity-increasing innovations and efficiency improvements.
- **Faltering Global Human Prosperity** – characterized by slowing global economic growth and diminishing human material living standard improvement, which have engendered deteriorating human cultural circumstances.
- **Deteriorating Human Cultural Circumstances** – characterized by increasing political instability, economic fragility, and societal volatility, which have impeded industrial development.
- **Counterproductive Human Responses** – characterized by increasing frustration, anger, and violence, which have exacerbated deteriorating human circumstances and undermined industrial development.

These increasingly unfavorable inhibiting trends, which have accelerated during the new millennium, will become increasingly debilitating during the coming decades.

"But when the resources begin to run dry, the consequences will be catastrophic. Already [2012], since 1990 at least 18 violent conflicts worldwide have been triggered by competition for resources."[10] (Moyo)

Chapter 5:
Industrialism1 – Industrialism Emerges

> England and the Netherlands rose in fortune as they developed their domestic mineral resources and those of their colonies, took over the great trade route established by the Spanish, and founded the trade companies...[1] (Lovering)

Industrialism1 – humanity's first industrial revolution – originated in Great Britain (England, Scotland, and Wales) during the mid-18th century (1750), spread to Belgium, Sweden, and the Netherlands during the mid/late 18th century, then spread to second-generation industrializing nations during the early/mid-19th century, before culminating with Scarcity1 in 1875.

The driving force behind Industrialism1 was an emerging industrial class – located primarily in Great Britain, and to a lesser extent in the other industrial pioneers – who endeavored to create unprecedented real wealth and human prosperity, through the factory-based mass production of industrial and consumer products.

Eighteenth century British industrialists represented a new social stratum – neither commoners nor aristocrats – many of whom became increasingly wealthy through the private ownership of NNR reserves, NNR-based infrastructure and machines, and NNR-derived economic output.

Industrialists were forward thinking, risk taking, and ingenious individuals who sought solutions to problems through innovation and efficiency improvement – and through the ever-increasing exploitation of Earth's fossil fuels, metals, and nonmetallic minerals.

Industrialism1 Operating Environment

Great Britain's extremely favorable natural environment, which had enabled British agrarian and mercantilist successes between the 14th and 17th centuries, also enabled the establishment of a cultural environment that encouraged the further exploitation of Britain's natural environment – this time focused on NNR-based industrial production.

Owing to Britain's comparatively favorable operating environment, Industrialism1 became the era of British industrial supremacy, "The industrial hegemony of Great Britain during the nineteenth century was due to the happy juxtaposition of coal, iron, cheap skilled labor, and cheap transportation to the great world markets."[2] (Lovering)

Industrialism1 Natural Environment

While Great Britain's 18th century Earth resource endowments paled in comparison to those of larger nations such as Russia, America, and China, they were sufficient at the time to enable Britain to launch humanity's Industrial Revolution.

Habitat Britain's temperate maritime climate provided a sufficiently productive growing season to enable the British Agricultural Revolution – a prerequisite to the Industrial Revolution. Too, the damp, mild climate in Northwest England was ideal for spinning cotton.

British waterways were proximate to domestic sources of coal, industrial metals, and other NNRs, and to major British cities, which became the hubs of industrial activity. Moreover, the extensive navigable British coastline and internal waterways provided shipping lanes and ports for both merchant ships and military vessels. Finally, Britain's island status offered enhanced stability and security.

Renewable Natural Resources Abundant arable land and fresh water supplies were the fundamental enablers of the British Agricultural Revolution, which provided the wealth surplus that enabled Britain to launch Industrialism1. In addition, rapidly flowing British rivers and streams provided the energy that powered Britain's early factories.

Nonrenewable Natural Resources Great Britain possessed the highest quality coal in Europe, and abundant supplies of iron ore, lead, copper, tin, and limestone, which were the primary NNR inputs to early industrial economies. Additionally, Britain's expanding colonial empire and extensive global trade network provided access to industrial raw materials that were unavailable domestically.

Industrialism1 Cultural Environment

The differences between Great Britain's 18th century cultural environment and those of other nations were significant. For the first time in human history, prosperity could be determined by human ingenuity and initiative – not by accident of birth or by the whims of Nature.

By the mid-18th century, intellectual freedom had become well established in Great Britain. Enlightened thinking, which had emerged among Britain's increasingly literate and educated population during the Late Middle Ages, encouraged the free exchange of ideas within an increasingly secular societal framework.

Scientific evidence rather than religious or monarchal dogma had become the basis for human decision making and action. Applying the scientific method toward improving the human condition prompted myriad discoveries and inventions.

Individual liberty had also become increasingly pervasive during the centuries prior to Industrialism1. Britain's parliamentary government (representative democracy), the rule-of-law (enforcement of contracts and private property), and the abandonment of manorialism and feudalism (personal freedom) following the English civil war fostered the proliferation of human rights.

Moreover, government encouragement of entrepreneurism (private ownership), domestic trade (elimination of domestic tolls and tariffs), international trade (protected shipping lanes), and technological innovation (patent protection) created an economic environment within which human ingenuity could thrive.

Finally, the 18th century British cultural environment nurtured the development of a (relatively) free-market-based economic system characterized by entrepreneurism, private property, free trade, and limited government intervention.

Britain's established merchant base, global trade network, and domestic markets for manufactured goods, in combination with its emerging colonial empire and emerging banking system – operating within the context of Britain's (relatively) laissez-faire economic system – enabled risk-taking entrepreneurs to finance their commercial ventures,

> The ability of financial institutions, such as banks and private companies to amass substantial amounts of money was crucial to the development of large-scale, machine-intensive industries. As the need for such investments grew, merchants and banks in England were willing and able to provide these funds, more so than in other countries.[3] (Sass)

Land wealth, the exclusive domain of the aristocracy, was superseded by industrial wealth, created by entrepreneurs who owned factories and machines – within a cultural environment that enthusiastically encouraged the application of their ingenuity toward the ever-increasing exploitation of Earth's NNRs.

Industrialism1 Enablers

> In real terms the price of coal to consumers in London fell by 40% over the course of the Industrial Revolution, at a time when coalfield annual output expanded 18-fold.[4] (Clark and Jacks)

Within the context of an extraordinarily favorable global natural environment and increasingly favorable national cultural environments, the industrial pioneers were well positioned to capitalize upon relative NNR abundance and rapid industrial productivity growth during Industrialism1.

Industrialism1 NNRs

> The industrial revolution made coal and iron the most valuable mineral resources a county could have within its borders.[5] (Lovering)

Industrial humanity's early NNR requirements were extremely modest by today's standards, owing to the limited scope and scale of industrial activity during the mid-18th century.

Economically viable NNR supplies were likewise relatively modest, given the rudimentary developmental stage of the mining industry and the limited geographic scope of industrial-scale mining activity at the time.

Both NNR requirements and economically viable NNR supplies increased rapidly during Industrialism1, however, as human industrialism proliferated – with respect to both geography and innovation.

Industrialism1 NNR Demand

The rapid geographic proliferation of human industrialism and the myriad discoveries, inventtions, and other innovations that occurred during Industrialism1 spawned corresponding increases in humanity's NNR requirements – NNR uses and NNR users – during the period.

NNR Uses Given that all nations, including the industrial pioneers, were almost exclusively agrarian at the inception of Industrialism1, early NNR-related applications typically involved increasing agricultural output and broadening the newly emerging industrial base – particularly in the area of textile production.

Additionally, Industrialism1 discoveries and innovations enhanced the overall quality of human life – in areas such as transportation, refrigeration, home lighting, sanitation, communications, and healthcare.

NNR Users Populations that exploited NNRs on an industrial scale at the dawn of Industrialism1 generally occupied Great Britain, Belgium, Sweden, and the Netherlands. The combined population of these nations in the year 1750 was approximately 14 million, which accounted for less than 2% of the global human population at the time.

Table 5-1: Global Industrialization Status as of 1875 [million people]

Year	Industrialized	Industrializing	Pre-industrial	Total
By 1750	0 (0%)	14 (1.9%)	706 (98.1%)	720 (100%)
By 1875	41 (3.0%)	291 (22.0%)	993 (75.0%)	1,325 (100%)

Sources: Kremer and Populstat.[6]

By the end of Industrialism1 in 1875, at least 15 additional nations – including America, France, Germany, Russia, Austria-Hungary, and Japan – had joined the industrial pioneers in launching industrialization initiatives.

Nearly 41 million people (3% of the global population) occupied nations that were predominantly industrialized by that time. Over 290 million people (22% of the global population) occupied nations that were in the process of industrialization, which left nearly 1 billion people (75% of the global population) who were still predominantly pre-industrial farmers or hunter-gatherers.

Notably, the total population of nations occupied by industrial-scale NNR users – the global industrialized and industrializing population – numbered less than 350 million by the end of Industrialism1.

Industrialism1 NNR Supply

Virtually untapped reserves of high quality/low cost NNRs, both domestic and foreign, ensured rapid development for the industrial pioneers and the emerging second-generation industrializing nations during Industrialism1.

NNR Mix Industrial humanity's mix of NNR "building blocks" was extremely limited at the inception of Industrialism1, consisting of coal as the primary NNR energy source, basic industrial metals – iron, copper, lead, tin, and zinc – and basic nonmetallic minerals (industrial and construction minerals) such as cement, clay, gypsum, lime, sand & gravel, stone, and sulfur.

By the culmination of Industrialism1, the mix of NNRs being exploited on an industrial scale had expanded beyond basic industrial metals to include various alloys and specialty metals such as antimony, boron, arsenic, manganese, nickel, mercury – and steel.

Additionally exploited nonmetallic minerals included abrasives, barite, feldspar, fluorspar, graphite, soda ash, and sodium sulfate. And "rock oil" was emerging as a viable substitute for whale oil in kerosene lamps.

NNR Sources Given the extremely limited and primitive overland transportation infra-structure that existed in 1750, economically viable NNR supplies, especially those pertaining to bulky NNRs such as iron ore and coal, were almost exclusively sourced domestically – and in close proximity to processing and manufacturing facilities.

Accordingly, Great Britain, owing to its relatively abundant domestic NNR reserves, attained industrial supremacy during Industrialism1. During the 19th century:[7]

- Annual British coal extraction ranged between 60 percent and 90 percent of global totals.
- Annual British iron ore extraction represented 33 percent to 50 percent of global totals.
- Annual British copper and tin extraction averaged 50 percent of global totals.
- Annual British zinc extraction exceeded 25 percent of global totals.
- Britain was the world's leading producer of lead.

By the mid-19th century, however, the industrial pioneers – including Great Britain – had become increasingly reliant on imported NNRs, as their extensively depleted domestic NNR reserves failed to completely address their ever-increasing requirements.

Hewett made the following observation in 1929 regarding shifting European sources of economically viable NNRs between the early 17th century and the early 20th century,

> …it is impressive to note the shift in the last 300 years in the outstanding sources of iron from Sweden to England, then to Germany, and since the war [WW1] to France through the transfer of Lorraine. Similarly, districts in Norway, England, and Spain were successively outstanding sources of copper, and in England, Germany, and Spain, of lead.[8]

With respect to the increasingly NNR-deficient industrial pioneers, sources of NNR imports expanded initially to neighboring European nations, generally through trade, and ultimately to the rest of the world, through trade and colonial expropriation.

NNR Supplies As noted previously, initially available NNR supplies were extremely modest, owing to the limited scope and scale of industrial activity, and to the rudimentary stage of mining industry development at the inception of Industrialism1. As industrialism proliferated during the period, and NNR exploitation tools and techniques improved, NNR extraction, production, and utilization increased commensurately.

Table 5-2: Select Global NNR Extraction/Production Quantities and Growth Rates 1750 and 1875

NNR	1750	1875	1750-1875 CAGR
Coal (MT)	7,000,000	235,000,000	2.85%
Iron Ore (MT)	260,000	16,000,000	3.35%
Copper (MT)	10,000	115,000	1.97%
Lead (MT)	15,000	250,000	2.28%
Zinc (MT)	5,000	180,000	2.91%
Tin (MT)	4,500	21,000	1.24%
Cement (MT)	165,000	2,700,000	2.26%
Salt (MT)	220,000	6,000,000	2.68%
Sulfur (MT)	27,500	850,000	2.78%
Average CAGR			**2.48%**

Sources: Hewett, Lovering, and other.[9]
MT = metric tonnes.

With respect to the nine Core-20 NNRs for which relatively reliable data are available, global extraction/production increased significantly during Industrialism1 – at a 2.48% rate (on average) compounded annually. Specifically:

- Annual cement production increased by over 16 times – from 165,000 MT (metric tonnes) to 2,700,000 MT – or 2.26% compounded annually,
- Annual coal extraction increased by nearly 34 times – from 7 million MT to 235 million MT – or 2.85% compounded annually, and
- Annual iron ore extraction increased by nearly 62 times – from 260,000 MT to 16,000,000 MT – or 3.35% compounded annually.

Owing to rapidly increasing NNR extraction, production, and utilization during Industialism1:

- Global human prosperity improved at previously inconceivable rates – global GDP (economic output) increased by 1.19% compounded annually, while global pc GDP (the average material living standard) increased by 0.71% compounded annually, and
- Extensively depleted NNR reserves within the industrial pioneers – particularly Great Britain – culminated in Scarcity1.

Scarcity1 – Nature's Initial Warning

From 1750 to 1850, the United Kingdom mined over 50 percent of the world's lead; from 1820 to 1840, she produced 45 percent of the world's copper; from 1850 to 1890, she increased her iron production from one-third to one-half of the entire world output. It is interesting to note that this rapid exploitation of mineral reserves led to peak production for each of these minerals, followed by the inevitable decline that must be expected to accompany increasing costs with depth and by gradual exhaust-tion of the mineral deposits.[10] (Lovering)

Relative domestic NNR abundance among the industrial pioneers had prevailed throughout most of Industrialism1, and had enabled robustly improving prosperity – especially for Great Britain. By the latter years of Industrialism1, however, relative domestic NNR abundance had been displaced by increasingly pervasive domestic NNR scarcity.

Persistent and increasing depletion of their relatively modest NNR reserves had caused increasing domestic NNR shortfalls – and increasing NNR import reliance – for the industrial pioneers. By 1875, Great Britain was import-reliant with respect to all major industrial metals and coal – the fundamental enablers of industrial development at the time:[11]

- British zinc extraction peaked in approximately 1800 (first imports in the late 1700s).
- British copper extraction peaked in 1861 (first imports in 1826).
- British lead extraction peaked in 1870.
- British tin extraction peaked in 1871 (first imports in the 1850s).
- British iron ore extraction peaked in 1882 (first imports in 1865).

The result was industrial humanity's first episode of permanent NNR scarcity – Scarcity1 – which occurred between the mid/late 1860s and the early/mid 1870s. Scarcity1 was a geologically-induced phenomenon from which Great Britain and the other industrial pioneers would never fully recover.

By offering a localized preview of the inevitable fate that awaited industrial humanity, Nature had issued its initial warning to rapidly industrializing *Homo sapiens*. At the time, however, humankind was preoccupied with industrial growth, and paid little attention to the inherent limitations regarding the fundamental enablers of that growth. Scarcity1 and Nature's initial warning went unheeded.

The world was so vast and unexploited, and industrial humanity's 19th century NNR requirements were insignificant compared with Earth's seemingly unlimited NNR supplies. Had the concept of global NNR scarcity been considered, it would have been dismissed as a concern for thousands of years in the future.

It never occurred to anyone during the latter years of Industrialism1 that the permanently-debilitating, geologically-induced reality being imposed upon Great Britain and the other industrial pioneers – increasingly pervasive domestic NNR scarcity – would inevitably occur globally, and much sooner than anyone living in 1875 could have imagined.

Industrialism1 Industrial Productivity

For most of humanity's history, advances in technology, productivity, and real income per capita came very slowly and sporadically. But with the development of modern science in the 17th century and the quickening of technological innovation that it sparked, the stage was set for significant improvements in productivity.[12] (Wallace)

During Industrialism1, Nature's reinforcing "geological tailwind" – global NNR abundance – amplified human ingenuity efficacy. That is, an expanding array of NNR "building blocks" combined with generally decreasing NNR price trends encouraged the development and deployment of highly-impactful, productivity-increasing innovations and efficiency improvements – which produced extraordinary industrial productivity growth during the period.

Mining Sector Productivity

With the notable exception of the steam engine, NNR exploitation tools and techniques employed during the early years of Industrialism1 were generally labor-intensive and involved minimal mechanization – and therefore did little to improve mining sector productivity.

Visual inspection of Earth's surface (prospecting) was the primary NNR exploration technique employed during the mid/late 18th century, "Companies were mainly opportunistic, employing prospectors and limited exploration organization. Almost all discoveries were made at the surface in outcrops of bedrock, without the need for indirect technologies."[13] (Jébrak)

And given the nascent stage of mining and metallurgy development, early NNR extraction and processing techniques were also extremely rudimentary – consisting primarily of surface mining at shallow depths and smelting of the basic industrial metals.

As Industrialism1 and the fledgling mining industry evolved into the 19th century, however, mining sector productivity growth became increasingly robust. Newly-developed, increasingly-impactful NNR mining tools and techniques were increasingly based on science rather than intuition,

> The scientific approach of geology was developed during the nineteenth century, especially in Europe and America, and has been summarized several times (Ellenberger, 1994; Gohau, 1990; Rabinovitch, 2000). Geological principles slowly took prominence in the prospecting process. (For a long time, mineral deposits were considered an act of God, or the effect of exotic processes. Lower Canada was considered by some specialists during the reign of Louis XIV to be of poor mining potential because of the lack of warm sun, which was supposed as generating the gold deposits.) The book Principles of Geology by Charles Lyell in 1833 constituted a milestone for the emergence of a new discipline: the application of scientific knowledge to an industrial process…[14] (Jébrak)

Specific innovations that fostered mining sector productivity growth during Industrialism1 include Banská Štiavnica (the world's first mining school), the steam engine, the geological map, cyanidation, the miner's safety lamp, mass spectrometry, Portland cement, the power drill, petroleum refining, open hearth steel making, and dynamite.

Overall Industrial Productivity

> For the first 50 years after the beginnings of the Industrial Revolution in Britain around 1760, labour productivity grew at an average annual rate of around 0.5 percent, but it then accelerated to more than 1 percent in the 19th century.[15] (Wallace)

Overall industrial productivity growth, while initially modest, increased significantly during Industrialism1.

Table 5-3: Great Britain Industrial Productivity Growth 1760-1873

Productivity Indicator	1760-1780	1780-1831	1831-1873
Labor Productivity	.32%	.87%	1.05%
Total Factor Productivity	.13%	.53%	.58%

Source: Derived from Crafts[16]; compound annual growth rates.

Labor productivity growth more than tripled between early Industrialism1 and late Industrialism1 – increasing from 0.32% compounded annually between 1760 and 1780, to 1.05% compounded annually between 1831 and 1873.

And total factor productivity growth more than quadrupled between early Industrialism1 and late Industrialism1 – increasing from 0.13% compounded annually between 1760 and 1780, to 0.58% compounded annually between 1831 and 1873.

Relatively modest industrial productivity growth during the early years of Industrialism1 was likely attributable to the fact that "the initial impact of a GPT [General Purpose Technology] is either negligible or even possibly negative and that the delay before TFP [Total Factor Productivity] growth rises appreciably may be considerable."[17] (Crafts)

For example, "steam had a relatively small and long-delayed impact on productivity growth when benchmarked against later technologies such as electricity or ICT [Information and Communication Technology]".[18] (Crafts)

Specifically, "[t]he real price of steam power stayed high for many decades and, consequently, the build up of steam horsepower was very gradual with only 160,000 horsepower in use in 1830. At this time for most of the economy steam was irrelevant."[19] (Crafts)

Accordingly, "…it is unwarranted to expect that major technological breakthroughs will lead to more or less simultaneous increases in productivity."[2] (Mokyr)[20] (Crafts)

Still, the productivity-increasing innovations and efficiency improvements introduced during Industrialism1 revolutionized the production and provisioning of goods services. Craft guilds and the "putting out" system were displaced by factory-based mechanized production, which dramatically increased the variety, quantity, and quality of products and services available to industrializing populations, while simultaneously decreasing costs and prices.

Specific innovations and efficiency improvements that contributed to the comparably exceptional industrial productivity growth rates achieved during Industrialism1 include:[21]

Table 5-4: Industrialism1 Innovations and Efficiency Improvements

- The spinning jenny, which could spin eight cotton threads at one time.
- The spinning frame (water frame), which produced thousands of cotton threads at one time.
- The spinning mule, which combined the spinning jenny and the water frame, and revolutionized the quality of cotton thread.
- The power loom, which increased worker productivity by a factor of 40.
- The cotton gin, which increased worker productivity by a factor of 50.
- The steam engine, which enabled deeper mining, and countless stationary and mobile steam powered applications including the steam locomotive, the steam boat, and the steam ship.
- Innovations in iron processing such as the substitution of coke (coal) for charcoal (wood); and processes such as puddling, rolling, and hot blast, which enabled iron (and ultimately steel) to become a ubiquitous building material.
- The emergence of coal as the primary energy source – both for industrial applications (powering machinery and smelting metals) and for household uses (cooking and heating) – which dramatically increased industrial productivity and improved human quality of life.
- The introduction of mechanized machine tools such as the lathe, milling machine, and metal planer, which dramatically increased both the quantity and quality of factory produced goods.
- The development and proliferation of transportation infrastructure such as paved roads, canals, and railroads, which enabled the cost-effective transportation of NNRs and NNR-derived machines and products.
- The mass production of industrial materials such as Portland cement, sulfuric acid, and sodium carbonate (soda ash), which enabled affordable concrete, glass, and paper products.

Arguably the most transformative innovation introduced during Industrialism1 – and almost certainly during humanity's three-million-year history – was our capacity to exploit NNRs on an industrial scale.

Industrialism1 Outcomes

The new evidence confirms what has come to be called 'trend acceleration.' Somewhere around the 1820s Britain passed through a secular turning point. Growth in national income was much lower before than after: for example, Harley estimates the growth in per capita income at 0.33 percent per year 1770-1815 and 0.86 percent per year 1815-1841.[2] The doubling of the growth rate is apparent, too, in the indices of industrial production, which grew annually at 1.5 or 1.6 percent before 1815 and at 3.0 or 3.2 percent afterwards.[3] ... The turning point is even more dramatic in the standard of living: the adult, male, working-class real wage failed to increase between 1755 and 1819, but from 1819 to 1851 rose at an annual rate of 1.85 percent.[22] (Williamson)

Global human prosperity improved gradually during the early years of Industrialism1, owing to:

- Britain's lack of focus on industrialization during the late 18th and early 19th centuries, "Britain tried to do two things at once – industrialize and fight expensive wars, and she simply did not have the resources to do both. During the 60 years following 1760, Britain was at war for 36…" Accordingly, "British growth before the 1820s looks odd when set beside the conventional dating of the industrial revolution. There is no evidence of improvement in the standard of living among the working classes until the 1820s."[23] (Williamson)
- The paucity of industrialization initiatives launched by other resource-rich nations during the 18th century, "Prior to 1815 the German people lived in scores of small principalities which strove jealously against one another in an essentially feudal agricultural society. At this time all Europe seemed satisfied to sit back and continue its vegetable culture. Central Europe was held in bondage by poor communications, provincialism, selfishness, lack of co-operation, and illiteracy."[24] (Lovering)

By the 1820s, however, as relative peace and stability returned to Great Britain and much of the rest of the world, several "second-generation" nations – notably America, Germany, and France – launched industrialization initiatives. Human prosperity improved measurably and perceptibly, particularly in Great Britain, for the first time in human history. And a middle class emerged, also for the first time in human history.

Yet by 1875, owing to increasingly pervasive domestic NNR scarcity (Scarcity1), prosperity was diminishing among the industrial pioneers – particularly Great Britain, "Following the industrial revolution, trend growth in real [British] GDP per person peaked at about 1.25 percent per year in the mid-nineteenth century."[25] (Crafts and Mills)

And emerging second-generation industrializing nations – most notably America and Germany – were challenging Britain for global industrial supremacy.

Industrialism1 Human Prosperity

The improvement in human prosperity achieved during Industrialism1, particularly for Great Britain and the other industrial pioneers, was unprecedented in human history. For the first time since the emergence of genus *Homo*, rapidly increasing economic output (GDP) was sufficient to support both a significantly increasing human population and measurable improvement in the average human material living standard.

Humanity's industrial foundation, which was established during Industrialism1, consisted of an increasingly robust primary (mining) sector and secondary (manufacturing) sector. Tertiary (service) sector initiatives launched during the period generally supported primary sector and secondary sector activities.

Consumer products – luxury items for the elites and mass-produced, factory-built goods for the masses – became increasingly prevalent. And increasingly affluent middleclass population segments, whose demand for mass-produced consumer goods would drive industrialism into the 20th century and beyond, also proliferated during Industrialism1.

Industrialism1 Global Human Prosperity

Owing to industrialization initiatives launched by the industrial pioneers during the mid/late 18th century and by second-generation industrializing nations during the early/mid-19th century, global human prosperity metrics improved significantly during Industrialism1.

Table 5-5: Industrialism1 Global Human Prosperity Metrics

Human Prosperity Indicator	1750	1875	CAGR
Global Economic Output (GDP) [billion]	$129	$568	1.19%
Average Material Living Standard (pc GDP)	$178	$429	0.71%

Source: DeLong;[27] 1990 International $.

During Industrialism1 (1750-1875):

- Global GDP (economic output) increased by more than a factor of four – from an estimated $129 billion to $568 billion; the corresponding compound annual growth rate was 1.19%.
- Global pc GDP (the average material living standard) increased by a factor of 2.4 – from an estimated $178 to $429; the corresponding compound annual growth rate was 0.71%.

Industrialism1 British Prosperity

> In the nineteenth century, Great Britain was successively the world's largest producer of lead, copper, tin, iron, and coal. During that period she was the wealthiest nation in the world.[26] (Lovering)

At the inception of our industrial era in 1750, Britain's GDP accounted for 2.6% of global GDP. By 1875, British GDP had increased to 8.1% of the global total – a 3.1 times increase in global GDP share.[28]

In 1750, British pc GDP already stood at 2.6 times the global average, owing to the comparatively high British material living standard attained during the Second Agricultural Revolution, and to the economic foundation established during Britain's pre-industrial mercantilist era. By 1875, following a century of industrialization, however, British pc GDP had further increased to an extraordinary 4 times the global average.[29]

Despite its relatively small size and modest NNR reserves, Great Britain achieved dramatically increasing prosperity and retained global industrial supremacy during the 19th century, owing to increasing NNR imports from its extensive global trade network and its expanding colonial empire. These foreign NNR sources offset, albeit at greater costs, Britain's increasingly pervasive domestic NNR scarcity.

Historical Human Prosperity Comparisons

> In the modern age, we take for granted that the US will grow at 3.5% a year, and that the world economy grows at 4% to 4.5% a year. However, these are numbers that were unheard of in the 19th century, during which World GDP grew under 2% a year.

> Prior to the 19th century, annual World GDP growth was so little that changes from one generation to the next were virtually zero.[30] (The Futurist)

It is impossible to overstate the beneficial impact that industrialism has had on human prosperity. The lifestyles that we in the industrialized world consider "normal" – and a birthright – are anything but normal from humanity's historical perspective.

During humanity's 3,000,000-year hunter-gatherer era, human prosperity improved imperceptibly for millennia at a time. During humanity's 12,000-year agrarian era, human prosperity improvement remained negligible, and was certainly imperceptible on an intergenerational basis – especially for the general population.

During Industriialism1, however, human prosperity improved at rates that were both measurable and perceptible intergenerationally – and that were sufficient to benefit increasingly broad segments of the general population.

Table 5-6: Historical Human Prosperity Improvement Rates

Prosperity Indicator	HG Era	Agrarian Era	Industrialism1
Global GDP	Imperceptible	0.051%	1.19%
Global pc GDP	Imperceptible	0.006%	0.71%

Source: DeLong[31], Compound Annual Growth Rates.

During Industrialism1, as compared with humanity's agrarian era:

- The annual growth rate in global GDP (economic output) increased by a remarkable 23 times, from 0.051% to 1.19%.
- The annual growth rate in global pc GDP (the average material living standard) increased by a spectacular 118 times, from 0.006% to 0.71%.

That is, every year between 1750 and 1875, the increase in global economic output was 23 times greater (on average) than had been the case every year for the 12,000 years prior to 1750; and improvement in the average human material living standard was 118 times greater every year (on average) than had been the case every year for the 12,000 years prior to 1750!

Industrialism1 Human Cultural Circumstances

As the benefits attainable from industrialization became increasingly apparent during the early/mid-19th century, populations within other (primarily) Western nations endowed with similarly favorable natural environments established similarly favorable cultural environments, and launched similarly successful industrialization initiatives.

Most of these industrializing nations employed the Western Industrialization Model, which is characterized by varying combinations and degrees of:

- Political freedom – e.g., rule-of-law, individual liberty, private property, and "Bill of Rights" freedoms;
- Economic freedom – e.g., free markets, free trade, and entrepreneurism; and
- Societal freedom – e.g., freedom of expression, freedom of movement, freedom of religion, voluntary cooperation, and tolerance.

The Western Industrialization Model fosters the spontaneous development and deployment of productivity-increasing innovations and efficiency improvements, as the means by which to maximize economic output – and thereby optimize human prosperity and human cultural circumstances.

The benefits accruing to industrializing nations that employed the Western Industrialization Model were undeniable,

> This potential comparative advantage was increasingly realized across the nineteenth century, as ocean freight rates declined, as railroads linked port to interior, and as trade boomed. The result was large volumes of manufactured goods exported from what we will call the industrial core and, in exchange, large volumes of primary commodities imported from what we will call the poor periphery. (Benetrix, et al.)[32]

Industrialism1 Political Circumstances

Governments of industrializing nations typically encouraged and protected their fledgling domestic industrial enterprises by minimizing regulations on domestic commercial enterprises, by imposing tariffs on foreign goods, and by subsidizing domestic producers,

> In spite of being the world's foremost advocate of free trade, Britain found many ways to 'discourage' foreign commercial enterprise." For example, "…in 1750 the British Parliament passed a law to close all the mills and furnaces in the colonies in order to protect British manufacturers.[33] (Lovering)

Nations that failed to industrialize were typically constrained by governments that continued to impose onerous regulations on domestic commercial ventures, and often maintained exploitive control over internal economic and societal affairs. Wars – both trade wars and actual wars – also impeded industrial development, especially during the early years of Industrialism1,

> Meanwhile, war, blockades, and embargoes diminished international trade, inflating the relative prices of agricultural and raw material importables in the home market while lowering the price of manufactured exportables deflected from world markets.[34] (Williamson)

Notwithstanding instances of nationalism, protectionism, and cronyism, however, something akin to laissez-faire political circumstances generally prevailed within successfully industrializing nations between 1750 and 1875. Human ingenuity and initiative were encouraged by the rule-of-law, private property rights, and individual freedom.

Industrialism1 Economic Circumstances

> England's economy was based primarily on manufacturing and trade during most of the nineteenth century.[35] (Lovering)

The Second Agricultural Revolution had enabled Great Britain to create a sufficient real wealth surplus by the mid-18th century to fund the initial investments in mining, factories, machinery, and transportation infrastructure required to launch humanity's first industrial revolution.

Savings and investment, which were understood to be the basis for sound economic growth – i.e., previously created surplus wealth was invested in successful commercial ventures, thereby creating future wealth – were encouraged in Great Britain during Industrialism1,

> Feinstein's estimate of the rate of [British physical] capital formation also drifts upwards during the period [1760-1850]: in constant prices, the share of gross domestic investment in national income rises from about 9 percent in the 1760s to almost 14 percent in the 1850s; the rate of capital accumulation rises from 1 percent 1761-1800 to 1.7 percent per year 1801-1860; the capital per worker growth rate rises from 0.11 percent per year 1761-1830 to 0.88 percent per year 1830-1860.[36] (Williamson)

Great Britain's established banking system, commercial markets, and global trade network provided the economic framework within which abundant British industrial capital inputs could be profitably converted into infrastructure, machinery, product, and energy outputs. As a result, Britain became the production engine of the world during Industrialism1.[37]

Industrialism1 Societal Circumstances

Surplus farmers – a product of rural crowding (population pressure) and labor-saving agricultural innovations developed during the Second Agricultural Revolution – migrated to urban industrial centers to seek work in newly emerging factories.

Concurrently, an increasingly affluent middle class evolved, an extremely affluent industrial class evolved, and the elite class, who presided over successful industrializing nations, garnered tremendous economic, political, and military power.

Industrialism1 Human Responses

Undoubtedly the most profound cultural change that occurred during Industrialism1 was humanity's fundamental rethinking of the world – and of humanity's role in it. The primary thoughtway within industrializing nations became "unlimited human potential".

This notion was derived from the emerging cornucopian worldview;[38] which perceived no natural limits to human success, or to the global proliferation of human industrialism. The only perceived impediments to achieving universal human prosperity through global industrialism were constrained human ingenuity and human initiative.

Newly industrializing populations therefore viewed Nature (NNRs) as something to be harnessed – through human ingenuity (industrial productivity) – as the means by which to achieve continuously improving human prosperity.

Accordingly, it was presumed without question that, notwithstanding periodic shortages owing to temporary demand/supply imbalances, globally available, economically viable NNRs would remain sufficiently abundant to perpetuate human industrialism indefinitely.

By the end of Industrialism1 in 1875, increasingly exuberant, NNR-enabled, industrial humanity was evolving from exceptional to "exemptional". The notion that we uniquely ingenious *Homo sapiens* are exempt from the ecological laws of Nature that govern all "lesser" species was becoming ingrained in our cultural DNA.

Chapter 6:
Industrialism2 – Industrialism Proliferates

> The consequence of changing production technology was the rise of technological systems (Hughes, 1983, 1987). Again, some rudimentary systems of this nature were already in operation before 1870: railroad and telegraph networks and in large cities gas, water supply, and sewage systems were in existence. These systems expanded enormously after 1870, and a number of new ones were added: electrical power and telephone being the most important ones. The second Industrial Revolution turned the large technological system from an exception to a commonplace.[1] (Mokyr)

Industrialism2 – industrial humanity's second industrial revolution – spanned an often tumultuous century, from the 1870s (1875) to the 1970s (1973). Essentially an extension of Industrialism1, Industrialism2 was primarily a "Western" phenomenon featuring more industrializing nations, more NNR applications, more NNR "building blocks", more NNR sources, more NNR exploitation tools and techniques – and the eventual global proliferation of human industrialism.

During Industrialism2, industrialization initiatives were launched or accelerated by an increasing number of opportunistic nations, in which increasingly favorable cultural environments encouraged the aggressive exploitation of Earth's extraordinarily favorable natural environment.

Second-generation industrializing nations included America, Germany, and France, followed by Austria-Hungary, Russia, Japan, Canada, Australia, Italy, Spain, and most of the rest of Western Europe, followed by most of Eastern Europe.

In addition to seeking improved prosperity, which the industrial pioneers had clearly achieved during Industrialism1, second-generation industrializing nations were also driven to industrialize by fear – fear of being left behind.

By the mid-19th century, it had become obvious to the pre-industrial world that industrialism provided irrefutable economic, political, and military advantages to the industrial pioneers, especially Great Britain. The British Empire had continued to expand during the 19th century, and Britain's dominion over the seas was unquestioned at the time.

The need to challenge British industrial supremacy – or at least avoid becoming a colony – was a compelling motivator for second-generation industrializing nations. The major European powers and other nations that were able to launch industrialization initiatives during the mid/late 19th century, did so.

In essence, the second-generation industrializing nations had no choice – a military balance of power required an economic balance of power.

Industrial humanity also shifted its primary focus during Industrialism2 – from establishing the basic industrial foundation to manufacturing mass-produced, factory-built products targeted at increasingly affluent, middleclass, mass-market consumers.

In retrospect, despite the "disaster years" – the three decades between 1914 and 1945 that featured WW1, the global flu pandemic, the Great Depression, and WW2 – Industrialism2 proved to be industrial humanity's golden age. Global human prosperity – enabled by abundant globally available, economically viable NNRs – improved at previously inconceivable rates.

By the end of Industrialism2 in 1973, most Western nations were industrialized or becoming industrialized, and several Eastern nations, particularly Japan and the Asian Tigers – Taiwan, South Korea, Hong Kong, and Singapore – were in the process of industrialization or re-industrialization.

Humankind had landed a man on the moon, and our goal of achieving universal human prosperity through global industrialism appeared to be within reach – until increasingly pervasive global NNR scarcity (Scarcity3) became a reality.

Industrialism2 Operating Environment

> Thus, the latter half of the nineteenth century found central Europe with a well-developed transportation system, a skilled industrial population, plentiful supplies of excellent steam and coking coal, a huge reserve of satisfactory iron ore close to adequate transportation, all within a region where the artificial barriers caused by political boundaries had been eliminated.[2] (Lovering)

The most successful second-generation industrializing nations – with America being foremost – enjoyed both extremely favorable natural environments and extremely favorable cultural environments.

Moreover, all second-generation industrializing nations benefitted from the foundation that had been laid by the industrial pioneers during Industrialism1, and from the fact that the increasingly NNR-deficient pioneers had become vulnerable to emerging NNR-rich competitors.

Industrialism2 Natural Environment

Great Britain and the other industrial pioneers – the victims of Scarcity1 – occupied relatively small geographies and had extensively depleted their domestic NNR reserves by the end of Industrialism1. Accordingly, they had begun to experience faltering prosperity by the early years of Industrialism2,

> The United Kingdom is often considered to have been the hardest hit [by the Long Depression]; during this period it lost some of its large industrial lead over the economies of Continental Europe.[3] While it was occurring, the view was prominent

that the economy of the United Kingdom had been in continuous depression from 1873 to as late as 1896...[3] (Wikipedia)

The slowdown experienced by the industrial pioneers provided the needed catch-up opportunity for second-generation industrializing nations, some of which were far better endowed with natural capital and human capital.

Most second-generation industrializing nations – particularly Russia, America, Canada, Australia, Germany, and Austria-Hungary – were much larger than the industrial pioneers. Most possessed larger economically viable NNR reserves, abundant water resources and farmland, and favorable geographical attributes such as navigable terrain, inland waterways, and saltwater ports.

Also contributing to the success of second-generation industrializing nations was the emergence of NNRs that had not been exploited on an industrial scale during Industrialism1 – including steel and various alloys, aluminum, NPK (nitrogen, potassium, and phosphorous) fertilizer components, and petroleum (oil and natural gas).

These and other newly-exploited NNRs would revolutionize human prosperity during Industrialism2, in applications pertaining to agriculture, mining, energy, infrastructure, manufacturing, construction, transportation, communications, healthcare, consumer products, recreation – and war.

The second-generation industrializing nations that exploited their domestic natural environments most effectively – Germany and America – would equal or exceed Great Britain with respect to both economic output and industrial prominence by the beginning of WW1.

Industrialism2 Cultural Environment

"The great mineral resources of Russia were developed slowly in the nineteenth century."[4] (Lovering) [Note that industrial success is contingent upon both a favorable natural environment AND a favorable cultural environment.]

With respect to successful second-generation industrializing nations, sufficiently favorable (but varied) natural environments, enabled the establishment of sufficiently favorable (but varied) cultural environments, within which to launch or accelerate industrialization initiatives.

National unification initiatives – which fused provinces, fiefdoms, and city-states into national entities – created cohesive nation-states, which were better able to compete industrially than fragmented and often contentious sub-national entities.

Unification initiatives proliferated during the transition years between Industrialism1 and Industrialism2 – Italy (1861), America (reunification in 1865), Canada (1867), Austria-Hungary (1867), Italy (1871), Germany (1871), and later, Australia (1901). It was generally the case that national unification preceded successful industrial development.

It was also common for central governments to encourage industrialization within their respective nations – as the means by which to increase their global political and military power, and to increase tax revenues flowing into government coffers.

Government encouragement sometimes entailed ensuring relatively free markets and free trade, but more often involved protecting fledgling domestic commercial enterprises from foreign competition through tariffs, subsidies, monopolies, and cartels.

All second-generation industrializing nations – including America and Germany – engaged in various forms of domestic industrial protection and subsidization, which while serving the interests of the favored domestic industries, typically disadvantaged the general public by increasing prices and limiting choices,

> A protective tariff, of course, 'protects' one group at the expense of another. The higher price transfers an unnecessary load to some other part of the national economy.[5] (Lovering)

Last, but certainly not least, increasingly favorable national cultural environments nurtured human ingenuity, which was manifested by increasingly rapid industrial productivity growth.

Industrial productivity growth fostered the development of an expanding array of new NNR-based applications – and a corresponding increase in NNR requirements – and encouraged the development of increasingly impactful NNR exploitation tools and techniques with which to address those requirements.

Industrialism2 Enablers

> Growing industrialization, with its huge demand for raw materials, growing populations, and a desire for a higher standard of living were the immediate causes for the intensified search for resources [NNRs].[6] (Youngquist)

During Industrialism2, unparalleled human ingenuity enabled humankind to discover, invent, and produce more of everything – which engendered more NNR uses, NNR users, NNR "building blocks", NNR sources, and NNR exploitation tools and techniques. The consequence was ever-increasing global NNR exploitation, as the means by which to address industrial humanity's ever-increasing NNR requirements.

Industrialism2 NNRs

Humanity's NNR requirements increased rapidly during Industrialism2, owing to the rapidly increasing rate of industrial development during the late 19th century and the early/mid-20th century. Globally available, economically viable NNR supplies increased commensurately, owing to the rapidly expanding scope and scale of the global mining industry during the period.

Continuously decreasing NNR exploitation costs and price trends, enabled by continuously increasing global NNR quality, afforded relative global NNR abundance during Industrialism2 – until the end of the period.

Industrialism2 NNR Demand

The plethora of new innovations introduced during Industrialism2 combined with the rapid pace of global industrial expansion, dramatically increased humanity's requirements – uses and users – for NNRs and NNR-derived infrastructure, machines, products, energy, and services.

NNR Uses Rapid gains in the quantity and quality of NNR-based innovations during Industrialism2 increased both the productivity of and the output from the burgeoning industrial sector, and thereby improved the quality-of-life for increasingly affluent consumers.

Major Industrialism2 innovations ranged from telecommunications, the internal combustion engine, electrification, human flight, radio communications, and the automobile assembly line, to the electron microscope, the digital circuit, and the microprocessor.

Significant quality-of-life improving products introduced during the period included electrical appliances such as the vacuum cleaner, iron, toaster, washing machine, dishwasher, refrigerator, and microwave oven, and electronic entertainment devices such as the phonograph, radio, and television.

Many NNR-based applications developed during Industrialism2 – such as the telephone, the incandescent lamp, nylon, air travel, the digital computer, and the mobile telephone – benefitted both industry and consumers.

NNR Users "Prior to 1939, about 80 percent of the production of the twenty-eight chief minerals of commerce was consumed by the industries of only eight nations: the United States, Germany, France, the United Kingdom, the Soviet Union, Japan, Belgium, and Italy."[7] (Lovering)

The fact that most Western nations had fully industrialized during Industrialism2 significantly increased the industrialized segment of the global population by the end of the period. Conversely, despite industrialization initiatives launched by several (smaller) Eastern nations during the post-WW2 period, the industrializing segment of the global population had decreased significantly by the end of Industrialism2.

Table 6-1: Global Industrialization Status as of 1973 [million people]

Year	Industrialized	Industrializing	Pre-industrial	Total
By 1750	0 (0%)	14 (1.9%)	706 (98.1%)	720 (100%)
By 1875	41 (3.0%)	291 (22.0%)	993 (75.0%)	1,325 (100%)
By 1973	838 (21.3%)	129 (3.3%)	2,975 (75.4%)	3,942 (100%)

Sources: Kremer, Populstat, and World Bank.[8]

By 1973, over 21% of Earth's 3.9 billion human population occupied nations that could be considered industrialized, approximately 3% occupied nations that were in the process of industrialization, and over 75% of global humanity remained pre-industrial agrarian or hunter-gatherer.

Notably, the total population of nations occupied by industrial-scale NNR users – the global industrialized and industrializing population – had increased from less than 350 million to nearly 1 billion by the end of Industrialism2.

Industrialism2 NNR Supply

An expanding NNR mix, a broadening array of global NNR sources, and increasing globally available, economically viable NNR supplies were generally sufficient to address industrial humanity's ever-increasing NNR requirements during Industrialism2 – until Scarcity3.

NNR Mix During Industrialism2, industrial humanity's NNR mix expanded considerably beyond coal, basic industrial metals, and basic industrial and construction minerals, to include alloys, super alloys, specialty metals, catalysts, reagents, and synthetic fertilizers.

Oil and natural gas became increasingly important components of humanity's energy mix. Steel and aluminum came into common use as primary industrial metals, in addition to specialty metals such as chromium, cobalt, magnesium, molybdenum, nickel, platinum, rhenium, titanium, tungsten, vanadium, and uranium. The NNR-based fertilizers – urea (nitrogen), potash, and phosphate rock – were also first exploited on an industrial scale during this period.

These newly-exploited NNR "building blocks" broadened the range of available products, improved product quality, and decreased product costs and prices – and encouraged the development and deployment of an expanding array of productivity-increasing innovations and efficiency improvements.

NNR Sources "The Victorian era [mid/late 19th century] was the first large industrial global mining boom, supported by a colonial structure. For the first time, major financial and industrial groups were able to explore for ore all around the world."[9] (Jébrak)

During Industrialism2, NNR exploitation became a global phenomenon – out of necessity – and colonial possessions offered a decided advantage to nations that presided over colonial empires,

> In all the areas controlled by the great colonial empires of France, Belgium, Holland, and England, the commerce and capital of the mother country were favored and both German capital and German commerce found themselves in an inferior competitive position.[10] (Lovering)

By the early years of Industrialism2, increasingly pervasive domestic NNR scarcity within the industrial pioneers had significantly increased the importance of foreign NNR sources. Fortunately, decreasing international transportation costs and newly developed NNR exploitation tools and techniques had dramatically increased the economic viability associated with imported NNRs.

An expanding array of international mining ventures, which were established during the latter years of Industrialism1 and the early years of Industrialism2, capitalized on these positive developments,

> ...new companies formed in all the mining countries, especially in the British Empire. Many of these groups were destined to become leaders of the twentieth century: BHP was formed in 1863, Rio Tinto in 1873, Peñarroya in 1881, Gold Fields in 1887, Asarco in 1899, Inco in 1902, Cominco in 1906 and Dome mines in 1910 (Schodde and Hronsky, 2006).[11] (Jébrak)

Some second-generation industrializing nations – most notably America – also became significant sources of newly mined and refined NNRs during Industrialism2. By the end WW2 (1945), America had become the undisputed global leader with respect to NNR extraction and production:[12]

- Annual US coal extraction accounted for 49 percent of global extraction – US oil extraction for 68 percent and US natural gas extraction for 87 percent of global extraction totals respectively.
- Annual US iron ore extraction represented 56 percent of the global total, US copper 48 percent, US zinc 47 percent, US tin 46 percent, US lead 36 percent, and US bauxite 29 percent – the US also produced 67 percent of global steel and 52 percent of global aluminum.
- Annual US phosphate rock extraction accounted for 50 percent of the global total, and US potash extraction for 41 percent.
- Annual US cement and gypsum production stood at 35 percent of total global production, while US sulfur extraction accounted for 72 percent of the global total.

However, as had been the case with the industrial pioneers during Industrialism1, second-generation industrializing nations were increasingly forced to supplement their dwindling domestic NNR reserves with imported NNRs – which opened previously untapped global NNR frontiers,

> The geography of metal production changed significantly. Due to the opening of vast unexplored regions and advances in communications technologies, Africa and South America were explored by Western government agencies and mining companies. The BRGM [French Geological Survey] began mapping West Africa, and the USSR explored Northern Siberia. The United Nations were strongly involved in mineral exploration and contributed to several discoveries, especially in Latin America (Petaquilla, Los Pelombres).[13] (Jébrak)

By the end of Industrialism2 – owing to increasingly pervasive domestic NNR scarcity within all first-generation and second-generation industrializing nations – every continent except Antarctica was being extensively mined for NNRs. And, unsurprisingly, the exporting nations had become aware of the criticality – and value – associated with their NNR reserves,

Immediately following the decolonization era, nationalizations became increasingly common after 1960, leading to the expropriation of several foreign companies (32 between 1960 and 1969), particularly in South America (Chile, Peru, Bolivia, Brazil, Venezuela), Africa (Zaire, Zambia, Guinea, Madagascar, Mauritania), India and Indonesia. The acquisition of mines and on-site processing facilities by the state ended the colonial monopoly.[14] (Jébrak)

Most importantly, the inordinately high and persistently increasing NNR price trends being experienced by the end of Industrialism2, clearly indicated that Earth's untapped, high quality/low cost NNR frontiers were dwindling.

NNR Supplies Overall, industrialism2 was a period of relative global NNR abundance, during which annual global NNR extraction, production, and utilization increased extraordinarily.

Table 6-2: Select Global NNR Extraction/Production Quantities and Growth Rates 1875 and 1973

NNR	1875	1973	1875-1973 CAGR
Potash (MT)	450,000	18,900,000	3.89%
Phosphate Rock (MT)	300,000	111,000,000	6.22%
Coal (MT)	235,000,000	3,074,000,000	2.66%
Oil (Gbbls)	0.01	21.37	8.14%
Iron Ore (MT)	16,000,000	832,000,000	4.11%
Copper (MT)	115,000	6,920,000	4.27%
Lead (MT)	250,000	3,440,000	2.71%
Zinc (MT)	180,000	5,710,000	3.59%
Tin (MT)	21,000	238,000	2.51%
Nickel (MT)	1,000	710,000	6.93%
Chromium (MT)	2,500	2,030,000	7.08%
Manganese (MT)	25,000	9,740,000	6.28%
Cement (MT)	2,700,000	702,000,000	5.84%
Salt (MT)	6,000,000	155,000,000	3.37%
Sulfur (MT)	850,000	48,200,000	4.21%
Average CAGR			**4.79%**

Sources: Hewett, Lovering, USGS, BP Statistical Review, and IEA.[15]
MT = metric tonnes; Gbbls = gigabarrels.

With respect to the 15 Core-20 NNRs for which reliable data are available, global extraction/production increased at an extraordinary 4.79% rate (on average) compounded annually during Industrialism2 – versus 2.48% during Industrialism1. Examples of the extraordinary increases in NNR extraction and production that occurred during Indus-trialism2:

- Global phosphate rock extraction increased from 300 thousand metric tonnes in 1875 to 111 million metric tonnes in 1973 – a growth rate of 6.22% compounded annually.
- Global oil extraction increased from 10 million barrels in 1875 to over 21.37 billion barrels in 1973 – a growth rate of 8.14% compounded annually.
- Global iron ore extraction increased from 16 million metric tonnes in 1875 to 832 million metric tonnes in 1973 – a growth rate of 4.11% compounded annually.
- Global cement production increased from 2.7 million metric tonnes in 1875 to 702 million metric tonnes in 1973 – a growth rate of 5.84% compounded annually.

The extraordinary increases in global NNR utilization during Industrialism2 enabled similarly extraordinary increases in global human prosperity during the period (1875-1973):

- Global GDP (economic output) increased at 3.29% compounded annually – versus 1.19% compounded annually during Industrialism1, and
- Global pc GDP (the average material living standard) increased at 2.16% compounded annually – versus 0.71% compounded annually during Industrialism1.

The increases in global NNR utilization and resultant improvement in global human prosperity during the post-WW2 rebuilding period were particularly impressive – and never to be equaled. A compound annual growth rate of 6.5% in global NNR extraction/production between 1945 and 1973 yielded:[16]

- Spectacular global GDP (economic output) growth of 4.84% compounded annually, and
- Equally spectacular global pc GDP (the average material living standard) growth of 3.04% compounded annually.

The post-WW2 rebuilding period, which proved to be industrial humanity's "heyday", would also prove to be short lived,

> The second globalization corresponds to the post-war reconstruction era, between 1945 and 1971-1975, especially in Europe and Japan. The economic growth was largely driven by the automotive industry, along with other consumer goods that relied on electricity. This created an enormous demand, not only for basic metals such as copper, iron and bauxite-aluminum, but also for rare metals such as platinum, chromium and titanium, which were needed mainly by industries involved in aeronautics, nuclear power, spatial exploration and electronics. ... It was the glory years (Snow and Juhas, 2002). But then the US recorded its first global deficit in 1971 and the oil crisis exploded in 1973"[17] (Jébrak)

Industrialism2 culminated with Scarcity3, a geologically-induced NNR scarcity episode that signaled permanent NNR scarcity for the industrialized West – and the inception of increasingly pervasive NNR scarcity for the world as a whole.

Fortunately for industrialized Western nations and for Eastern nations that launched industrialization initiatives following WW2, several "final NNR frontiers" remained to be exploited during Industrialism3.

Industrialism2 NNR Scarcity

The extraordinary prosperity improvement enjoyed by industrial humanity during Industrialism2 was marred by two increasingly severe (and ominous) NNR scarcity episodes:

- Scarcity2 occurred between 1914 and 1916, by which time European NNR reserves had been extensively depleted, particularly in the run-up to and during WW1. Permanent European (regional) NNR scarcity ensued.
- Scarcity3 occurred between 1969 and 1980, by which time American and other Western NNR reserves had been extensively depleted, particularly during WW2 and the post-WW2 rebuilding period. Permanent Western (super-regional) NNR scarcity ensued.

The consequences from these two NNR scarcity episodes – initially for Europe, and ultimately for the industrialized West – included increasing reliance on costlier and riskier imported NNRs, faltering prosperity, and diminishing industrial prominence.

Scarcity2 – European NNR Scarcity "The gradual decline in European metal production [during the early years of Industrialism2] brought with it the threat of a return to the Dark Ages. The threat might have been realized had not new sources of mineral wealth been found in central Europe and, a little later, in Mexico and South America."[18] (Lovering)

Europe's share of total global mining peaked at approximately 60% during the early 1860s (notably, at about the time that Europe's share of global GDP peaked).[19] In 1875, approximately 56% of global (metals) mining occurred in Europe; by 1914, Europe's share of global mining had decreased to 29%; by 1945, to 15%; and by 1973, to 7%.[20]

While Europe's declining share of global mining was partially attributable to increasing mining activity in areas such as North America, South America, Africa, Oceania, and Asia, the decline was largely attributable to Europe's rapidly depleting NNR reserves,

> No one can review the record of European metal mining without being impressed (1) by the shifts in supply from one outstanding source to another during the past 125 years [1800-1925], (2) by the declines in production from most of the outstanding sources, and (3) by the declines in grades of ore treated.[21] (Hewett)

Great Britain, which, during Scarcity1, had been among the first nations to experience the adverse effects imposed by permanent domestic NNR scarcity – diminishing prosperity and industrial prominence – continued to feel the effects during Scarcity2,

> Britain had reached her peak in domestic mineral production [during the 19th century], except in coal [which peaked in 1913], and one of the factors in her commercial greatness had changed. She no longer had an abundance of cheaply mined high-grade ore close to manufacturing centers; and concomitant with increasing cost of mineral production, German, French, and American competition made itself felt in foreign markets.[22] (Lovering)

Other major victims of Scarcity2 included France, Italy, Spain, and Germany, which lacked significant NNR endowments, owing to unfavorable geology (Spain) or to relatively small geographies.

NNR extraction peaks became increasingly prevalent among European nations in the run-up to Scarcity2 (prior to WW1). Spanish iron ore extraction peaked in 1908; Austrian iron ore extraction peaked in 1913 – and Germany became a net importer of iron ore in 1898. German zinc extraction peaked in 1905, and Spanish copper and lead extraction peaked in 1912.[23]

According to Lovering's previously referenced Industrial Development Cycle analysis, in which he tracked industrial development through five stages, increasingly pervasive domestic NNR scarcity was seriously impeding industrial development in Europe's most powerful nations – Great Britain and Germany – prior to WW2:

> …in 1938, Rhodesia was in stage 1 [acceleration], Canada was entering stage 2 [inflection between acceleration and deceleration], the Soviet Union was near the end of stage 2 [pre-peak deceleration], the United States was nearly through stage 3 [peaking], **Germany was in stage 4 [post-peak decline], and Great Britain was in stage 5 [advanced post-peak decline].[24] (emphasis mine)**

Adversely impacted European central governments responded to their nations' deteriorating circumstances with increasing desperation,

> The immediate [1929] outlook for an increase in metal production in Europe is not encouraging, iron possibly being excepted. Whether her statesmen would admit it or not, much of European diplomacy seems to reflect concern over a downward tendency of production and attempts to extend control over it. It is small wonder that continental Europe is turning rapidly toward cartels and understandings – first, iron and steel, next mercury, aluminum and zinc, with lead and copper in the near distance.[25] (Hewett)

Nature's Second Warning As was the case with Scarcity1 and Nature's first warning, Scarcity2 – permanent European NNR scarcity – and Nature's second warning went essentially unheeded. The nearly universal lack of concern was due primarily to the rapid resolution of Scarcity2 – given the availability of abundant economically viable NNR imports from colonies and global trading partners.

Scarcity3 – Western NNR Scarcity Western industrialization initiatives launched during Industrialism1 and Industrialism2, which were initially enabled by domestically-sourced NNRs, were increasingly enabled by imported NNRs from colonies and resource-rich trading partners located in Canada, Australia, Latin America, Africa, and Asia.

By the end of Industrialism2, however, many of the high quality/low cost NNR reserves located within these foreign sources had been extensively depleted.

American Scarcity3 "The story [of America's industrialization] has been a spectacular one, and our material well-being is proof of the bounty won from the ground. But the record tells us too that [US] production of some metals is now [1979] declining and production of others grows less rapidly than our needs.

As a result, we are becoming more and more an importing country, less and less a producer and exporter of minerals. The pattern is familiar because it is one seen in the history of essentially all industrial countries – as their mining districts become depleted, foreign sources have to fill their needs."[26] (Skinner)

Unsurprisingly, Britain's experience with domestic NNR scarcity was replicated in America – with an approximate three-generation time lag. In 1873, approximately 17% of global (metals) mining occurred in the US. By 1914, the percentage had doubled to 35 percent; by 1945, it had further increased to 38 percent. By 1973, however, US mining had decreased to 18 percent of the global total.

America's share of total global mining activity peaked at nearly 40% in 1940[27] (notably, at about the time that America's share of global GDP peaked).[28]

Hewett had raised the specter of increasingly pervasive American NNR scarcity in 1929,

> Measured by district production curves, many of our [US] outstanding [mining] districts of a few years ago are showing signs of exhaustion, and we are sustaining or increasing national totals by turning quickly to new sources of lower grade. If science and technique can keep up the pace, we have no cause for concern. Personally, I doubt that they can much longer.[29]

Hewett was correct...

As had been the case with Great Britain during the 18th and 19th centuries, America's period of rapid industrial development during the 19th and 20th centuries had ravaged its domestic NNR reserves, thereby causing annual US extraction/production peaks during Industrialism2 with respect to the majority of industrially critical NNRs.

Table 6-3: Industrialism2 US Peak NNR Extraction/Production Years

Peak US Extraction Year	
Bismuth: Never Mined	Cobalt: 1958
Tantalum: Never Mined	Niobium: pre-1959
Graphite: 1907	Rubidium: pre-1959
Silver: 1916	Tellurium: 1960
Manganese: 1918	Thorium: 1961
Bauxite: 1943	Titanium Mineral Concentrates: 1964
Magnesium Metal: 1943	Indium: 1966
Mercury: 1943	Magnesium Compounds: 1966
Mica: 1943	Helium: 1967
Strontium: 1943	**Potash: 1967**
Arsenic: 1944	Sodium Sulfate: 1968

Table 6-3: Industrialism2 US Peak NNR Extraction/Production Years (cont.)

Peak US Extraction Year	
Fluorspar: 1944	Cadmium: 1969
Tin: 1945	Selenium: 1969
Antimony: 1948	**Zinc: 1969**
Iron Ore: 1953	**Oil (Conventional): 1970**
Lithium: 1954	**Lead: 1970**
Tungsten: 1955	**Steel: 1973**
Chromium: 1956	Vermiculite: 1973

Sources: USGS and ASPO;[30] **Core-20 NNR = Bold.**

Unsurprisingly, Lovering's Industrial Development Cycle analysis indicated that increasingly pervasive domestic NNR scarcity had begun to adversely impact US industrial development prior to WW2,

> ...in 1938, Rhodesia was in stage 1 [acceleration], Canada was entering stage 2 [inflection between acceleration and deceleration], the Soviet Union was near the end of stage 2 [pre-peak deceleration], **the United States was nearly through stage 3 [peaking]**...[31] **(emphasis mine)**

Global Scarcity3 "By the 1970s, the development of airborne geophysics had produced a peak in the [NNR] discovery rate all around the world..."[32] (Jébrak)

Scarcity3 was the first geologically-induced NNR scarcity episode that adversely affected human prosperity at the global level. Moreover, Scarcity3 marked the inception of increasingly pervasive NNR scarcity at the global level.

Industrial humanity's significantly increasing NNR requirements during WW2 and the post-WW2 rebuilding period had compelled the global mining industry to exploit lower quality/higher cost NNRs, which caused significantly increasing NNR price trends during the 1970s,

> AN EXTRAORDINARY increase in commodity prices occurred in 1973-74. Even leaving aside crude oil as a special case, primary commodity prices on one index more than doubled between mid-1972 and mid-1974...[33] (Cooper and Lawrence)

Interestingly, Scarcity3-induced NNR price trend increases would have been even more substantial and protracted in the absence of above-ground NNR reserves that were brought to market during the mid-1970s,

> The metal prices were additionally depressed by large sales between mid-1973 and mid-1974 from the US government's strategic stockpiles, and in late 1974 from excessive commercial stocks in Japan that had been built up in the preceding year (Cooper and Lawrence, 1975).[34] (Radetzki)

Moreover, while the 1970s oil shocks certainly exacerbated the effects of Scarcity3, oil was hardly the only NNR to experience a significant price trend increase during Scarcity3, nor was oil the catalyst for Scarcity3, "Energy prices rose significantly only at the end of 1973, later than the prices of other commodities..."[35] (Radetzki)

Fortunately for industrial humanity, the Scarcity3-induced NNR price trend increases were transitory. Inordinately high NNR prices during the 1970s caused NNR demand destruction and resultant decreasing NNR prices by the early 1980s – but not before the inordinately high NNR prices had caused a decade of national and global economic recessions.

On the supply side, increasing NNR price trends also triggered an extensive NNR exploration effort by the global mining industry. Earth's final NNR frontiers were targeted as a result, which temporarily alleviated global NNR supply shortages.

By the end of Industrialism2, however, it had become clear (to some) that Scarcity3 had revealed a fundamental change with respect to global NNR demand/supply dynamics,

> The sharp increase in commodity prices in 1973 was cause for widespread anxiety and even alarm. It was for many a new and unusual development that seemed to support a number of fears that were current concerning the exhaustion of resources and the acceleration of inflation.[36] (Cooper and Lawrence)

Nature's Squeeze Scarcity3 marked a pivotal geologically-based transition – from relative global NNR abundance (Nature's Stimulus) to increasingly pervasive global NNR scarcity (Nature's Squeeze).

Nature's Squeeze is the irreversible geologic/economic process by which increasingly pervasive global NNR scarcity – as manifested by permanently increasing price trends associated with an increasing number of NNRs – causes faltering global human prosperity, deteriorating human cultural circumstances, and the unraveling of human industrialism.

The transition from Nature's Stimulus to Nature's Squeeze, which occurred in conjunction with Scarcity3, was unambiguously indicated by permanently reversing secular (long term) NNR price trends:

- Generally decreasing NNR price trends, caused by Nature's Stimulus, were observed by Hewett in 1929, "Since 1800 the trend of prices for the common metals, measured not only by monetary units but by the cost of human effort, has been almost steadily downward in all the countries considered."[37]
- Generally increasing NNR price trends, caused by Nature's Squeeze, were observed by Jacks in 2018, "real commodity prices of both energy and non-energy commodities have been on the rise from 1950..."[38]

Nature's Third Warning Notwithstanding the disaster years, Industrialism2 proved to be industrial humanity's golden age; it was also arguably the most profoundly impactful century in human history. The human experience had literally evolved from horses and buggies to lunar landings in less than 100 years.

The extraordinarily favorable global natural environment that prevailed during Industrialism2 had enabled the establishment of increasingly favorable cultural environments within a multitude of industrializing nations. The result was approximately 100 years of historically unprecedented human prosperity improvement.

Yet the culmination of Industrialism2 marked the most profoundly impactful inflection point in industrial human history – and in human history more broadly.

With the advent of Scarcity3 and Industrialism3, global human prosperity has begun to falter. That is, while global GDP (economic output) and global pc GDP (the average material living standard) have continued to increase during Industrialism3, they have increased at decreasing rates – the trend in global human prosperity improvement has decelerated.

Through Scarcity3, Nature issued its third warning – a fundamental discrepancy exists between humanity's anthropocentric perspective regarding the future of human industrialism and ecological (geological) reality.

However, as was the case with Nature's previous warnings regarding the inevitably catastrophic consequences associated with increasing NNR scarcity, Nature's third warning went essentially unheeded.

Anthropocentric humanity's concerns regarding Scarcity3 were generally focused on its cultural environment manifestations – the "oil shocks", economic recessions, and "stagflation" during the mid/late 1970s – rather than on the broader implications of increasingly pervasive global NNR scarcity for the future of human industrialism and industrial humanity.

Industrialism2 Industrial Productivity

Technical change was especially apparent with the introduction of electricity and its applications, and included communications (the telephone and telegraph), transport, and much more. The introduction of the railroad led to a steep decline in the costs of moving freight, and there were further dramatic drops in the costs of ocean shipping following the introduction of steamships. Data from O'Rourke and Williamson imply a drop in costs of transport between the U.S. and Europe from about 80 per cent of the price of the commodity to less than 20 percent during that period [early Industrialism2].[39] (International Monetary Fund)

Nature's increasingly-reinforcing "geological tailwind" – relative global NNR abundance – further amplified human ingenuity efficacy during Industrialism2. That is, our expanding mix of NNR "building blocks" combined with generally decreasing NNR price trends encouraged the development and deployment of myriad highly-impactful, productivity-increasing innovations and efficiency improvements during the period. The result was rapid industrial productivity growth.

Mining Sector Productivity

While reliable mining sector productivity data is not available prior to 1970, mining sector productivity research pertaining to the pre-1970 period "does provide strong circumstantial evidence that the positive, cost-reducing elements of productivity must, for the most part, have grown sufficiently strongly to have offset the negative, cost-increasing effects of depletion (Barnett & Morse 1963; Manthy 1978; Barnett 1979; Humphreys 2013)."[40] (Humphreys)

Notwithstanding a brief lapse in innovation during the disaster years, NNR exploration, extraction, and refining tools and techniques improved extraordinarily during Industrialism2 – evolving from rudimentary during the early years, to scientifically-based, automated, and computerized by the end of the period,

> It is a common assumption that wartime yields growth in the mining industry. The downturn of the economy from 1918 to 1945, marked by two World Wars, clearly shows that this is not the case. A lack of investment in knowledge and exploration, and the slowing rise in the consumption of metals, led to a period with few innovations in mining and mineral exploration. However, fundamental discoveries in physics, mainly in the Western world, and chemistry, mainly in the communist world (Goldschmidt, 1937; Suess, 1988), were preparing the ground for the revolution in the second part of the twentieth century in the new fields of geophysics and geochemistry.[41] (Jébrak)

Industrialism2 NNR Exploration During Industrialism2, NNR exploration evolved from an intuitive, labor-intensive process suitable for discovering easily detectable NNR deposits at Earth's surface, to a set of scientifically-based principles and processes designed to locate previously undetectable subsurface NNR deposits.

Productivity-increasing NNR exploration innovations that contributed to this evolution include:

- Spectroscopy – mineral analysis based on the absorption and emission of electromagnetic radiation.
- Geophysics – quantitative analysis of Earth processes pertaining to mineral formation and location.
- Airborne geological survey techniques.
- Stratigraphy and sedimentology – the study of rock layers and sediments and their formation.
- Radiometry – mineral analysis using electromagnetic radiation.
- Lithogeochemistry – mineral analysis based on chemical composition.
- Computer analysis of NNR formations and field data.

As a consequence of these and other NNR exploration-related innovations developed during Industrialism2, "(g)eological reasoning began to challenge surface prospecting as new deposits were discovered hidden underground."[42] (Jébrak)

Industrialism2 NNR Extraction The size, scale, and complexity with respect to mining operations increased significantly during Industrialism2, as did the size, scale, and complexity with respect to NNR mining equipment.

Productivity-increasing NNR extraction-related innovations deployed during Industrialism2 include the steam shovel, compressed air drilling, nitroglycerine, and rotary drilling. Dynamite, which had been invented in 1867, became essential to the "drill and blast" mining technique employed increasingly during Industrialism2.

The continuous miner, which extracts "soft" NNRs such as coal, in the absence of explosives, and the hard rock tunnel boring machine, which extracts NNRs from hard rock formations, also in the absence of explosives, became commercially viable during the 1940s and 1950s.

These and other massive, complex, and costly machines are indicative of the NNR extraction-related productivity revolution that occurred during Industrialism2. As an example of the tangible benefits attributable to this revolution, drilling technology employed in 1907 produced a drilling rate of 3.5 meters/hour; by 1973 the drilling rate had increased to 65 meters/hour.[43]

Industrialism2 NNR Refining NNR refining innovations and efficiency improvements deployed during Industrialism2 increased the effectiveness with which targeted NNRs are separated from their naturally-occurring states, thereby improving output-to-input ratios (industrial productivity growth).

For example, "(t)he gradual improvement in oil refining allowed the production of three times as much gasoline from a barrel of oil in 1940 as was possible twenty years before."[44] (Jébrak)

Other productivity-increasing, NNR refining-related tools and techniques developed during Industrialism2 include:

- Wilfley tables, which perform gravity separation for NNRs such as stone, gravel, and sand;
- Froth flotation, which separates and concentrates NNRs such as copper, lead, and zinc;
- The Hall-Heroult process, which economically separates aluminum from its bauxite ore ["In 1856 aluminum cost $90 per pound, but by 1886, thanks to the Hall-Heroult process (as it is known today), its price plummeted to thirty cents per pound."[45] (Sass)]; and
- The Haber Bosch process, which "fixes" nitrogen for use in fertilizers by producing ammonia from methane feedstock.

As a consequence of these and other NNR exploration, extraction, and refining innovations,

> ...mine size increased dramatically over the twentieth century, being both facilitated by, as well as creating opportunities for, the deployment of larger and larger equipment. Almost certainly, it was a major contributor to improvements in mine productivity.[46] (Humphreys)

Finally, transformative mining sector efficiency improvements pertaining to human capital also emerged during Industrialism2. In addition to an increasingly skilled workforce,

> ...it seems highly probable that a key element in boosting [mining sector] productivity lies in the ability of management to pull all the various factors of production, capital, labour and intermediate products together in an effective and disciplined fashion.[47] (Humphreys)

Overall Industrial Productivity

Despite the disaster years from WW1 to WW2, industrialized and industrializing nations achieved extraordinary – albeit varying – industrial productivity growth during Industrialism2, at rates that far-exceeded those achieved during Industrialism1.

Table 6-4: Industrialized and Industrializing Nation Labor Productivity* Growth 1870-1973

Productivity Indicator	1870-1913	1913-1950	1950-1973
US Labor Productivity	2.0%	2.4%	2.5%
5-Country** Labor Productivity	1.6%	1.6%	5.3%

*Labor productivity is defined as real GDP per hour worked.
**The five countries are France, Germany, Japan, Netherlands, and the UK.
Source: Wallace[48]; compound annual growth rates.

Between 1870 and 1913: "By the latter part of the 19th century the countries of western Europe, the United States, and Japan enjoyed a marked and sustained rate of improvement in productivity generally exceeding that of Britain, the earlier leader."[49] (Wallace)

Between 1870 and 1950: "Data for 10 additional industrialized countries indicated that much the same range of productivity growth rates prevailed for the smaller western European countries and for Canada and Australia. But much of the rest of the world had not yet begun to experience sustained growth of productivity and real per capita income."[50] (Wallace)

Between 1950 and 1973: "Growth of productivity in countries other than the United States accelerated greatly after World War II. The five-country average rate of growth in labour productivity more than tripled in the 1950–73 period compared with the preceding 80 years."[51] (Wallace)

Also between 1950 and 1973: "Of even wider importance, most nations outside the original industrialized group also began to record substantial increases in labour productivity beginning around 1950. What fragmentary information is available indicates that generally low rates of productivity growth were the norm in those countries before 1950. So World War II was a true watershed, in that after the immediate postwar period of reconstruction, most nations were able to accelerate their productivity gains markedly."[52] (Wallace)

While the US maintained leadership in industrial productivity growth during the early/middle years of Industrialism2, many/most other industrialized and industrializing nations surpassed the US during the post-WW2 period.

Nations that had been devastated by WW2 were rebuilt during the post-war years with the assistance of newly established global institutions and conventions such as the World Bank (WB), International Monetary Fund (IMF), and the General Agreement on Tariffs and Trade (GATT) – and with American financial aid, technology transfers, and physical capital transfers (most of which was state-of-the-art).

The Paradox of Industrial Productivity

Productivity-increasing innovations and efficiency improvements developed and deployed during our industrial era have demonstrably increased the effectiveness with which NNRs are utilized – that is, such innovations have dramatically increased the units of economic output derived from each unit of NNR-based economic input.

Concurrently, these innovations have dramatically increased annual NNR extraction and utilization, and have thereby dramatically accelerated NNR reserve depletion. This phenomenon – Jevons' Paradox – was first documented by economist William Stanley Jevons in 1865,[53] with respect to coal utilization in steam engines.

A broad array of innovations had occurred in steam engine technology during the hundred years between the 1760s, when James Watt introduced the first commercially viable steam engine, and the 1860s. These innovations had significantly increased steam engine efficiency – i.e., the work performed per steam engine per ton of coal burned.

Predictably, increases in steam engine efficiency caused commensurate increases in the number of steam engine applications, in the number of steam engines sold, and in the total extraction and utilization of coal to fuel these steam engines. Paradoxically, human ingenuity applied to steam engine innovation had caused an extraordinary increase – on the order of 30 times – in annual global coal extraction during the period.

The critical point is that Jevons' Paradox applies to all NNRs. Human ingenuity applied to industrial products and processes, which often produce extraordinary increases in NNR utilization effectiveness "per unit", typically increase – often extraordinarily – the number of units sold, and thereby cause extraordinary increases in total NNR quantities extracted and utilized.

Viewed from the ecological perspective – paradoxically, in the process of improving our CURRENT prosperity through the development and deployment of highly-impactful, productivity-increasing innovations, we simultaneously undermine our FUTURE prosperity and hasten our demise, through accelerated NNR depletion.

Industrialism2 Outcomes

> That the earth could maintain a thousand billions of people as easily as a thousand millions is a necessary deduction from the manifest truths that, at least so far as our agency is concerned, matter is eternal and force must forever continue to act.[54] (Henry George in 1879)

Henry George's comment captures the spirit of exuberance that prevailed during Industrialism2. No challenge was beyond the capacity of human ingenuity and initiative; no problem was unsolvable. Viewed from the anthropocentric perspective, the potential for industrial *Homo sapiens* was literally unlimited!

Early Industrialism2 The pre-WW1 years of Industrialism2 featured exceptional human innovation and global industrial proliferation, as rapidly improving prosperity in America and other second-generation industrializing nations more than offset faltering prosperity among the industrial pioneers. Accordingly, global human prosperity improved at historically unprecedented rates during the period.

It was also during the pre-WW1 years that global industrial leadership – and NNR extraction leadership – passed from Great Britain to America,

> Thus in 1900 Great Britain gave place to the United States as the world's foremost producer of the two minerals most essential to our industrial economy [coal and iron ore].[55] (Lovering)

Middle Industrialism2 The middle years of Industrialism2 – the "disaster years" between WW1 and WW2 – featured a series of natural and human-caused global disasters, specifically WW1, the 1918/19 global influenza pandemic, the Great Depression, and WW2.

Remarkably, despite this formidable series of catastrophes, the rate at which global human prosperity improved during the disaster years exceeded that of Industrialism1. More remarkably, both American industrial supremacy and the rate of American prosperity improvement peaked during this otherwise dismal period.

Late Industrialism2 The latter years of Industrialism2 – the post WW2 rebuilding period – featured renewed rapid global industrial development and human prosperity improvement and renewed human optimism and innovation.

The post-WW2 years were characterized by pent up demand for improved material living standards, which had been suppressed for decades during the disaster years. The resultant rebuilding boom produced the greatest prosperity surge in human history – and severely taxed already extensively depleted Western NNR reserves.

The latter years of Industrialism2 also marked the emergence of the industrializing East, with the birth of the Japanese "economic miracle" and the launching of industrialization initiatives by the Asian Tigers.

Interestingly (and ominously), the rate of global human prosperity improvement peaked during the latter years of Industrialism2, which culminated with Scarcity3 and the first "oil shock". Industrial humanity had experienced its "heyday" during the latter years of Industrialism2.

Industrialism2 Human Prosperity

> We found that, in U.S. history, each generation has passed to the next improved conditions of natural resource availability and economic productivity. Moreover, the phenomena of accumulated knowledge, scientific advances, and self-generating technological change have more than overcome tendencies of increasing costs for utilization and exhaustion of specific resources.[56] (Smith)

The rate of global human prosperity improvement achieved during Industrialism2 far exceeded that of Industrialism1. And while prosperity improvement achieved by America and other NNR-rich, second-generation industrializing nations generally exceeded global averages, such was typically not the case for the increasingly NNR-deficient industrial pioneers – and for Europe more broadly.

Industrialism2 Global Human Prosperity

Owing to the industrialization initiatives launched by myriad (primarily Western) nations during the early years of Industrialism2, and by several (primarily Eastern) nations during the latter years of Industrialism2, global human prosperity improved extraordinarily during the period, despite the disaster years.

Table 6-5: Industrialism2 Global Human Prosperity Metrics

Human Prosperity Indicator	1875	1973	CAGR
Global GDP (billion)	$568	$13,530	3.29%
Global pc GDP	$429	$3,484	2.16%

Sources: DeLong and World Bank;[57] 1990 International $.

During Industrialism2 (1875-1973):

- Global GDP (economic output) increased by nearly 24 times – from an estimated $568 billion to $13,530 billion; the corresponding compound annual growth rate was an extraordinary 3.29%.
- Global pc GDP (the average material living standard) increased by approximately 8 times – from an estimated $429 to $3,484; the corresponding compound annual growth rate was a remarkable 2.16%.

Most remarkable was the 1945-1973 post-WW2 rebuilding period, during which "...the world economy embarked upon a quarter century of sustained and unprecedentedly rapid economic growth"[58] (Krueger)

Global GDP (economic output) increased by an astounding 4.84% compounded annually during the period, while global pc GDP (the average material living standard) increased by an equally astounding 3.04% compounded annually – rates that would never be equaled.

And while the rate of global human prosperity improvement achieved during Industrialism1 dwarfed that of humanity's agrarian era, it paled in comparison to the rate achieved during Industrialism2.

Table 6-6: Historical Global Human Prosperity Improvement Rates

SW Indicator	Agrarian Era	Industrialism1	Industrialism2
Global GDP	0.051%	1.19%	3.29%
Global pc GDP	0.006%	0.71%	2.16%

Sources: DeLong and World Bank[59]; compound annual growth rates.

During Industrialism2, as compared with Industrialism1:

- The compound annual growth rate in global GDP (economic output) nearly tripled, from 1.19% to 3.29%.
- The compound annual growth rate in global pc GDP (the average material living standard) more than tripled, from 0.71% to 2.16%.

America Attained Industrial Supremacy

By the late 1920s, the United States, with six percent of the world population, was producing 70 percent of the world's oil, almost 50 percent of its copper, 46 percent of its iron, and 42 percent of its coal.[13] The ability to produce and use these basic industrial materials and energy resources was the key to the phenomenal rise of the United States.[60] (Youngquist)

America's then-abundant Earth resources were being exploited aggressively by the inception of Industrialism2 – the inevitable consequence was extraordinary improvement in American prosperity during the period.

Table 6-7: Industrialism2 American Human Prosperity Metrics

Human Prosperity Indicator	1875	1973	CAGR
US GDP (million)	$159,500	$5,690,900	3.71%
US pc GDP	$3,506	$26,851	2.10%

Source: Measuring Worth;[61] 2012 USD.

During Industrialism2 (1875-1973):

- America's GDP (economic output) increased by an extraordinary 35.6 times – from an estimated $159.5 billion to $5,690.2 billion; the corresponding compound annual growth rate was an equally extraordinary 3.71%.
- America's pc GDP (average material living standard) increased by 7.7 times – from an estimated $3,506 to $26,851; the corresponding compound annual growth rate was an extremely robust 2.10%.

American GDP accounted for 8.6% of global GDP in 1875; the percentage doubled to 16.7% by 1914, and further increased to an extraordinary 26.1% by 1945 (By some estimates, 1945 US GDP exceeded 40% of the global total.[62]) – before decreasing to 20.6% of global GDP by 1973.[63]

A similar trend occurred with respect to American pc GDP, which stood at 2.7 times the global average in 1875, increased to 3 times the global average by 1914, and further increased to a remarkable 4.4 times the global average in 1945 – before decreasing to 3.7 times the global average in 1973.[64]

Interestingly, while American industrial supremacy persisted throughout Industrialism2, and beyond, American prosperity had already begun to falter during the latter years of the period.

US GDP growth peaked during the 1914-1945 period at 4.32% compounded annually, and US pc GDP growth peaked at 3.17% compounded annually during the same period.

Ironically, while the compound annual growth rates pertaining to both US GDP and US pc GDP peaked during the disaster years of Industrialism2, it not the case that these were America's "best years" with respect to quality of life.

America's extraordinary prosperity improvement during the disaster years was largely attributable to the production of war materiel in support of WW2. In essence, America's highest quality/lowest cost NNRs were utilized to arm the Allies against the Axis powers, rather than to improve the quality of American life.

Europe Faltered while Japan Emerged

Western Europe (including Great Britain) clearly dominated the industrializing world in 1875, accounting for approximately 33% of global GDP. This percentage remained relatively constant until the beginning of WW1 in 1914, owing to successful industrialization initiatives launched by Germany, France, Italy, and other Western European nations.[65]

Western Europe's industrial dominance during the early years of Industrialism2 is further illustrated by the region's prodigious share of global industrial production,

> By 1900, the leader in industrial production was Britain with 24% of the world total, followed by the US (19%), Germany (13%), Russia (9%) and France (7%). Europe together accounted for 62%.[66] (Wikipedia)

Increasingly NNR-deficient Western Europe saw its economic dominance wane during the disaster years, however, as its share of global GDP decreased steadily until it reached parity with America at 26% by the end of WW2. Europe's share of global GDP further decreased during the post-WW2 period, reaching approximately 25% of the global total by the end of Industrialism2.[67]

Japan, on the other hand, commenced (or revived) its "economic miracle" during the post-WW2 rebuilding period. Japanese GDP increased extraordinarily – from 1.9% of global GDP in 1945 to 6.8% in 1973. Similarly, Japanese pc GDP increased from only 60% of average global pc GDP in 1945 to 2.4 times the global average in 1973.[68]

Japan's emergence as a future industrial power was a precursor to the many transitions that occurred with the transition from Industrialism2 to Industrialism3 – in this case, the West-to-East transition with respect to rapid industrial development and human prosperity improvement.

Industrialism2 Human Cultural Circumstances

Our extraordinarily favorable global natural environment – which featured seemingly unlimited high quality/low cost NNR reserves – fostered an attitude of limitlessness and exuberance during Industrialism2, particularly in the West, and most particularly in America.

By the latter years of Industrialism2, the prevailing attitude among most industrialized and industrializing populations was that things had never been better – and that our political, economic, and societal circumstances would continue to improve rapidly for the indefinite future.

Industrial humanity had successfully emerged from the disaster years following WW2, and was enjoying industrialism's "heyday". We had proven that all problems could be solved by human ingenuity – and that we industrial *Homo sapiens* were "exemptional". Or so we thought...

Industrialism2 Political Circumstances

While support for individual rights and free trade during the early years of Industrialism2 varied considerably among industrialized and industrializing nations, central government attitudes toward industrialists were generally conciliatory at best and impartial at worst.

British and American central governments played limited roles with respect to industrial development, typically acting as facilitators. Such governments sought to establish favorable cultural environments within which domestic commercial enterprises would prosper, enormous wealth would be created, and global political power would accrue to the incumbent ruling elites.

By the inception of WW1, however, the positive relationships between governments and industry had become strained. "Big business" was increasingly portrayed and perceived as an exploiter of the working class, and workers – the voting public – turned to increasingly interventionist central governments to redress their grievances.

Given the "emergency powers" ceded to – or seized by – most central governments during WW1 and the Great Depression, it was a natural progression for the role of government to expand from that of a referee to that of a guarantor of "welfare" for all citizens.

The surplus wealth required to promise previously inconceivable social welfare benefits – and to buy popular support and increased government influence in the process – seemed to exist within an increasing number of successful industrialized and industrializing nations by the middle years of Industrialism2. And so, the "welfare state" was born.

Subsequently, given the incremental "emergency powers" ceded to – or seized by – most central governments during WW2, it was a natural progression for the role of government to expand from that of a guarantor of basic human rights for all citizens to that of a guarantor of "security" for all citizens.

The surplus wealth required to promise previously inconceivable levels of security from all external threats, real and imagined – and to buy popular support and increase government influence in the process – seemed to exist within an increasing number of successful industrialized and industrializing nations by the post-WW2 years of Industrialism2. And so, the "warfare state" was born.

Industrialism2 Economic Circumstances

During the course of Industrialism2, central governments used their expanding political powers to intervene increasingly in the economic affairs of their respective nations. As a result, the economic systems within most industrialized and industrializing nations became increasingly intertwined with their political systems – inextricably intertwined in many cases.

Relatively free-market, laissez-faire, entrepreneur-driven economies that had become commonplace during Industrialism1 and the early years of Industrialism2, evolved into increasingly regulated, planned, and controlled economies, which were "managed" by political and corporate elites and their cadres of bureaucrats.

Government intervention into national economic affairs was justified (rationalized) as the means by which to "overcome free market limitations", "smooth business cycles", "promote economic fairness", and "ensure the equitable distribution of economic opportunities and benefits".

In less extreme cases, which existed in most Western European nations and America, the political/economic unions produced "mixed economies". Central governments intervened according to Keynesian economic principles in attempts to stimulate economic growth during economic downturns and suppress economic growth when economies became "overheated".

The stated goals with respect to such government intervention were to mitigate cyclical economic fluctuations, and to ensure continuously improving human prosperity within an environment of perpetually low unemployment and low inflation.

In extreme cases, which existed in the communist Soviet Union, fascist Germany, and communist China, horrific multi-decade experiments involving coercive central economic planning and control were conducted, during which tens of millions of people died from starvation (or extermination), as a result of central government resource misallocation and mismanagement.

Viewed from the ecological perspective, while the merits of central government intervention in national economic affairs will be forever debated, it is clear that such intervention neither constrained the proliferation of human industrialism nor suppressed industrial humanity's enormous and ever-increasing NNR appetites.

By the post-WW2 rebuilding period, rekindled Western prosperity improvement and emerging Eastern prosperity improvement had convinced anthropocentric humankind that achieving universal human prosperity through global industrialism was not only inevitable, but imminent.

Anthropocentric humankind failed to understand, however, that the extraordinary global NNR abundance that had prevailed during most of Industrialism2 – and that had enabled industrial humanity to prosper lavishly, despite our often egregiously wasteful malinvestment of industrial and financial capital – was in the process of transitioning to increasingly pervasive global NNR scarcity.

Industrialism2 Societal Circumstances

During the early years of Industrialism2, industrial success was attained by societies that encouraged human ingenuity – resourcefulness, technological innovations, efficiency improvements, and productivity enhancements. Personal attributes such as self-reliance, accountability, fiscal responsibility, and a strong work ethic were actively encouraged.

The result of this supportive societal environment was a "can do" attitude among the populations of second-generation industrializing Western nations such as Germany and America, who were thereby able to successfully exploit the extremely favorable natural environments within which they found themselves.

Yet, as had been the case with shifting Western political and economic attitudes, the prevailing societal attitudes of self-reliance and self-assurance also shifted during the disaster years – to self-doubt; our confidence in ourselves had been shaken. Moreover, enormous industrial wealth had produced equally enormous, and divisive, wealth disparities – our confidence in "the system" had been shaken as well.

Following WW2, however, with the restoration of peace and (relative) stability, industrial humanity attempted to resurrect the aura of self-confidence and self-assurance that had prevailed during the early years of Industrialism2. Surviving the disaster years had re-instilled humanity's faith in itself and its institutions.

Industrialism2 Human Responses

The atmosphere of exuberance that emerged during Industrialism2 – as industrial humanity's self-perception evolved from exceptional to "exemptional" – fostered the belief that that "every generation will have it better than the last". And while this belief was battered during the disaster years, it was not broken. Industrial humanity emerged from WW2 fully intending to pick up where it had left off prior to WW1.

By the end of Industrialism2, however, populations occupying many industrialized Western nations were beginning to feel the adverse effects of Nature's Squeeze (increasingly pervasive global NNR scarcity).

Prosperity improvement within these nations had peaked, and cultural circumstances were deteriorating. Political instability, economic fragility, and societal volatility emerged as a consequence – to which impacted populations responded with increasing frustration, anger, and violence.

Viewed from the ecological perspective, rapidly improving global human prosperity – and industrial humanity's resultant optimism and innovation – which had been enabled by global NNR abundance during our Old Normal (Industrialism1 and Industrialism2), had become geologically impossible with the inception of increasingly pervasive global NNR scarcity during our New Normal (Industrialism3).

Chapter 7:
Industrialism3 – Industrialism Unravels

> Global rates of growth in both population and GDP have slowed over time with highest average growth rates experienced in the 1970s and lowest growth rates since 2000.[1] (UNEP)

Industrialism3 – industrial humanity's third and final industrial revolution – commenced in 1973. Through the first two decades of the 21st century, Industrialism3 has been characterized by Eastern industrialization and Western deindustrialization – within the broader context of unraveling industrialism at the global level.

Eastern Industrialization Whereas Industialism1 and Industrialism2 were primarily Western phenomena, Industrialism3 has been primarily an Eastern phenomenon,

> Since 1960 Asia, the largest and most populous of the continents, has become richer faster than any other region of the world. ... Of course, this growth has not occurred at the same pace all over the continent. The western part of Asia grew during this period at about the same rate as the rest of the world, but, as a whole, the eastern half (ten countries: China, Hong Kong, Indonesia, Japan, Korea, Malaysia, the Philippines, Singapore, Taiwan Province of China, and Thailand) turned in a superior performance...[2] (IMF)

With the exception of China, which is a large, resource-rich nation, the newly industrializing Eastern nations are severely NNR deficient. And even China does not possess sufficient domestically available, economically viable NNRs with which to achieve global industrial supremacy.

Consequently, the most significant competitive advantage enjoyed by industrializing Eastern nations during Industrialism3, has been their "low cost" status – as had been the case for successfully industrializing Western nations during Industrialism1 and Industrialism2.

Relatively low wages and low or nonexistent benefit, entitlement, regulatory, and compliance costs have afforded commercial enterprises located within the industrializing East an unassailable competitive advantage over business rivals located within "high cost" Western nations.

The success of the Eastern Industrialization Model has been evidenced by the rapid pace of Eastern industrial development during Industrialism3, and by the extraordinary prosperity improvement achieved by Eastern populations – success that has been enabled by correspondingly extraordinary increases in global NNR extraction, utilization, and reserve depletion.

Western Deindustrialization As was the case with industrialization, the West has taken the lead with respect to deindustrialization. Notably, however, the transition from industrializing savings-based, production-oriented, manufacturing economies to deindustrializing debt-based, consumption-oriented, service economies, has not been made intentionally,

> The idea that developed countries must inevitably move toward a post-industrial or service economy related to a 'knowledge economy' is one of the most popular beliefs concerning economic development. It is also a dangerous misconception because the 'service economy' is nothing other than a 'statistical artifact' (Kaske, 1991) or 'statistical illusion' (Jansson, 2009).[3] (Soilen)

Western deindustrialization has occurred by default, owing to increasingly unfavorable, geologically-imposed, economic circumstances. It is not coincidental that Western nations such as Great Britain and America experienced peak mining activity, increasingly pervasive domestic NNR scarcity, deindustrialization, faltering prosperity, and diminishing global prominence in rapid succession.

Quite the contrary, it would be peculiar if circumstances were otherwise,

> The result of this strategic shift from production to service is now clear for all to see. It has led to a weaker competitive position for the majority of Western countries vis-à-vis the new Asian economic powers, first of all China.[4] (Soilen)

Unraveling Industrialism Unsurprisingly, owing to Scarcity4 and the Great Recession, deindustrialization has become a global phenomenon,

> However it is measured, there is no escaping the fact that in the last few decades deindustrialisation has been experienced by virtually all developed countries, and also by a growing number of developing countries.[5] (Skuflic and Druzic)

Increasingly pervasive global deindustrialization is being caused by increasingly pervasive global NNR scarcity – Nature's Squeeze. Far from being a lofty "post-industrial" goal to which industrialized nations should aspire – deindustrialization is an indicator of "unraveling toward collapse".

Industrialism3 Operating Environment

"As the material standard of living grows, mineral and metal demand also expands. This pattern has been followed by all developing countries in history."[6] (ICMM) [The ICMM inverted cause and effect – a growing material living standard is enabled by mineral and metal utilization – NNR utilization precedes human prosperity improvement.]

Achieving improved prosperity through industrialization has taken on special significance for industrializing Eastern nations. Most Eastern nations were decimated by WW2 or by internal strife during Industrialism2, and/or had suffered under colonial rule by one or more Western powers during the period.

Eastern industrialization aspirations therefore transcend prosperity improvement and catching up with the industrialized West. Through industrialization, Eastern nations seek to break permanently from the past, and ensure that they will never again be subject to poverty, oppression, and foreign exploitation.

Despite their laudable intentions, however, our increasingly unfavorable global operating environment – which is characterized by increasingly pervasive NNR scarcity, diminishing industrial productivity growth, faltering human prosperity, and deteriorating human cultural circumstances – can no longer perpetuate industrial success for the industrialized West, much less enable industrial success for the industrializing East.

Industrialism3 Natural Environment

Imported NNRs – and imported NNR-derived infrastructure, machines, products, and energy – have been the primary enablers of Eastern industrialization during Industrialism3. Even large nations such as Russia, China, and India – which are far more favorably endowed with NNRs than Japan, the Asian Tigers, and the Tiger Cubs – are heavily reliant on imported NNRs and NNR-derived economic output.

Unfortunately, increasing NNR import reliance by an increasing number of industrialized and industrializing nations, within the context of a global natural environment characterized by increasingly pervasive NNR scarcity, is a formula for increasing global conflict – not for long term industrial success.

Industrialism3 Cultural Environment

In contrast to their Western counterparts, Eastern cultural environments have typically featured:

- Government economic leadership, rather than entrepreneurial economic leadership.
- Planned economies, rather than market-based economies.
- Centralized, highly structured societies, rather than decentralized, loosely organized societies.
- An emphasis on societal order, rather than on individual rights.
- An emphasis on societal conformance, rather than on individual initiative.

And although cultural environments vary among industrializing Eastern nations, most employ a common set of practices designed to facilitate industrial success:

- Jumpstart the industrialization process by capitalizing on 200+ years of Western industrial experience, industrial infrastructure development, and accumulated investment capital.
- Employ extensive government intervention to facilitate domestic industrial development and discourage unsolicited foreign interference.
- Promote societal stability and order as prerequisites to effective long term planning and investment.
- Overcome domestic industrial capital deficiencies by sourcing and optimizing imported natural capital and physical capital.
- Focus on human capital development.

- Develop export-driven, manufacturing-based economies – i.e., import NNRs, maximize added value through low cost production processes, and export price/performance superior finished goods.
- Imitate and improve – embrace "better, faster, and cheaper" – initially; invent and discover later.

Both Western and Eastern cultural environments have proven extraordinarily successful at facilitating industrial development and human prosperity improvement. Our success in both cases has been enabled, however, by our ever-increasing exploitation of Earth's finite, non-replenishing – and now extensively depleted – NNR reserves.

Industrialism3 Enablers

> Over the period since 1850, the oft-cited *Economist* index of commodity prices[7] dropped by around 80 per cent relative to overall prices. However, overall mineral resource prices have increased relative to the prices of manufactures over the past half-century.[7] (Australian Government/Treasury)

The extraordinarily favorable "enabling" trends that prevailed during Industrialism1 and Industrialism2 – relative global NNR abundance and rapid industrial productivity growth – have been displaced during Industrialism3 by increasingly unfavorable "inhibiting" trends – increasingly pervasive global NNR scarcity and diminishing industrial productivity growth.

Industrialism3 NNRs

> There are some important factors that create serious concerns about to what extent mineral production can be expanded at the same rates as in the past. Two key factors are the increasing *geological* and *geographical distance* to minerals. Past mining has concentrated on picking the 'low-hanging fruit' and depleted those resources that were of the highest quality, easiest to extract and closest to consumers.

> Future mining will face an increasing geological distance. This means mining deposits of lower ore grade, which are found in deeper and less accessible layers in the planet's crust. Deposits are to be found at greater geographic distance from centres of consumption and in less accessible environments (e.g. offshore).[8] (Humphreys)

Our extraordinary NNR requirements – driven by new NNR uses and new NNR users – have increased unabated during Industrialism3,

> At the end of this period [1995], the general feeling among exploration geologists was that the world was going to suffer a prolonged mining recession (Snow and Juhas, 2002). This turned out to be largely untrue because their vision of the world was limited to traditional developed countries and did not include the upcoming exceptional rise of China and India, two countries situated well below the radar at the time.[9] (Jébrak)

Yet, globally available, economically viable NNR supplies have failed increasingly to completely address our enormous and ever-increasing NNR requirements during the period – i.e., to enable China, India, and the rest of the world to "live like Americans".

The United Nations estimates that global NNR utilization during the year 2010 totaled 51 billion metric tonnes. Had Earth's human population been able to use NNRs at North American levels during 2010, global NNR utilization would have totaled 145 billion metric tonnes – nearly 3 times the actual total.[10]

Given that historically unprecedented NNR prices crashed the global economy in 2008 (Scarcity4), during which industrial humanity extracted approximately 50 billion metric tonnes of NNRs, the notion that we might somehow extract anywhere close to 145 billion metric tonnes of economically viable NNRs during a single year – then, now, or ever, especially on a persistent basis – is ludicrous.

Industrialism3 NNR Demand

Continuously increasing NNR requirements from the industrialized West combined with rapidly increasing NNR requirements from the industrializing East have caused extraordinarily increasing global NNR requirements during Industrialism3.

NNR Uses NNR-based innovations introduced during Industrialism3 have typically involved medical technology, electronics, composite materials, computerization, information processing, miniaturization, robotics, data communications, wireless communications, semiconductors, superconductors, infrastructure, and power generation.

Specific innovations – and the NNRs that enable them – have covered a wide range of industrial sectors and applications,

> A revival of the nuclear industry occurred in response to reduced carbon footprints — in spite of local disasters and green party activists — and required new supplies of uranium in addition to boron, zirconium, barium, hafnium and cobalt.

> The aerospace industry needed new metals, such as rhenium and niobium, as well as more of the traditional metals, such as nickel, aluminum and chromium.

> The production of electricity from wind turbines triggered strong growth in the demand for permanent magnets, which use rare earth metals (praseodymium, neodymium, samarium), and the transport of this power required large quantities of classic metals (aluminum, iron, manganese, chromium, nickel, copper), and less abundant products (carbon, vanadium, gallium, indium, cobalt, molybdenum).

> Photovoltaic production required selenium, tellurium and silicon, and even precious metals were needed for connectors (gold, silver) and catalysis (palladium, platinum).

> Energy storage metals included lanthanum, lead, tantalum, manganese, cobalt, nickel and lithium (Bihoux and De Guillebon, 2010), the latter of which also became a key component of the car industry.

Most of these new energy-related technologies require greater amounts of metals per kilowatt than traditional non-renewable energy sources such as petroleum or coal. Up to 45 elements were considered of interest by the metal industry during this period [1995-2012], up from only ten during the first globalization [1870-1914] (Eggert, et al., 2008).[11] (Jébrak)

NNR Users By 2019, less than 20% of Earth's 7.7 billion human inhabitants occupied nations that could be considered industrialized, while slightly more than half occupied industrializing nations, and nearly one third occupied nations that were primarily pre-industrial.

Table 7-1: Global Industrialization Status as of 2019 [million people]

Year	Industrialized	Industrializing	Pre-industrial	Total
By 1750	0 (0%)	14 (1.9%)	706 (98.1%)	720 (100%)
By 1875	41 (3.0%)	291 (22.0%)	993 (75.0%)	1,325 (100%)
By 1973	838 (21.3%)	129 (3.3%)	2,975 (75.4%)	3,942 (100%)
By 2019	1,363 (17.7%)	3,978 (51.6%)	2,372 (30.8%)	7,714 (100%)

Sources: Kremer, Populstat, World Bank, and Cairn.[12]

Notably, the total population of nations occupied by industrial-scale NNR users – the global industrialized and industrializing population – has increased extraordinarily during Industrialism3, from approximately 1 billion to over 5 billion. This number will increase continuously going forward, as the nearly 2.4 billion people who occupied pre-industrial nations in 2019 attempt to industrialize.

Industrialism3 NNR Supply

As it now stands, much of modern technology depends on metals whose supplies are uncertain and whose market transactions are largely opaque; in concert, this produces a supply situation that may prove difficult to sustain.[13] (Nassar)

Industrial humanity's NNR mix has remained unchanged during Industrialism3, and targeted NNR sources, while shifting geographically, have decreased in terms of both quantity and quality.

Moreover, while global NNR extraction, production, and utilization have increased extraordinarily during Industrialism3, global NNR scarcity has become increasingly pervasive.

NNR Mix NNR byproducts – such as specialty metals, high tech metals, and super alloys – have been employed increasingly during Industrialism3 in an expanding array of high technology applications. Their continued availability and affordability are of increasing concern.

Table 7-2: Byproduct NNRs

Primarily Targeted Metal	Byproduct Metals
Aluminum	Gallium and Vanadium
Copper	Arsenic, Antimony, Cobalt, Gold, Molybdenum, PGMs, Rhenium, Selenium, Silver, Tellurium, and Thallium
Iron Ore	Niobium, REMs, Scandium, and Vanadium
Lead	Arsenic, Bismuth, Cadmium, Cobalt, Gallium, Germanium, Indium, Silver, Thallium, and Vanadium
Lithium	Cesium and Rubidium
Nickel	Cobalt, PGMs, Selenium, and Tellurium
PGMs	Rhodium and Ruthenium are byproducts of Platinum and Palladium; Iridium and Osmium are byproducts of Platinum
Tin	Indium, Niobium, and Tantalum
Zinc	Arsenic, Bismuth, Cadmium, Cobalt, Gallium, Germanium, Indium, Silver, and Thallium
Zirconium	Hafnium and Thorium

Source: Nassar.[14]

Metals such as arsenic, bismuth, cadmium, cesium, germanium, gallium, hafnium, indium, scandium, selenium, thallium, and tellurium (with the exception of one mine in China) are mined exclusively as byproducts – i.e., they are only recovered in the process of exploiting their respective primarily targeted metal or metals.

Prices and availability associated with byproduct metals are therefore contingent upon the demand/supply dynamics pertaining to their respective primarily targeted metals – thereby calling into question the availability of sufficient economically viable supplies of byproduct metals in the future,

> The growth in technological innovation that has occurred over the past decades has, in part, been possible because an increasing number of metals of the periodic table are used to perform specialized functions. However, there have been increasing concerns regarding the reliability of supply of some of these metals. A main contributor to these concerns is the fact that many of these metals are recovered only as by-products from a limited number of geopolitically concentrated ore deposits, rendering their supplies unable to respond to rapid changes in demand.[15] (Nassar)

NNR Sources "'We took the nice, simple, easy stuff first from Australia, we took it from the U.S., we went to South America. Now we have to go to the more remote places.'" Glencore CEO, Ivan Glasenberg explaining to the *Financial Times* why his firm operates in the Congo and Zambia." (His point: "Complicated more expensive extraction of metals from increasingly harder to find, lower grade ore bodies in almost inaccessible and hostile parts of the world is going to affect our lifestyles.")[16] (Glasenberg and Mills)

Glasenberg's comments highlight the three major shifts that occurred during Industrialism3 with respect to targeted NNR sources – West to East, lower risk to higher risk, and lower cost to higher cost.

The following data from the 2016 United Nations analysis of global NNR sourcing and utilization, *Global Material Flows and Resource Productivity*, reveal the West-to-East shift in global NNR sourcing during Industrialism3.

Table 7-3: Global NNR* Sourcing Shares

Region	1970	2010
Africa	7.9%	7.0%
Asia and Pacific	**24.3%**	**52.9%**
E. Europe, Caucuses, C. Asia	14.7%	5.8%
Europe	**20.9%**	**10.5%**
Latin America	9.4%	10.7%
North America	**19.6%**	**9.7%**
West Asia	3.2%	3.4%

Source: UNEP.[17] *Includes biomass

Between 1970 and 2010, North American and European shares of global NNR* sourcing halved, while the Asia and Pacific share doubled. Moreover, "Latin America, West Asia and Africa all saw growth in total DE [domestic extraction] of greater than 100%, at compounding annual growth rates of 3.1%, 2.9% and 2.5% respectively."[18] (UNEP)

New mining ventures have also targeted, out of necessity, environmentally inhospitable and politically unstable areas, "Exploration began in several new regions, such as Siberia, Eastern China, Mongolia and some parts of Africa."[19] (Jébrak)

Additionally, NNR-rich nations have exerted increasing control over foreign access to their domestic NNR reserves and mining operations,

> A new period emerged in 1973 with the arrival of the oil crisis — an attempt by resource rich developing countries to gain more power on a global basis. It could be interpreted as the logical consequence of the decolonization that progressively developed during the previous period.[20] (Jébrak)

Finally, mine expropriations became increasingly prevalent toward the end of Industrialism2 and the beginning of Industrialism3,

> Thirty-two expropriations occurred between 1960 and 1969 in Chile, Peru, Zaire, Zambia and Guinea, particularly for copper and aluminum. Other expropriations occurred between 1970 and 1976, especially for iron (Mauritania, Brazil, India, Venezuela and Chile), phosphates (Morocco) and tin (Bolivia, Indonesia).[21] (Jébrak)

NNR Supplies "Over the past four decades [1970-2010] global material use has thus tripled, growing on average by 2.7% annually."[22] (UNEP)

Diagram 7-1: Global NNR* Extraction/Utilization 1970-2010

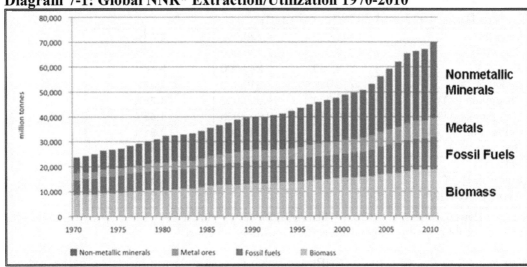

Source: UNEP;[23] *includes biomass.

"All four material groups have grown over the past four decades [1970-2010]. Biomass extraction grew by 2%, fossil fuels by 1.9%, metal ores by 2.8% and non-metallic minerals by 4% per year on average."[24] (UNEP)

These extraordinary increases in global NNR extraction and production have been caused primarily by historically unprecedented demand from industrializing Eastern nations, particularly China, where NNR demand increased by nearly 40 times between 1970 and 2008.[25]

Yet, while annual global NNR extraction and production quantities have increased extraordinarily during Industrialism3 – to nearly 8 billion tonnes of coal, over 4 billion tonnes of cement, and nearly 2.5 billion tonnes of iron ore during 2019 – annual global NNR extraction/production growth rates have decreased significantly during the period – to rates considerably lower than those achieved during Industrialism1, AND significantly lower than those achieved during Industrialism2.

Table 7-4: Select Global NNR Extraction/Production Quantities and Growth Rates 1973 and 2019

NNR	1973	2019	1973-2019 CAGR
Potash (MT)	18,900,000	41,300,000	1.71%
Phosphate Rock (MT)	111,000,000	227,000,000	1.57%
Coal (MT)	3,074,000,000	7,921,000,000	2.08%
Oil (Gbbls)	21.37	34.66	1.06%
Natural Gas (TCF)	46.63	140.41	2.43%
Aluminum (MT)	12,100,000	63,200,000	3.66%
Iron Ore (MT)	832,000,000	2,450,000,000	2.38%
Copper (MT)	6,920,000	20,400,000	2.38%

Table 7-4: Select Global NNR Extraction/Production Quantities and Growth Rates 1973 and 2019 (continued)

Lead (MT)	3,440,000	4,720,000	0.69%
Zinc (MT)	5,710,000	12,700,000	1.75%
Tin (MT)	238,000	296,000	0.48%
Nickel (MT)	710,000	2,610,000	2.87%
Chromium (MT)	2,030,000	14,000,000	4.29%
Manganese (MT)	9,740,000	19,600,000	1.53%
Cement (MT)	702,000,000	4,100,000,000	3.91%
Gypsum (MT)	61,500,000	140,000,000	1.80%
Salt (MT)	155,000,000	283,000,000	1.32%
Sulfur (MT)	48,200,000	80,000,000	1.11%
Average CAGR			**2.06%**

Sources: Hewett, Lovering, USGS, BP Statistical Review, and IEA.[26]
MT = metric tonnes; Gbbls = gigabarrels; TCF = trillion cubic feet.

With respect to the 18 Core-20 NNRs for which reliable data are available, global extraction/production has increased anemically during Industrialism3, at a 2.06% rate (on average) compounded annually – versus 4.79% during Industrialism2, and 2.48% during Industrialism1.

Predictably, diminishing global NNR utilization growth has caused faltering global human prosperity improvement during Industrialism3:

- The compound annual growth rate in global GDP (economic output) has decreased considerably – from 3.29% during Industrialism2 to 2.91% during Industrialism3, and
- The compound annual growth rate in global pc GDP (the average material living standard) has decreased significantly – from 2.16% during Industrialism2 to a lackluster 1.40% during Industrialism3.

Industrialism3 NNR Scarcity

Much of the earth has been pounded by prospectors and geologists. The entire world is readily accessible today by remote sensing and most of it by physical means. Much of the world has been surveyed by satellite imaging, airborne magnetometry and radiometry; surface geochemical surveys and regional-scale geological mapping have been carried out over large portions of the earth.

Many areas have seen very intensive exploration. Until the early 1990s, the diminishing returns of exploration efforts relative to funds expended was largely confined to the most heavily explored regions of the world—southern Africa, North America, and Australia—although most of the world's greatest orebodies had been discovered decades earlier, no matter where they were located.

Beginning in about 1993, exploration became a truly global effort as the Soviet Union collapsed and opened up to new exploration, as Africa and Latin America became much more easily accessible, and as global sources of exploration capital became available to thousands of junior exploration companies that spread their mineral search all over the world.

This global search temporarily increased the success rate of global exploration efforts as new lands opened up in the 1990s, but in recent years exploration seems to have become increasingly unsuccessful again. Specifically, the massive increase in exploration budgets during the commodities boom from 2003 to 2008 was not mirrored by a massive increase in metals discovery during this period.

Quite the opposite.[27] (Beaty)

Permanent NNR Price Trend Reversals Decreasing NNR price trends during times of relative global NNR abundance – Industrialism1 and Industrialism2 – enabled industrial humanity to enjoy rapidly improving prosperity during the period.

By the mid-20th century, however, many of Earth's NNR reserves had become extensively depleted – the high quality/low cost NNRs had been extracted. Accordingly, the price trends associated with these NNRs were reversing permanently from decreasing to increasing.

For example, the iron ore price trend reversed in 1906, oil reversed in 1933, phosphate rock reversed in 1955, copper reversed in 1961, salt reversed in 1965, and clays reversed in 1967.

As global NNR reserves were further depleted during Industrialism3 and NNR quality continued to decrease, the price trends associated with nearly all remaining NNRs reversed permanently as well,

> Note that there is significant variation in the long-term trends, with metal prices…falling steadily until mid-1970s, and rising quite rapidly thereafter.[28] (Erten and Ocampo)

Permanent Global NNR Scarcity Our persistent and ever-increasing depletion of Earth's finite and non-replenishing NNR reserves since the inception of our industrial era produced its inevitable result during Industrialism3 – permanent global NNR scarcity.[29]

Global NNR Scarcity Evidence

"…a rising long-term price for a commodity indicates increasing scarcity of supply relative to demand. This is what we should expect with minerals as depletion progresses."[30] (USGS) As the USGS correctly observes, the primary indicator of relative global NNR scarcity is a secular (long term) NNR price trend.[31]

The following four analyses, which evaluate long term NNR price data at both the individual NNR level and the aggregate NNR level, provide indisputable evidence of increasingly pervasive global NNR scarcity – permanently increasing NNR price trends associated with an increasing number of NNRs – during Industrialism3:

- The **Global Oil Scarcity Analysis** examines evolving price trend dynamics and relative scarcity with respect to oil between 1861 and 2019.
- The **Aggregate Global NNR Scarcity Analysis** examines evolving price trend dynamics and relative scarcity with respect to the Core-20 NNRs between 1900 and 2019.
- The **Global NNR Scarcity Status Analysis** provides current (2019) global scarcity status with respect to the vast majority (81) of NNRs that enable our industrialized way of life.
- The **Critical NNR Scarcity Analysis** provides current (2019) global scarcity status with respect to four NNR subsets for which increasing global scarcity poses the greatest threat to human industrialism.

Global Oil Scarcity Analysis The 160-year oil price curve and its corresponding quadratic trendline exemplify the evolution of relative global NNR scarcity during our industrial era.

Diagram 7-2: Relative Global Oil Scarcity

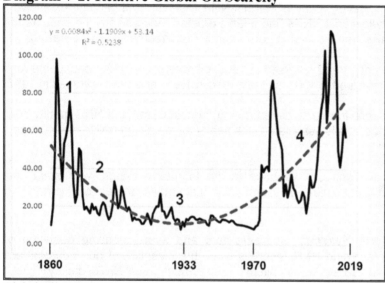

$$y = 0.0084x^2 - 1.1909x + 53.14$$
$$R^2 = 0.5238$$

Global Oil Scarcity Trendline (and Oil Price Trendline) = Dashed Line.
Oil Price Curve = Solid Line.[32]

1 During the early 1860s when oil was initially exploited on an industrial scale, humanity's oil requirements, while extremely modest by today's standards, were increasing rapidly. And initially discovered oil, which was relatively complex and costly to extract and refine, was in limited supply. Accordingly, oil prices were high – oil was **initially scarce**.

2 Despite humanity's rapidly increasing oil requirements during the late 19th century and early 20th century, the secular oil price trend decreased, as higher quality/lower cost oil deposits were exploited, and significantly improved oil exploitation tools and techniques were developed and deployed – oil was **relatively abundant**.

94

3 The oil price trendline (dashed line) reached its minimum in 1933 – the secular oil price trend reversed permanently from decreasing to increasing – and oil **transitioned permanently** from relatively abundant to increasingly scarce.

4 Since the mid-20th century, humanity's oil requirements have been enormous and ever-increasing, while Earth's extensively depleted high quality/low cost "conventional" oil deposits are being abandoned in favor of remaining lower quality/higher cost "unconventional" deposits – e.g., deep water oil, heavy oil, tar sands, and shale oil. Accordingly, the secular oil price trend has increased – oil is **increasingly scarce**.

Aggregate Global NNR Scarcity Analysis As illustrated by the Global NNR Scarcity Index[33] – an indicator of aggregate relative global NNR scarcity between 1900 and 2019 – the aggregate global NNR scarcity trend transitioned permanently from "relative NNR abundance" to "increasing NNR scarcity" during the mid-20th century.

Diagram 7-3: Global NNR Scarcity Index 1900-2019

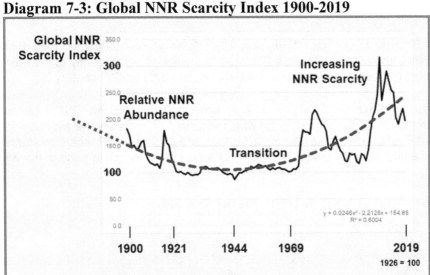

Global NNR Scarcity Index Trendline (and Composite NNR Price Curve Trendline) = Dashed Line. Composite NNR Price Curve = Solid Line.[34]

The Global NNR Scarcity Index is derived from long-term, criticality-weighted, inflation-adjusted price data pertaining to the Core-20 NNRs, a diverse mix of 20 widely-deployed NNRs that are indispensable to the perpetuation of human industrialism – oil, iron ore, cement, natural gas, crushed stone, copper, coal, phosphate rock, aluminum, clays, chromium, potash, zinc, salt, manganese, sulfur, lead, nickel, gypsum, and tin.

Key dates and intervals:

Prior to 1900, available price data pertaining to oil, coal, iron ore, copper, lead, zinc, nickel, tin, phosphate rock, and sulfur reveal decreasing price trends during the mid/late 19th century, indicating **relative global NNR abundance** during the pre-1900 period.[35]

Between 1900 and 1944, the Global NNR Scarcity Index (dashed line) decreased by 33%, from 152 to 102, indicating **relative global NNR abundance** during the 44-year period.

Between 1900 and 1969, the Composite NNR Price Curve (solid line) decreased by 45%, from 182.2 to 100.6, indicating **relative global NNR abundance** during the 69-year period.

Between 1944 and 1969, the Global NNR Scarcity Index reached its minimum of 102 (1944) and the Composite NNR Price Curve reached its minimum of 100.6 (1969), indicating a **permanent transition** from relative global NNR abundance to increasing global NNR scarcity during the mid-20th century (between 1944 and 1969).

Between 1944 and 2019, the Global NNR Scarcity Index increased extraordinarily – by nearly 150% – from 102 to 248, indicating permanent **increasingly pervasive global NNR scarcity** during the most recent 75-year period.

Between 1969 and 2019, the Composite NNR Price Curve increased by nearly 96%, from 100.6 to 197.1, indicating permanent **increasingly pervasive global NNR scarcity** during the most recent 50-year period.

The Global NNR Scarcity Index and Composite NNR Price Curve clearly indicate that aggregate global NNR abundance (Nature's Stimulus) transitioned permanently to increasingly pervasive global NNR scarcity (Nature's Squeeze) during the mid-20th century.

Global NNR Scarcity Status Analysis The analysis provides current (2019) global scarcity status with respect to the 81 NNRs for which sufficient price data were available to establish meaningful long term price trends. (See Appendix C for NNR scarcity status definitions, a list of analyzed NNRs, and 2019 scarcity status with respect to each of the 81 analyzed NNRs.)

Diagram 7-4: 2019 Global NNR Scarcity Status Summary

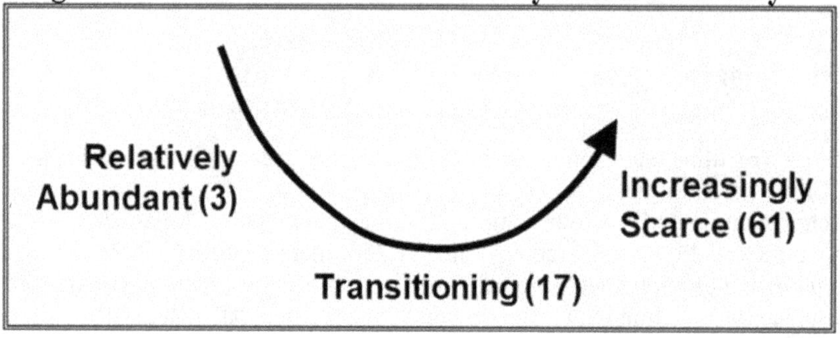

As of 2019:

- Decreasing secular price trends associated with only **3 of the 81 (4%) analyzed NNRs** – bauxite, industrial garnet, and peat – indicate **relative global abundance**.
- Reversing secular price trends associated with **17 of the 81 (21%) analyzed NNRs** – including cement, crushed stone, gypsum, and sulfur – indicate in-process **transitions** from relative global abundance to increasing global scarcity.

- Increasing secular price trends associated with an overwhelming 61 of the 81 (75%) analyzed NNRs – including aluminum, chromium, clays, coal, iron ore, lead, manganese, natural gas, nickel, oil, phosphate rock, potash, salt, tin, and zinc – indicate **increasing global scarcity**.

The findings of the Global NNR Scarcity Status Analysis confirm the findings of the Aggregate Global NNR Scarcity Analysis – increasingly pervasive global NNR scarcity.

Critical NNR Scarcity Analysis Sixty-six (66) of the 81 analyzed NNRs fall within one or more of the following four NNR subsets, which are especially critical to the perpetuation of human industrialism, and for which increasing global scarcity poses the greatest threat to human industrialism:

- **Core-20 NNRs** – 20 widely-deployed NNRs that are indispensable to the perpetuation of human industrialism.
- **High-Tech NNRs** – 42 NNRs that are widely expected to enable industrial humanity's technology-based future.
- **Conflict NNRs** – 33 NNRs that are most likely to engender international conflict among competing major global power centers during the coming years.
- **Practically Inexhaustible NNRs** – 23 NNRs, many of which are indispensable industrial and construction materials, for which economically viable (price/performance superior) substitutes typically do not exist.

Core-20 NNRs While all NNRs are critical to the perpetuation of our industrialized way of life, some NNRs are more critical than others. The Core-20 NNRs have proven to be indispensable in perpetuating human industrialism, both historically and currently.

As of 2019:

- **16 of the Core-20 NNRs (80%)** – aluminum, clays, chromium, coal, copper, iron ore, lead, manganese, natural gas, nickel, oil, phosphate rock, potash, salt, tin, and zinc – are **increasingly scarce** globally;
- **4 of the Core-20 NNRs (20%)** – cement, gypsum, stone (crushed), and sulfur – are **transitioning** from relatively abundant to increasingly scarce; and
- **None** of the Core-20 NNRs are **relatively abundant** globally.

No substitutes exist for these widely-deployed NNRs in their most critical applications, and no economically viable (price/performance superior) substitutes exist in their remaining applications.

The fact that every Core-20 NNR is either increasingly scarce or transitioning from relatively abundant to increasingly scarce explains the already debilitating effect that Nature's Squeeze is exerting on industrial humanity. And because suitable substitutes do not exist, successfully adapting to increasing global scarcity with respect to these indispensable NNRs is impossible.

As go the Core-20 NNRs, so goes global human prosperity – and human industrialism.

High-Tech NNRs "As the global economy grows and evolves in the 21st century, emerging technologies will require mineral commodities on a greater scale and in a larger number of applications than ever before."[35] (USGS)

For example, "…the number of materials used in printed circuit boards has grown from a handful to sixty over the last three decades [1990s to 2010s]." Moreover, "… a modern mobile phone may contain 500 to 1,000 different components."[36] (European Commission)

High-tech NNR applications – or "emerging technologies" – include solar energy, wind energy, electric vehicles (EV), energy storage, super alloys, and Industry 4.0 applications, which include smart factories, artificial intelligence, robotics, Internet-of-Things, nanotechnologies, 3D printing, and visualization software.

These and other high-tech applications, and their constituent NNRs, are widely expected to perpetuate our industrialized way of life for the indefinite future – while simultaneously reducing or eliminating our reliance on "low tech" and often "environmentally unfriendly" NNRs, such as fossil fuels. (See Appendix D for a list of High-Tech NNRs.)

As of 2019:

- **32 of the 42 high-tech NNRs (76%)** – aluminum, barite, boron, chromium, cobalt, copper, fluorspar, germanium, gold, graphite, hafnium, indium, iron ore, lead, lime, magnesium metal, manganese, molybdenum, nickel, phosphate rock, PGMs, potash, rhenium, silicon, silver, talc, tantalum, tellurium, tin, titanium metal, tungsten, zinc, and zirconium – are **increasingly scarce** globally;
- **10 of the 42 high-tech NNRs (24%)** – arsenic, bismuth, cadmium, gallium, lithium, mercury, REMs, selenium, sulfur, and vanadium – are **transitioning** from relatively abundant to increasingly scarce; and
- **None** of the 42 high-tech NNRs are **relatively abundant** globally.

By expanding the array of increasingly scarce NNRs upon which human industrialism depends, high-tech applications, to the extent that they come to fruition, will actually exacerbate the debilitating effects imposed by increasingly pervasive global NNR scarcity. Consequently, emerging high-tech applications are not industrial humanity's salvation.

Conflict NNRs None of the four major global power centers – Europe (EU), America, China, and Russia – is close to being NNR self-sufficient. Consequently, as domestic NNR scarcity and global NNR scarcity become increasingly pervasive, each global power center will employ all available means – including conflict – to obtain sufficient NNRs with which to perpetuate its industrial existence.

> Our analysis indicates that China relies on imports for over half of its consumption for 19 of 42 nonfuel minerals, compared with 24 for the United States—11 of which are common to both. It is for these 11 nonfuel minerals that competition between the United States and China may become the most contentious, especially for those with highly concentrated production that prove irreplaceable in pivotal emerging technologies.[37] (US National Academy of Sciences)

Thirty-three (33) NNRs are most likely to engender conflict among competing global power centers. These conflict NNRs are fossil fuels, metals, and nonmetallic minerals upon which multiple power centers are highly import-reliant, and for which current and/or prospective import sources are problematic. (See Appendix E for list of Conflict NNRs.)
As of 2019:

- **26 of the 33 conflict NNRs (79%)** – aluminum, antimony, barite, beryllium, boron, chromium, cobalt, copper, fluorspar, germanium, graphite, indium, iron ore, magnesium compounds, manganese, oil, PGMs, potash, rhenium, silicon, silver, tantalum, tin, titanium metal, zinc, and zirconium – are **increasingly scarce** globally;
- **6 of the 33 conflict NNRs (18%)** – arsenic, bismuth, gallium, lithium, REMs, and vanadium – are **transitioning** from relatively abundant to increasingly scarce; and
- **1 of the 33 conflict NNRs (3%)** – bauxite – is **relatively abundant** globally.

"Resource wars" over conflict NNRs (and other increasingly scarce NNRs) will almost certainly increase in the future, as Europe, America, and China further deplete their already extensively depleted domestic NNR reserves – and as Earth's rapidly dwindling "final frontier" NNR reserves become increasingly depleted,

> Many of the largest, highest grade, closest to surface, closest to market mineral deposits have been depleted or currently are in production. Over the next half century [2000-2050], the competition for land use among diverse sectors of an ever-increasing population will intensify.[38] (Doggett)

Conflict NNRs are ticking time bombs.

Practically Inexhaustible NNRs Twenty-three (23) NNRs, which represent over 25% of the approximately 90 NNRs that enable our industrial existence, are considered "practically inexhaustible" by the USGS, owing to their enormous and widely-dispersed global reserves. (See Appendix F for a list of Practically Inexhaustible NNRs.)

Global reserves associated with these 23 NNRs – most of which are construction and industrial materials – are typically difficult or impossible to quantify, and are characterized by the USGS as "large", "very large", "plentiful", "virtually unlimited", "adequate", or "ample".

While lacking the celebrity status typically accorded to high-tech NNRs, practically inexhaustible NNRs constitute the indispensable building blocks of our industrial infrastructure, and thereby serve as the foundation for human industrialism.

Because practically inexhaustible NNRs are widely-available in very large quantities, it is commonly assumed that they are relatively abundant globally – that is, their secular price trends are decreasing. For the vast majority of these NNRs, however, this is not the case.

As of 2019:

- **17 of the 23 practically inexhaustible NNRs (74%)** – asbestos, bromine, clays, dia-
  tomite, feldspar, kyanite, lime, magnesium compounds, magnesium metal, mica, pumice,
  salt, construction sand and gravel, industrial sand and gravel, silicon, talc, and wollas-
  tonite – are **increasingly scarce** globally;
- **4 of the 23 practically inexhaustible NNRs (17%)** – cement, gypsum, stone (crushed),
  and sulfur – are **transitioning** from relatively abundant to increasingly scarce; and only
- **2 of the 23 practically inexhaustible NNRs (9%)** – bauxite and industrial garnet – are
  relatively abundant globally.

Despite assurances from the USGS regarding their global abundance, the secular price
trends associated with three quarters of the practically inexhaustible NNRs are increasing,
which indicates increasing global scarcity.

Accordingly, given their essential and ubiquitous roles in construction and industrial
applications, increasing prices associated with these NNRs are already increasing the costs
of deploying indispensable infrastructure such as buildings, roads, railroads, waterways,
bridges, airports, ports, water distribution networks, food distribution networks, energy distribution networks, and communication networks worldwide.

Scarcity4 "The recent global economic crisis [Great Recession] was preceded by a
commodity price boom that was unprecedented in its magnitude and duration. The real prices
of energy and metals more than doubled in five years from 2003 to 2008..."[39] (Erten and
Ocampo)

Owing to industrialization initiatives launched by China and other industrializing nations
during the mid/late 20th century, in conjunction with the PPP-fueled consumption binge
embarked upon by many industrialized Western nations during the same period, industrial
humanity's NNR requirements increased to previously inconceivable levels during Indus-
trialism3.

NNR suppliers were compelled to exploit "final frontier" NNRs in their attempt to address
these unprecedented NNR requirements, the inevitable result of which was inordinately high
and persistently increasing NNR price trends during the first decade of the 21st century.
Scarcity4 ensued, which culminated in the Great Recession by the end of the decade.[40]

Nature's Fourth (and Final) Warning

> People tend to approach questions of Earth's resources in two ways. Aware that
> material consumption has grown exponentially since the Industrial Revolution, many
> seek answers in the history of technology and of economics over the past 2
> centuries. Those centuries have been times of technological triumph, so the answers
> tend to be optimistic and the conclusion that mineral resources are so many and so
> varied that a flexible economy and a responsive technology can offset any material
> limitation.

But technology has never had to face a real, global shortage of any material. For this reason, most geologists believe that the history of technology offers few guides, so they use a different line of reasoning and seek answers in the way materials occur on earth. ... Mineralogical and geochemical studies lead them to draw the less optimistic conclusion that resource challenges will be so abrupt and might be so costly that technology may not be able to evolve smoothly and produce antidotes for the shortages that will arise. Nature, not man, will dictate our use of resources.[41] (Skinner)

The two most recent NNR scarcity episodes, Scarcity3 and Scarcity4, delivered a devastating "one-two punch" to industrial humanity – especially to populations occupying high cost industrialized Western nations.

The adverse effects attributable to Scarcity3 were ultimately resolved by the exploitation of "final frontier" NNRs, which caused generally decreasing NNR price trends during the 1980s and 1990s – and enabled industrial humanity's "last hurrah" between 1982 and 2007.[42]

Regrettably, "final frontier" NNRs are not available to resolve the adverse effects attributable to Scarcity4; large, easily-accessible NNR deposits of high grade and purity no longer exist.

Scarcity4 – which marked the inception of permanent global NNR scarcity – was Nature's fourth (and final) warning...

NNR Scarcity Summary

Since the inception of our industrial era, we have experienced four major geologically-induced NNR scarcity episodes, each of which was more severe than the last in terms of its geographic scope, NNR price trend increases, and adverse effects on human prosperity.

Each of the four NNR scarcity episodes was characterized by:

- Extensive depletion of then-targeted NNR reserves.
- Broadly-based, multi-year NNR price trend increases.
- Inevitably peaking NNR demand – and NNR price trends.
- Rapidly decreasing NNR demand (demand destruction), and resultant diminishing human prosperity (economic recessions).
- Rapidly decreasing NNR price trends, owing to NNR demand destruction.

Scarcity1, which occurred between the mid/late 1860s and the early/mid 1870s, was a national-level phenomenon caused by the extensive depletion of basic industrial metals and coal reserves located in Great Britain and the other industrial pioneer nations.

Scarcity1 was resolved during the latter decades of the 19th century, through the exploitation of new NNR frontiers located in neighboring European nations and in Asian and African colonies. NNRs imported from these foreign sources enabled the industrial pioneers to maintain their industrial prominence during the 20th century, albeit at diminished levels.

Scarcity2, which occurred between 1914 and 1916, was a regional-level phenomenon caused by the extensive depletion of European industrial metals and coal reserves – particularly in the run-up to and during WW1.

Scarcity2 was resolved during the mid-20th century, through the exploitation of new NNR frontiers located Asia, Africa, Latin America, and Oceania, which had become economically viable owing to improved NNR mining tools and techniques, and to less costly global land and sea transportation.

Scarcity3, which occurred between 1969 and 1980, was a super-regional phenomenon caused by the extensive depletion of fossil fuel, industrial metals, specialty metals, and fertilizer reserves located in America and other (primarily Western) second-generation industrializing nations – particularly during and following WW2.

Scarcity3 was resolved during the latter decades of the 20th century, through the exploitation of new NNR frontiers located in less accessible regions of Asia, Africa, Latin America, North America, and Oceania. NNRs imported from these "final frontiers" enabled the industrial pioneers and second-generation industrialized nations to maintain their industrial prominence into the 21st century, albeit at diminished levels.

Scarcity4, which occurred between 1999 and 2008 (secondary peak in 2011), was a global phenomenon caused by extensive depletion of global fossil fuel, metals, and nonmetallic mineral reserves – particularly during industrial humanity's "last hurrah" between 1982 and 2007.

Scarcity4 was mitigated – but not resolved – during the second decade of the 21st century, through the increasing exploitation of NNRs from unconventional sources – e.g., shale oil and gas, mineralogically complex ores, and NNRs located in increasingly high cost and high risk (environmentally inhospitable, politically unstable, and difficult to access) areas,

> With the good ores being consumed over decades, miners are digging deeper and deeper for leaner and leaner grade ores day by day. The lean grade ores are also diversely complex in terms of mineralogical and mineral association characteristics. Efficient and economic separation of value minerals from these ores has become difficult with the traditional techniques.[43] (Somasundaran and Patra)

Increasing NNR Scarcity Severity The Composite NNR Price Curve clearly illustrates the increasing severity associated with each successive NNR scarcity episode (Scarcity1 predates comprehensive global NNR price data). [See Diagram 7-5]

During Scarcity2 (1914-1916), the Composite NNR Price Curve increased significantly, by 66% – from 107.9 to 179.0 – before settling back to 102.4 in 1921, after which it varied within a tight range between 86.3 and 112.8 until 1974.

During Scarcity3 (1969-1980), the Composite NNR Price Curve increased enormously, by 116% – from 100.6 to 217.5 – before settling back to 116.3 in 1999, the starting point for Scarcity4. (Note that the Scarcity3 peak of 217.5 exceeded the Scarcity2 peak of 179.0 by nearly 22%.)

Diagram 7-5: Post-1900 NNR Scarcity Episodes

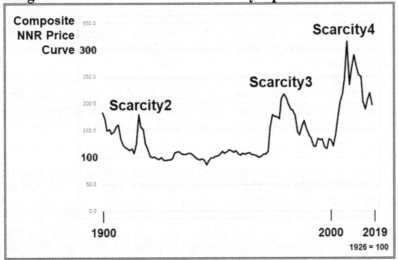

During Scarcity4 (1999-2008), the Composite NNR Price Curve increased spectacularly, by 171% – from 116.3 to 315.6 – before settling back to a "relatively low" 190.0 in 2016, which nearly equaled the Scarcity3 PEAK of 217.5. (Note that the Scarcity4 peak of 315.6 exceeded the Scarcity3 peak of 217.5 by 45%, and exceeded the Scarcity2 peak of 179.0 by 76%.)

Diagram 7-6: NNR Scarcity Episodes (Bannister)

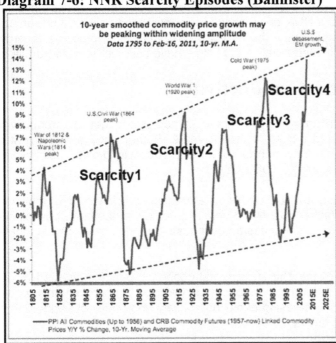

Research conducted by Barry Bannister of Stifel Nicolaus into historical commodity price trends confirms the above findings. Although Bannister's work considers both agricultural commodities and NNRs, the four increasingly severe NNR scarcity episodes – including Scarcity1 – are readily evident.

Source: Stifel Nicolaus (Bannister)[44]; "NNR Scarcity Episode" add-ons are mine.

NNR Quality, Not Quantity

It is critical to note that increasingly pervasive global NNR scarcity is a consequence of decreasing NNR "quality", not of decreasing NNR "quantities". Enormous quantities of all NNRs remain in Earth's crust – we will never "run out" of any NNR.

We are, however, "running short" of the high quality/low cost NNRs that have enabled the previously inconceivable prosperity to which those who occupy industrialized nations have become accustomed, and to which those who occupy industrializing and pre-industrial nations aspire,

> Leaner grades and finer dissemination of values in the more recently processed ores have made them more difficult to process economically and it expected that, future ore bodies will be similar or more demanding.[45] (Kota and Smart)

What remains are generally lower quality/higher cost NNRs – fewer, smaller, less accessible deposits of lower grade and purity – at a time when our NNR requirements are greater than ever!

> Ore 'complexity' has also increased during the same period of time [since 1980], with valuable components distributed sparsely and finely within the ore and often associated with a high content of impurities that are difficult to remove.[46] (Nyden and Skinner)

Predictably, as the exploitation costs associated with these lower-quality NNRs have increased since the mid-20th century, NNR price trends have increased as well. And, unsurprisingly, NNR-derived economic outputs – the infrastructure, machines, products, energy, and services that perpetuate our industrialized way of life – have become "less affordable".

Industrialism3 Industrial Productivity

> These authors [Gordon and Fernald] have hypothesized that a productivity slowdown has not occurred per se in recent years. Rather, they contend that a productivity *reversion* to the "new normal" of lower productivity growth, established in the early 1970s, has occurred.[47] (US BLS)

It is well understood that high quality/low cost NNRs are extracted early in the NNR depletion cycle, leaving only lower quality/higher cost NNRs for "eventually". It has been our expectation (hope) that human ingenuity – as manifested by industrial productivity – would indefinitely postpone "eventually".

That is, we have believed (hoped) that the incremental economic benefits afforded by an endless barrage of productivity-increasing innovations and efficiency improvements would perpetually delay and/or offset the increasing exploitation costs and prices associated with NNRs of continuously decreasing quality.

The result would be perpetual rapidly improving human prosperity – rapidly increasing economic output (GDP) and rapidly improving human material living standards (pc GDP) – essentially, a never-ending extension of our Old Normal.

This scenario has not occurred; nor will it.

Industrial productivity growth has diminished significantly during Industrialism3 – at both the sub-global and global levels – a phenomenon that has confounded most anthropocentric analysts. McKinsey notes, "Economists have proposed competing explanations for declining productivity growth and so far have failed to reach a consensus".[48]

The US Bureau of Labor Statistics concurs, "…not only has the productivity slowdown been one of the most consequential economic phenomena of the last two decades, but it also represents the most profound economic mystery during this time."[49]

Analysts from the Brookings Institution have simply given up, "Given that productivity has slowed down before—notably after 1973—many of these topics have been explored before as economists sought to explain the prior slowdown.[4] A single, clear rationale for the current slowdown is impossible to determine…"[50]

Diagram 7-7: Industrial Era Industrial Productivity Growth

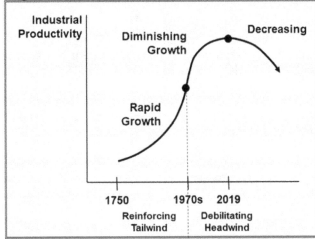

When viewed from the ecological perspective, however, the cause underlying diminishing industrial productivity growth is straightforward. Nature's increasingly-debilitating "geological headwind" – increasingly pervasive global NNR scarcity – has attenuated human ingenuity efficacy during Industrialism3.

That is, the absence of new NNR "building blocks"[51] combined with increasing NNR price trends[52] have discouraged the development and deployment of highly-impactful, productivity-increasing innovations and efficiency improvements during Industrialism3, thereby causing diminishing industrial productivity growth.

We are no less ingenious during our New Normal than we were during our Old Normal. It is simply the case that the direction of Nature's prevailing "geological wind" has shifted during our New Normal (Industrialism3) – from an increasingly-reinforcing tailwind, attributable to relative global NNR abundance, to an increasingly-debilitating and inevitably devastating headwind, attributable to increasingly pervasive global NNR scarcity.

"That true age of innovation – I'll call it the Golden Quarter – ran from approximately 1945 to 1971. Just about everything that defines the modern world either came about, or had its seeds sown, during this time."[53] (Hanlon)

Mining Sector Productivity

The second set of constraints on mineral development – referred to here as economic constraints – are a product of the fact that mineral resources deplete over time. That is to say, ores become lower in grade or more difficult to treat, whilst ore deposits are found at greater depth or in more remote locations.

To some degree, the upward pressure on industry costs which results from these trends can be offset by improvements in technology, and typically this has been the experience of the past 30 years. However, there is no law which says that this has to be the case and, for a number of mineral commodities, it would appear that the declining quality of reserves, combined with other factors like higher energy prices, are pushing up net production costs, notwithstanding continuing technological progress.[54] (Humphreys)

Innovations and efficiency improvements introduced by the mining industry during Industrialism3, while seemingly extraordinary, have failed to enable rapid productivity growth within the global mining sector.

Mining industry innovations, including "...better indirect methods of [NNR] detection, an improved geological understanding, lower drilling costs and deeper mining methods allowed deeply buried classical deposits in established districts to be developed..."[55] (Jébrak)

Yet, these and other recently developed NNR exploration, extraction, and refining tools and techniques have failed to constrain the increasing costs – and corresponding increasing price trends – associated with exploiting NNRs of continuously decreasing quality.

For example, the returns being generated on historically unprecedented global investments in NNR exploration – i.e., NNR exploration-related productivity – have diminished, and have actually gone negative in recent years.

- Between 1975 and 2000, each $1 billion invested in NNR exploration produced 15 moderate or larger (non-petroleum) NNR discoveries. By 2019, the number of discoveries had decreased to 5.[56]
- The average cost per (non-petroleum) NNR discovery increased from $63 million between 1975 and 2000, to $185 million between 2009 and 2018 – an increase of nearly 200%.[57]
- Between the years 2009 and 2018, the global investment in (non-petroleum) NNR exploration totaled $198 billion. During the same period, the value of new NNR discoveries totaled only $109 billion. Thus, each $1 invested in global NNR exploration between 2009 and 2018 generated only 55 cents in NNR discoveries – down from approximately $2 in NNR discoveries per $1 invested between 1975 and 2000. The global mining industry has "gone from value creation to value destruction".[58]

Richard Schodde, Executive Director of MinEx Consulting, succinctly summarized diminishing mining sector productivity growth, "The dramatic increase in [NNR exploration] expenditures post-2005 did not lead to a corresponding increase in the number of discoveries made."[59]

This assessment was corroborated by the Metals Economics Group, "…the substantial increase in exploration budgets over the past few years has not resulted in a proportionate rise in actual activity on the ground."[60]

Overall Industrial Productivity

Concerns about productivity are not, of course, confined to the mining industry. Slowing productivity is a widespread feature in many advanced economies. (OECD 2014; *Economist* 2016).[61] (Humphreys)

Industrial productivity growth trends at both the sub-global and global levels have followed a common evolutionary trajectory over the long term – from increasing, to diminishing, to rapidly diminishing (and even decreasing in some cases).

US Industrial Productivity Growth Throughout most of the 20th century, America led the world with respect to industrial innovation and efficiency improvement.[62] However, diminishing US industrial productivity growth during the past 50 years – since Scarcity3 – and rapidly diminishing US industrial productivity growth during the new millennium – since Scarcity4 – are undeniable.

Table 7-5: Annual US Labor Productivity Growth Rates 1920-2016

Productivity Metric	1920-1970	1970-2006	2006-1016
Output per Hour	2.82%	1.75%	0.97%
Output per Person	2.46%	1.75%	0.35%

Source: Derived from Gordon.[63]

"[US Labor] productivity growth has slowed by far more than can be explained by the waning contribution of education, from 2.8 percent per year during 1920-70 to 1.0 percent per year from 2006 to 2016."[64] (Gordon)

Even more alarming, "Overall, growth in output per capita exhibits a stunning seven-fold decline from 2.46 percent per year in 1920-70 to a mere 0.35 percent per year in 2006-16."[65] (Gordon)

Diminishing US industrial productivity growth was confirmed by a 2020 Brookings Institution (Hamilton Project) study (1948-2018), "Yet growth in [US] productivity has generally slowed over the past half century, except for a brief burst during the mid-1990s and early 2000s"[66] (Moss, et al.)

And the unfavorable US industrial productivity growth trend persists, "…since coming out of the Great Recession in 2009, [US] productivity growth has been flat or falling depending on which measure you look at."[67] (Voytek)

Underlying diminishing US industrial productivity growth is an extraordinary decrease in US R&D (research and development) productivity, an excellent proxy for US innovation,

> We find that research productivity for the aggregate US economy has declined by a factor of 41 since the 1930s, an average decrease of more than 5 percent per year.[68] (Bloom, et al.)

For example, "...the number of researchers required to double chip density today is more than 18 times larger than the number required in the early 1970s. At least as far as semi-conductors are concerned, ideas are getting harder to find. Research productivity in this case is declining sharply, at a rate of 7 percent per year."[69] (Bloom, et al.)

US R&D productivity has decreased precipitously in other areas as well,

> For agricultural yields, research effort went up by a factor of two between 1970 and 2007, while research productivity declined by a factor of 4 over the same period, at an annual rate of 3.7 %. For pharmaceuticals, research efforts went up by a factor of 9 between 1970 and 2014 while research productivity declined by a factor of 5, - an annual rate of 3.5%. ... Taking the U.S. aggregate number as representative, research productivity falls in half every 13 years...[70] (Wladawsky-Berger)

Industrialized Nation Industrial Productivity Growth The US is not alone with respect to diminishing industrial productivity growth,

> This slowdown in productivity growth is not unique to the United States: all of the major advanced economies have experienced similar declines in productivity growth.[71] (Moss, et al.)

The transition at the sub-global level between rapid industrial productivity growth during Industrialism2 and diminishing industrial productivity growth during Industrialism3, is clearly illustrated by the following analysis comprising the US and five other major industrialized nations (France, Germany, Japan, Netherlands, and UK).

Table 7-6: Annual Labor Productivity Growth Rates 1870-1984

Area\Period	1870-1913	1913-1950	1950-1973	1973-1984
United States	2.0%	2.4%	2.5%	1.0%
Five Countries	1.6%	1.6%	5.3%	2.8%

Source: Wallace.[72]

In both cases, the productivity growth rates achieved between 1950 and 1973 – the final years of Industrialism2 – were approximately twice the productivity growth rates achieved between 1973 and 1984 – the early years of Industrialism3:

- The US labor productivity growth rate, decreased from 2.5% per annum during the 1950-1973 period to 1.0% per annum during the 1973-1984 period, and
- The 5-country labor productivity growth rate, decreased from 5.3% per annum during the 1950-1973 period to 2.8% per annum during the 1973-1984 period.

A Total Factor Productivity (TFP) analysis (1954-2017) of five European nations (France, Germany, Italy, Spain, and UK), the USA, and Japan – which, at the time represented 45% of global GDP and 71% of high-income country GDP, "…shows that the seven countries are short-run synchronized, i.e., they share one common TFP cycle".[73] (Calcagnini, et al.)

Table 7-7: Annual Total Factor Productivity (TFP) Growth Rates 1954-2017

Country\Period	1954-2017	2008-2017
Germany	1.59%	0.20%
France	1.45%	(0.20%)
Italy	0.79%	(0.48%)
Japan	1.15%	0.42%
Spain	1.18%	(0.12%)
UK	0.53%	0.02%
US	0.71%	0.54%

Source: Calcagnini, G., Giombini, G. & Travaglini, G.[74]

- In all 7 cases, the longer term 1954-2017 annual TFP growth rate exceeded the more recent 2008-2017 annual TFP growth rate.
- In 6 of the 7 cases – the US being the exception – the 1954-2017 growth rate was more than twice the 2008-2017 TFP growth rate.
- In 3 of 7 cases – France, Italy, and Spain – the 2008-2017 annual TFP growth rate was actually negative, indicating absolute decreases in total factor productivity during the period.

The graphs accompanying the above data clearly indicate that these 7 major industrialized nations have experienced generally diminishing TFP growth since the inception of our New Normal (Scarcity3), and meager or even negative TFP growth since the Great Recession (Scarcity4).[75]

Global Industrial Productivity Growth All major industrialized nations – including developed East Asian nations – have experienced diminishing industrial productivity growth since the 1970s.

Table 7-8: Annual Labor Productivity Growth Rates 1950-2016

Area\Period	1950-1970	1970-1996	1996-2006	2006-2016
Developed East Asia	6.17%	3.47%	2.47%	1.45%
Western Europe (EU-15)	4.76%	2.73%	1.50%	0.55%
United States	2.61%	1.50%	2.38%	0.93%

Source: Gordon.[76]

Differences between the labor productivity growth rates achieved during the post-WW2 years of Industrialism2 and the rates achieved during the new millennium are especially compelling – and concerning:

- The US labor productivity growth rate decreased from 2.61% during the 1950-1970 period to 0.93% during the 2006-2016 period – a 64% decrease.
- The East Asia labor productivity growth rate decreased from 6.17% during the 1950-1970 period to 1.45% during the 2006-2016 period – a 76% decrease.
- The Western European labor productivity growth rate decreased from 4.76% during the 1950-1970 period to 0.55% during the 2006-2016 period – an 88% decrease.

Diagram 7-8: Annual Labor Productivity Growth Rates 1950-2016

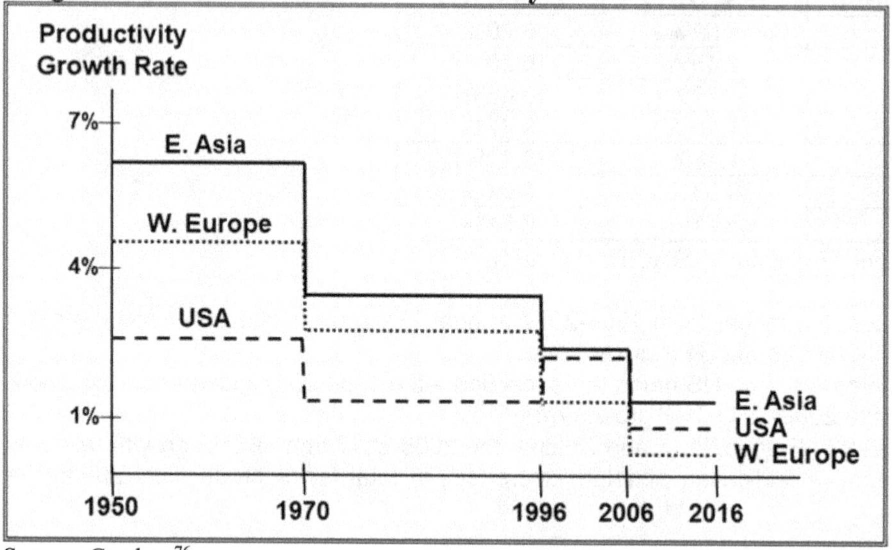

Source: Gordon.[76]

This particularly ominous trend is confirmed by a World Bank analysis of global industrial productivity growth between 1981 and 2018:

- The global productivity growth rate trend between 1981 and the Great Recession (2007), while fluctuating, was essentially flat – indicating constant productivity growth during the period.
- More recently, the global productivity growth rate has actually decreased – indicating negative productivity growth, "The GFC [Global Financial Crisis] resulted in lasting damage to global productivity growth, which remains 1.0 percentage point below its precrisis peak, at 1.8 percent in 2018, below both precrisis and longer-run averages"[77]

With respect to industrial productivity growth rate differentials between the industrialized West and the industrializing East,

> In advanced economies, productivity growth has experienced a long-run decline over the past 40 years, while in general, EMDE [Emerging Market Developing Economies] labor productivity growth has trended up over the same horizon until the global financial crisis (GFC). In EMDEs, labor productivity growth has declined from pre-crisis levels in the longest and most broad-based multiyear decline since the 1980s.[78] (World Bank)

110

Prior to the Great Recession (2007), the deindustrializing West fared worse than the industrializing East with respect to both increasingly pervasive NNR scarcity and diminishing industrial productivity growth. With the advent of the Scarcity4-induced Great Recession, however, the debilitating effects associated with these increasingly unfavorable trends became global.[79]

Industrialism3 Outcomes

> Americans were thereby undermining the American way of life by eliminating its environmental basis, just as countless other dominant species in other biotic communities have modified (adversely to themselves) the habitats upon which they depended.[80] (Catton)

During Industrialism3, secular trends associated with the enablers of human industrialism transitioned permanently from favorable to unfavorable:

- Relative global NNR abundance transitioned to increasingly pervasive global NNR scarcity, and
- Rapid global industrial productivity growth transitioned to diminishing global industrial productivity growth.

Predictably, permanently transitioning enablers of human industrialism caused corresponding permanent transitions with respect to the outcomes of human industrialism:

- Rapidly improving human prosperity transitioned to faltering human prosperity,
- Rapidly improving human cultural circumstances transitioned to deteriorating human cultural circumstances, and
- Constructive responses to our rapidly improving cultural circumstances transitioned to counterproductive responses to our deteriorating cultural circumstances.

Industrialism3 Human Prosperity

> ...until the 1970s, production, trade and employment grew strongly and steadily, in the global economy as well as in the different regions; since then, however, economic growth has been declining over the long run and has become unstable over the short and medium run.[81] (Schulmeister)

During Industrialism3, geologically-enabled exuberance has been displaced by geologically-imposed austerity. Earth's remaining low quality/high cost NNRs have failed increasingly to enable human prosperity improvement at rates that had been achieved through the utilization of high quality/low cost NNRs.

The result has been faltering global human prosperity.

Diagram 7-9: Industrial Era Global Human Prosperity Evolution

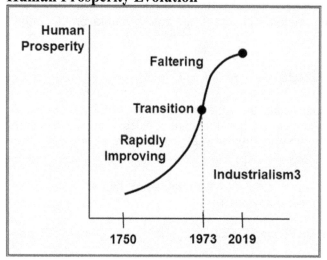

Industrialism3 Global Human Prosperity Improvement

During Industrialism3, between 1973 and 2019:

- Global GDP (economic output) more than tripled – from an estimated $13,530 billion to $50,685 billion; the corresponding compound annual growth rate was 2.91%.
- Global pc GDP (the average material living standard) increased by approximately 90% – from an estimated $3,484 to $6,606; the corresponding compound annual growth rate was 1.40%.

Table 7-9: Industrialism3 Global Human Prosperity Metrics

Prosperity Indicator	1973	2019	CAGR
Global GDP (billion)	$13,530	$50,685	2.91%
Global pc GDP	$3,484	$6,606	1.40%

Data Sources: World Bank and Macrotrends;[82] 1990 International $.

And while global human prosperity faltered significantly during the early years of Industrialism3, owing to Scarcity3, both global economic output growth and average human material living standard improvement rebounded considerably during industrial humanity's "last hurrah". With the advent of Scarcity4, however, global human prosperity faltered once again. (See Diagram 7-10)

- Between 1973 and 1982, during Scarcity3, global GDP (economic output) increased at an anemic 2.66% compounded annually, while global pc GDP (the average material living standard) increased at an even more anemic 0.85% compounded annually.

- Between 1982 and 2007, during which "final frontier" NNRs enabled industrial humanity's "last hurrah", global GDP (economic output) rebounded considerably, to 3.45% compounded annually, while global pc GDP (the average material living standard) rebounded as well – albeit to a still relatively anemic 1.71% compounded annually.

  Note, however, that the relatively robust rate at which global human prosperity improved during industrial humanity's "last hurrah" paled in comparison to the rate achieved during industrial humanity's "heyday", immediately following WW2.

  Between 1945 and 1973, global GDP (economic output) increased at an unprecedented 4.84% compounded annually, compared with 3.45% during the 1982-2007 period; and global pc GDP (the average material living standard) increased at an equally unprecedented 3.04% compounded annually, compared with 1.71% during the 1982-2007 period.

- Between 2007 and 2019, during Scarcity4 and the subsequent post-GR "non-recovery", the growth rate in global GDP (economic output) plummeted to 2.43% compounded annually, and the growth rate in global pc GDP (the average material living standard) plummeted as well, to 1.17% compounded annually.

Diagram 7-10: Industrialism3 Global Human Prosperity Improvement

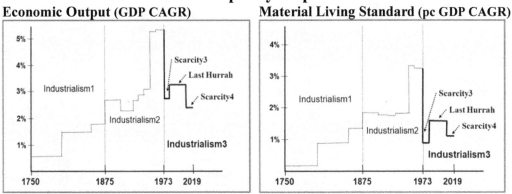

Economic Output (GDP CAGR) **Material Living Standard (pc GDP CAGR)**

Industrial Era Human Prosperity Comparisons

After nearly tripling from 1.19% during Industrialism1 to a 3.29% during Industrialism2, the compound annual growth rate in global GDP (economic output) decreased during Industrialism3 (through 2019), to 2.91% – a compelling indicator of faltering human prosperity during Industrialism3.

After tripling from 0.71% during Industrialism1 to 2.16% during Industrialism2, the compound annual growth rate in global pc GDP (the average material living standard) plummeted to 1.40% during Industrialism3 (through 2019) – an even more compelling indicator of faltering human prosperity during Industrialism3.

Table 7-10: Industrial Era Global Human Prosperity Improvement Rates

Prosperity Indicator	Industrialism1	Industrialism2	Industrialism3
Global GDP CAGR	1.19%	3.29%	2.91%
Global pc GDP CAGR	0.71%	2.16%	1.40%

Data Sources: Delong, World Bank, and Macrotrends.[83]

Perhaps the most compelling indicator of faltering global human prosperity during Industrialism3 is the precipitous decrease in human prosperity improvement experienced between the post-WW2 period (1945-1973) and Industrialism3 (1973-2019).

Table 7-11: Post-WW2 vs. Industrialism3 Global Human Prosperity Improvement Rates

Prosperity Indicator	Post-WW2	Industrialism3
Global GDP CAGR	4.84%	2.91%
Global pc GDP CAGR	3.04%	1.40%

Data Sources: World Bank and Macrotrends.[84]

The compound annual growth rate in global GDP (economic output) increased by an extraordinary 4.84% between 1945 and 1973, while global pc GDP (the average material living standard) increased by an equally extraordinary 3.04% compounded annually. These post-WW2 prosperity improvement rates were generally assumed at the time to represent industrial humanity's "new normal".

Diagram 7-11: Post-WW2 vs. Industrialism3 Global Human Prosperity Improvement

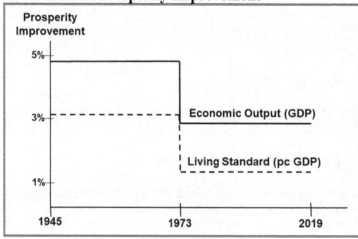

This assumption proved to be invalid, however, as the compound annual growth rate in global GDP plunged to 2.91% during Industrialism3, and the compound annual growth rate in global pc GDP likewise plunged to 1.40% during the period.

Data Sources: World Bank and Macrotrends.[84]

It is clear that global human prosperity improvement peaked during the post-WW2 rebuilding period, owing to:

- The permanent transition from relative global NNR abundance to increasingly pervasive global NNR scarcity, and
- The permanent transition from rapidly increasing global industrial productivity growth to diminishing global industrial productivity growth.

Industrialism3 Sub-Global Human Prosperity Improvement

While human prosperity has faltered at both the global and sub-global levels during Industrialism3, some nations – and regions – have fared better than others during the period. Specifically, low cost Eastern nations have generally enjoyed greater prosperity improvement than high cost Western nations.

Unfulfillable Promises Undoubtedly the most significant differences between the industrializing East and the industrialized (and deindustrializing) West are the increasingly onerous "societal overhead costs" – welfare state and the warfare state costs – that are severely impairing Western industrial competitiveness and success,

> America has become what this writer has termed "a warfare/welfare state." Almost two-thirds of the federal budget goes to the military, including veterans care, and to entitlements such as Medicare and Medicaid. We spend promiscuously on what Eisenhower dubbed "the Military Industrial Complex" and on what urban Populist Saul Alinsky described in The Professional Radical as "political pornography …a feeding trough for the welfare industry."[85] (*Forbes*)

During industrial humanity's era of relative NNR abundance, our Old Normal, industrialized and industrializing nations – primarily Western nations – created previously inconceivable amounts of NNR-derived real wealth; and prosperity within these increasingly wealthy nations improved accordingly.

The extraordinarily prosperous populations within these successful industrialized Western nations therefore felt at liberty to make two previously inconceivable promises to themselves and their posterity – universal social welfare (the welfare state), and universal national security (the warfare state).

Both promises entail enormous and continuously increasing financial obligations, the fulfillment of which requires enormous and continuously increasing amounts of NNR-derived real wealth.

Unbeknownst to the promisors, however, sufficient real wealth would not be available to permit them to fulfill their social welfare and national security promises, because sufficient globally available, economically viable NNRs would not be available to create the required real wealth.

Regrettably for these overly ambitious Western nations, increasingly onerous welfare state and warfare state costs have increasingly impaired their global industrial competitiveness – and success – during Industrialism3.

Ironically, but not surprisingly, Western welfare state and warfare state promises were made during the best of times for these nations – the times of peak NNR abundance and resultant peak prosperity improvement.

In hindsight – and when viewed from the ecological perspective – Western populations made promises to themselves and their posterity that could not possibly be fulfilled. These promises are now relentlessly draining the deteriorating economies of the nations that made them – a process that will continue until these promises are repudiated.

The West Versus the East In Great Britain, and in Europe more broadly, extensively depleted domestic NNR reserves have severely impaired human prosperity improvement during Industrialism3 (through 2019). And the situation in America, while slightly more favorable, has trended in the same unfavorable direction.

NNR-deficient Japan, owing to its low cost status and its highly trained and motivated workforce, fared significantly better than Western nations during both the post-WW2 period and the early years of Industrialism3. This competitive advantage was lost during the middle years of Industrialism3, however, as Japan became a high cost nation. Japanese prosperity has faltered since that time, at rates exceeding those of the West.

Countering the "faltering prosperity" trend, China has experienced historically unprecedented prosperity improvement during Industrialism3. China's extraordinary natural capital and human capital endowments, combined with its exceptional work ethic, have enabled the Chinese population to apply its extraordinary ingenuity toward successfully exploiting Earth's prosperity-enabling NNRs at historically unprecedented levels.

Table 7-12: Industrialism3 Sub-Global Human Prosperity Improvement Rates

Nation	Economic Output (GDP) CAGRs		Living Standard (pc GDP) CAGRs	
	Post-WW2	Industrialism3	Post-WW2	Industrialism3
Britain	3.05%	2.03%	2.56%	1.64%
America	3.29%	2.66%	1.72%	1.67%
Japan	5.78%	2.38%	5.22%	1.71%
China	3.38%	6.26%	1.77%	4.98%

Sources: World Bank and Measuring Worth.[86]

Industrialism3 British (and European) Prosperity As the first nation to industrialize, Great Britain was also the first nation to experience extensive domestic NNR depletion, and increasingly pervasive domestic NNR scarcity.

Britain was joined during the 19th century and early 20th century by the remainder of Europe – with respect to both industrialization and extensive NNR depletion. By the inception of Industrialism3, Europe, including Great Britain, had become critically deficient with respect to economically viable NNRs,[87]

> Europe has been actively mined over many centuries and many easy-to-access mineral deposits are mostly depleted. The major opportunities to access raw materials within the EU are in greater depths, in remote, but also in populated areas, in

former mine sites, in low grade deposits, and in small deposits where larger mining operations may not be feasible.[88] (European Commission)

The inevitable – and alarming – consequence, "The total EU28 contribution to overall [EU] materials supply can be estimated at around 9%. ... Therefore much of Europe's industry and economy is reliant on international markets to provide access to essential raw materials."[89] (European Commission)

Europe's reliance on foreign sources for over 90% of its NNR supplies is the fundamental cause underlying its rapidly faltering prosperity – and its rapidly diminishing global prominence.

Accordingly, Industrialism3 has been disastrous for NNR-deficient Europe with respect to human prosperity improvement – as exemplified by Great Britain. During 1973-2019, as compared with 1945-1973:

- The compound annual growth rate in British GDP (economic output) decreased from a respectable 3.05%, to a dismal 2.03%, and
- The compound annual growth rate in Britain's pc GDP (average material living standard) decreased from a robust 2.56%, to an anemic 1.64%.

Moreover, Britain's GDP as a percentage of global GDP decreased from 7.14% in 1945, to 4.35% in 1973, to 2.57% – slightly less than that of Brazil – in 2019. Europe's share of global GDP has experienced a similarly declining trajectory – from a spectacular 53.77% in 1945, to 37.78% in 1973, to 22.12% in 2019.[90]

Predictably, the roles of both Great Britain and Europe on the global stage have declined precipitously since WW2. Of the world's major power centers, NNR-starved Europe is furthest along the road to collapse. Absent an almost inconceivable series of serendipitous events (NNR exploitation miracles), Europe will remain at the forefront of industrial humanity's unraveling to global societal collapse.

Industrialism3 American Prosperity "The decade of the 1960s, at the beginning of which Kendrick's book was published, turns out in retrospect to have been the last of the five remarkable decades in which overall U.S. GDP growth raced along at close to four percent per year and labor productivity advanced at close to three percent per year.[1] The pace of advance has slowed in two phases, the first after 1970 [Scarcity3] and the second after 2006 [Scarcity4]. Taken together the two phases have reduced the annual growth rate of real GDP from 3.7 percent during 1920-70 to a mere 1.4 percent during 2006-16."[90a]

Although extremely well endowed with NNRs at the time of its "discovery", America neither was nor ever will be NNR self-sufficient. With respect to most NNRs, America's once-enormous reserves have been extensively depleted during the past 200 years, and now fail increasingly to address total US NNR requirements.

To the extent that the US attempts to perpetuate its "American way of life" going forward, increasing NNR imports from increasingly problematic sources is the price that must be paid.[91]

117

Diminishing US prosperity and global prominence, owing to increasing domestic NNR scarcity, were inevitable,

> ...by the late 19th century, the role of mining in Europe declined as the economic and political power passed to North America. The US in the late 19th and early 20th centuries then saw a dramatic increase – to be followed after World War 2 by the same dramatic decline experienced previously in Europe...[92] (ICMM)

"In 2016, the United States was reliant on imports for 80 non-fuel mineral commodities. It was fully dependent on imports for 20 of these commodities and more than 50 percent dependent on imports for another 30 commodities."[93] (Rand Corporation) America's NNR-dependence had not improved by 2019. (See Diagram 7-12)

With respect to the 92 NNRs and NNR-variants on which the USGS reported in 2019, the US was import reliant in 76 cases (83%):

- 100% import reliant in 17 cases, including manganese;
- 75%-99% import reliant in 17 cases, including bauxite (aluminum ore), potash, tin, and zinc;
- 50%-74% import reliant in 13 cases, including alumina (aluminum feedstock) and chromium;
- 20%-49% import reliant in 15 cases, including aluminum, copper, iron and steel, lead, nickel, and salt;
- Less than 20% import reliant in 14 cases, including cement, gypsum, phosphate rock, crushed stone, and sulfur.

In only 16 of the 92 cases (17%), including clays and iron ore, was the US NNR self-sufficient.

Accordingly, as is the case with NNR-deficient Great Britain, and Europe more broadly, American prosperity has faltered during Industrialism3. During 1973-2019, as compared with 1945-1973:

- The compound annual growth rate in US GDP (economic output) decreased from a relatively robust 3.29%, to 2.66%, and
- The compound annual growth rate in US pc GDP (average material living standard) decreased from a modest 1.72%, to a more modest 1.67%.

In addition, America's GDP as a percentage of global GDP decreased from an extraordinary 30.0% in 1945, to 22.71% in 1973, to 17.72% in 2019 – America's share of the global economic pie has been nearly halved in less than 75 years. Predictably, America's role on the world stage has also declined during Industrialism3.[94]

Increasingly NNR-deficient America lags Europe – possibly by a decade or so – with respect to natural environment and cultural environment deterioration. While America continues to enjoy global military superiority and primary global reserve currency status, these advantages are being abused, and are sources of increasing global resentment and tension.

Diagram 7-12: US NNR Import Reliance (2019)

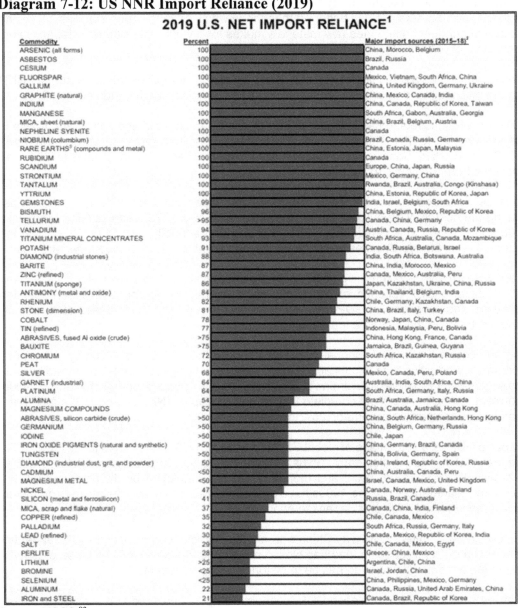

Source: USGS.[93]

Moreover, America's enormous welfare state and warfare state obligations will become increasingly problematic during the coming years, owing to America's inability to create sufficient NNR-based real wealth with which to fully discharge them.

Finally, as the most self-entitled global power center, America is likely to employ extreme measures to perpetuate its "American way of life" as Nature's Squeeze tightens – especially as it perceives increasing threats to its global military, political, and economic hegemony.

Industrialism3 Japanese Prosperity "A nation with a variety of minerals and energy supplies within its own borders is much better off than those which have to import supplies." "…being largely dependent on imported raw materials makes for a vulnerable situation. Japan is very much in that position."[95] (Youngquist)

Japan, which has always been extremely NNR-deficient, exemplifies the extraordinary NNR import reliance faced by smaller industrializing Eastern nations during Industrialism3,[96]

"The Asia-Pacific region has however shown by far the most rapid and consistent growth in its requirement for [NNR] imports, which increased more than fourfold between 1970 and 2010…"[97] (UNEP) Specifically, Japanese NNR import reliance stood at 66% in 2010, an increase from 51% only 10 years earlier.[98]

Despite its extreme domestic NNR shortcomings, Japan initiated its "economic miracle" during the post WW2 rebuilding period. Between 1946 and 1973, Japan's GDP (economic output) increased at a remarkable 5.78% compounded annually, and its pc GDP (average material living standard) increased at an equally remarkable 5.22% compounded annually.

Japanese prosperity faltered significantly during Industrialism3 however. Between 1973 and 2019, Japan's GDP (economic output) increased anemically, at only 2.38% compounded annually, and Japanese pc GDP (average material living standard) increased at an equally anemic 1.71% compounded annually.

Japan became a successful industrial power between the 1960s and 1980s by virtue of its extremely productive human capital, imported natural and physical capital, and readily available global financial capital. Japan's economic miracle peaked during the early 1990s, however, owing to its almost complete lack of natural capital (NNRs), and to the fact that it had lost its competitive advantage as a low cost nation.

Japan's GDP as a percentage of global GDP increased from 3.64% in 1945 to 7.97% in 1973, before peaking during the early 1990s at over 8%, and decreasing to 4.34% in 2019. Increasingly "stimulative" fiscal and monetary policies employed by Japan's political and economic leadership since the 1990s have predictably failed to revive the almost completely NNR-import-reliant, high cost Japanese economy.[99]

Industrialism3 Chinese Prosperity China's "economic miracle" commenced in 1978 under the leadership of Deng Xiaoping, and has blossomed during Industrialism3. Chinese prosperity improvement during this period has been historically unprecedented.[100]

Between 1952 and 1973, Chinese GDP (economic output) increased at a compound annual growth rate of 3.38%, and Chinese pc GDP (average material living standard) increased at 1.77% compounded annually – both metrics were well below the global averages during the period.

Between 1973 and 2019, Chinese GDP (economic output) increased at an extraordinary rate of 6.28% compounded annually, and Chinese pc GDP (average material living standard) increased at an equally extraordinary rate of 4.98% compounded annually – both of which were more than double the global averages during the period.

Moreover, China's share of global GDP tripled during Industrialism3, from 5.36% in 1973 to 17.43% in 2019.[101] And unlike Great Britain, Europe, America, and Japan, China experienced a dramatically expanding role on the global stage during the period.

Notably, however, the historically unprecedented scope and pace of China's industrial development efforts, combined with the fact that China has created the most extraordinary production-oriented, export-driven economy in the history of human industrialism, have engendered enormous Chinese NNR exploitation in a remarkably brief period of time,

> China's dramatic economic growth over the past few decades has increased demands for natural resources within and beyond the country itself in ways that are unprecedented in human history.[102] (UNEP)

Accordingly, owing to China's enormous and increasing NNR requirements during Industrialism3, and to the fact that China's high quality/low cost NNR reserves have been extensively depleted during the period, the industrializing giant has become heavily reliant upon imported NNRs during the new millennium,

> Despite being the number one mining nation in the world, China is facing a rapid depletion of its local mineral resources. Reserve-to-production (R/P) ratio, that represents the 'burn rate' of proven reserves of mineral commodities when applying current levels of domestic mine production, shows that China is in the 'red zone' for future supplies of nearly all crucial minerals.[103] (Mining.com)

Specifically,

> By 2008, China's net imports of metal ore and industrial minerals accounted for 25% of DMC [domestic material consumption] in this category, where only one decade before the corresponding figure was only 9%. Furthermore, China's dependency on foreign suppliers in this category is almost definitely much higher than the raw figure of 25% would indicate. This is because the traded commodities in this category are often highly concentrated compared to the form in which they are initially extracted.[104] (UNEP)

Moreover, "The other major feature to note…is China's transition from net exporter of fossil fuels to net importer. Net imports remain relatively small [in 2008] compared to domestic extraction, at around 6%, however the rate of growth over the period 2004 to 2008 was 22% p.a. [per annum] compounding."[105] (UNEP) [Note that by 2021, China was importing 74% of its oil and 45% of its natural gas.[106]]

While it is likely that China will discover additional economically viable NNRs within its borders, it is almost certain that China's future NNR requirements – and NNR import reliance – will remain enormous and ever-increasing. Hundreds of millions of Chinese have yet to fully industrialize, and China's Belt and Road Initiative will require enormous NNR quantities for decades to come.

China is therefore running a race against time, as it relies increasingly on imported NNRs to:

- Perpetuate its economic miracle, and thereby continuously improve Chinese prosperity, and
- Expand its economic (and military) influence, as an offset against America's waning global economic and military dominance.

In order to succeed in the near term, and thereby position itself to compete successfully for remaining globally available, economically viable NNRs in the future, China must execute its industrialization plans rapidly and flawlessly – or it will suffer the same fate as Japan.

Irrespective of its near term success, however, China's currently improving cultural environment will deteriorate during the coming decades, as a consequence of both increasingly pervasive domestic NNR scarcity and increasingly pervasive global NNR scarcity.

Signs of faltering Chinese prosperity are already evident. The compound annual growth rate in Chinese GDP from the Great Recession forward (2007-2019) was 5.61% – a considerable decrease from the 6.49% compound annual GDP growth rate achieved during the pre-recession period (1973-2007).

It is notable that Western nations, most of which had launched industrialization initiatives during our Old Normal (Industrialism1 and Industrialism2) – a period of relative global NNR abundance – generally enjoyed lengthy intervals of rapidly improving prosperity, which typically spanned well over a century.

Eastern nations, in comparison, most of which have launched industrialization initiatives during our New Normal [Industrialism3 (or late Industrialism2)] – a period of increasingly pervasive global NNR scarcity – are experiencing substantially compressed intervals of rapidly improving prosperity, which are typically measured in decades.

Industrialism3 Human Cultural Circumstances

The impact of the long-term democratic decline has become increasingly global in nature, broad enough to be felt by those living under the cruelest dictatorships, as well as by citizens of long-standing democracies. Nearly 75 percent of the world's population lived in a country that faced deterioration last year [2020].[107] (Freedom House)

The BTI [Bertelsmann Stiftung Transformation Index] 2022 finds evidence of a new low in terms of political and economic transformation. Poor governance has exacerbated this development. Moreover, the regulatory framework governing the market and competition is neither free nor fair in most countries. Corruption, clientelism and mismanagement by the established elites stand in the way of economic development and social participation.[108]

"Worse still, the rules of this game are obstructing public efforts to deal with the common challenges now threatening the peace and stability of our highly interconnected world."[109] (UNCTAD)

And finally, "Novel layers of uncertainties are interacting to create new kinds of uncertainty—a new uncertainty complex —never seen in human history."[110] (UNDP)

The Anthropocentric Ideal During our Old Normal – Industrialism1 and Industrialism2 – industrial humanity's exuberance gave birth to an "anthropocentric ideal". Continuously improving cultural circumstances – increasingly favorable political, economic, and societal trends – would enable humankind to achieve universal prosperity through global industrialism.

The continuously improving cultural circumstances envisioned by the anthropocentric ideal featured:

- Political stability, characterized by transparent and enlightened governance, to be conducted through participatory liberal democracies, which would stress freedom, human rights, and rule-of-law.
- Economic resilience, characterized by market-based economies that would foster increasing wealth creation, within the context of fiscal prudence, savings and investment, entrepreneurism, and a stable long term planning horizon.
- Societal cohesion, characterized by intra-national and international cooperation, tolerance, and peaceful coexistence.

Ecological Reality With the transition during Industrialism3 from relative global NNR abundance to increasingly pervasive global NNR scarcity, the anthropocentric ideal, which was almost certainly a utopian fantasy in any event, became geologically impossible. Rather, industrial humanity has experienced generally deteriorating cultural circumstances since the 1970s:

- Increasing political instability, characterized (and caused) by increasingly opaque and repressive governance, which is conducted through increasingly authoritarian regimes – even within alleged "democracies". Small, well-connected cliques of "ruling elites" have resorted increasingly to autocratic governing techniques – e.g., propaganda, surveillance, censorship, and extrajudicial legal activities – as the means by which to oppress the general public, control the public discourse, and silence dissent.
- Increasing economic weakness, characterized (and caused) by increasing deindustrialization – the transition from savings-based, production-oriented, manufacturing economies to debt-based, consumption-oriented, service economies. Resultant diminishing industrial production growth and real wealth creation have fostered increasing global economic fragility.
- Increasing societal volatility, characterized (and caused) by social fragmentation and inequality, which have become epidemic at both the national and global levels.

Political Instability

"Political instability also deteriorated, with 51 countries recording a fall in peacefulness in this indicator while only 26 improved in the past year [2021]. This indicator is now at its worst level since 2008."[111] (*Global Peace Index*)

"There has been an erosion in public confidence in democratic institutions and an increase in social and political polarization in both rich and poor countries across the globe, which has contributed to a rise in authoritarianism."[112] (Fund for Peace)

"Today, we are witnessing the unravelling of the international arms control architecture and a gradual backtracking on established arms control agreements, which have supported global stability, restraint, and transparency."[113] (United Nations)

Global political instability, as attributable to phenomena such as the increasing incidence of fragile – failed and failing – states, and increasingly authoritarian – oppressive, corrupt, opaque, unaccountable, and invasive – governments, has increased dramatically during Industrialism3.

Fragile States The Fund for Peace maintains the Fragile States Index (FSI), which rates 178 nations with respect to 12 indicators pertaining to state fragility. In their 2019 report, 18 nations were considered "sustainable", and 41 nations were considered "stable". Eighty-eight (88) nations received "warning" ratings, and 31 nations received "alert" ratings.[114]

While one third (59) of the nations received either "stable" or "sustainable" FSI ratings, two thirds (119) received either "warning" or "alert" ratings. Interestingly, nearly all NNR "final frontiers" are located in Asian, African, and Latin American nations that received either "warning" or "alert" FSI ratings.

Also of note, America appears to be among the leaders with respect to increasing national fragility,

> Of the 20 most worsened countries in the 2019 FSI, nine of those countries were also among the 20 most worsened countries in the 2018 FSI. Three of those countries — namely, Brazil, the United States, and Venezuela — have been among the 20 most worsened countries for each of the three most recent FSIs.[115] (Fund for Peace)

Moreover, increasing US fragility appears to be apolitical,

> In the previous year's FSI [Trump presidency], the United States was the most worsened due to the cascading effects of COVID-19, which included growing social and political polarization, economic downturn, rising political violence, and group grievance. Every country can have a bad year. But a resilient country usually improves the following year. In 2021 [Biden presidency] the United States worsened yet again.[116] (Fund for Peace)

Authoritarian Governments TheGlobalEconomy.com tracks various "quality of governance" data, which is sourced from over 200 nations and territories worldwide. The following quality of governance indicators have trended from bad to worse during past two and a half decades:[117]

- The Political Stability Index (World Bank), which decreased from -0.01 in 1996 to -0.07 in 2019 – with -2.5 indicating very unstable, +2.5 indicating very stable, and 0 indicating neutral – reveals dramatically increasing global political instability.
- The Rule of Law Index (World Bank), which decreased from -0.01 in 1996 to -0.04 in 2019, reveals a significant decrease in global rule-of-law.
- The Control of Corruption Index (World Bank), which decreased from -0.02 in 1996 to -0.04 in 2019, reveals noticeably increasing global government corruption.
- The Corruption Perceptions Index (Transparency International), which decreased from 47 in 2001 to 43 in 2019 – with 100 indicating "no corruption" – also reveals noticeably increasing global government corruption.
- The Voice and Accountability Index (World Bank), which decreased from -0.01 in 1996 to -0.04 in 2019, reveals significantly decreasing popular participation in governance processes worldwide.

Freedom House publishes *Freedom in the World*, an annual report on political rights and civil liberties, consisting of ratings and assessments pertaining to 195 countries worldwide. Their 2021 report concludes,

> As a lethal pandemic, economic and physical insecurity, and violent conflict ravaged the world in 2020, democracy's defenders sustained heavy new losses in their struggle against authoritarian foes, shifting the international balance in favor of tyranny. Incumbent leaders increasingly used force to crush opponents and settle scores, sometimes in the name of public health, while beleaguered activists—lacking effective international support—faced heavy jail sentences, torture, or murder in many settings.[118]

Accordingly, "These withering blows marked the 15th consecutive year of decline in global freedom. The countries experiencing deterioration outnumbered those with improvements by the largest margin recorded since the negative trend began in 2006. The long democratic recession is deepening."[119]

Moreover, our deteriorating political circumstances did not improve in 2021,

> The present threat to democracy is the product of 16 consecutive years of decline in global freedom. A total of 60 countries suffered declines over the past year, while only 25 improved. As of today, some 38 percent of the global population live in Not Free countries, the highest proportion since 1997. Only about 20 percent now live in Free countries.[120]

Increasing political corruption, lack of accountability, and a general disregard (or outright contempt) for those whom they purport to serve, have amplified the effects of the elitist power-grab, and have thereby increased global political instability,

"Corruption erodes trust in government and undermines the social contract. This is cause for concern across the globe, but particularly in contexts of fragility and violence, as corruption fuels and perpetuates the inequalities and discontent that lead to fragility, violent extremism, and conflict."[121] (World Bank)

Christopher O. Clugston

Confirming the World Bank assessment, "Freedom House research, including *Freedom in the World*, has documented the global decline in government accountability, transparency, and rule-of-law, as authoritarian leaders ignore the most basic elements of due process, misuse the justice system to persecute their critics, and perpetuate impunity for corruption and abuses of power."[122]

For example, "Based on worldwide economic data compiled in 2001-2002, the World Bank estimated that the amount of money paid in bribes globally was some $1 trillion."[123] (United States Institute of Peace) It is unlikely that this amount decreased during the ensuing 20 years.

Censorship and surveillance are population control techniques employed by authoritarian regimes to monitor and silence critics. Both censorship and surveillance have increased dramatically during Industrialism3 – owing in no small part to the proliferation of the Internet and social media – and further contribute to public distrust and political instability,

> Traditional censorship was basically an exercise of cut and paste. Government agents inspected the content of newspapers, magazines, books, movies, or news broadcasts, often prior to release, and suppressed or altered them so that only information judged acceptable would reach the public. For dictatorships, censorship meant that an uncooperative media outlet could be shut down or that unruly editors and journalists exiled, jailed, or murdered.

> Starting in the early 1990s, when journalism went online, censorship followed. Filtering, blocking and hacking replaced scissors and black ink.[124] (Bennett and Naim)

"Governments went from spectators in the digital revolution to sophisticated early adopters of advanced technologies that allowed them to monitor journalists, and direct the flow of information."[125] (Bennett and Naim)

Most disconcerting is the fact that "liberal democracies" are also heavily involved in these practices, "National security policies place the US and other mature democracies in the same discussion as countries, like Russia, that see the internet as both a threat and a means of control."[126] (Bennett and Naim)

An international study conducted by researchers from the University of Pretoria, SA found that,

> In many countries strong trends toward nation-wide monitoring, sometimes even calling on the support of search engines such as Google, Internet café owners and Internet service providers, were noted. In some countries serious invasion of individual privacy are noted, e.g. not even being able to send anonymous emails, and government security infiltration of online networks.[127] (Bitso, et al.)

And, the scope of government monitoring and censorship activities is broad based,

> Although mostly websites are targeted, censoring of social media websites, chat groups, and Internet telephony service (e.g. Skype) also occurs. In some countries

126

Internet censorship is formerly regulated by the government; in others there are no formal legal structures but very strong surveillance and enforcement actions.[128] (Bitso, et al.)

Again, "liberal democracies" are also heavily involved, "Although a democratic country, the United Kingdom seems to have very strict rules on Internet censorship and especially Internet surveillance, owing to a strong concern for national security."[129] (Bitso, et al.)

Finally, victims of censorship and surveillance are often dealt with harshly, "Actions against those considered in breach of regulations and legislation differs widely between countries. It can range from a fine, police custody, imprisonment, intimidation and even alleged murder."[130] (Bitso, et al.)

Economic Fragility

After almost three decades of remarkable progress since the end of the Second World War, economic conditions started to deteriorate in the 1970s. Economic growth slowed down in all parts of the world during the second half of the 1970s and the first half of the 1980s. Before the oil price shock of 1973, the annual growth of world gross product had been at 5.3 per cent, while during the rest of the 1970s, annual world growth reached only 2.8 per cent.[131] (UN/DESA)

Fast-forward to today, after over half a century of purportedly remedial government fiscal and monetary policies,

As the major shareholders of the global economic regime remain antipathetic to the required changes in the rules, norms and policies, and trust in government, at all levels, continues to deteriorate, the world economy today bears an eerie resemblance to the early 1930s, when, in the face of unresolved debt problems, growing inequality and political polarization, the siren calls of central bankers and economic thinkers helped usher in a global depression that led to a world war.[132] (UNCTAD)

The IMF accurately summarized our deteriorating global economic circumstances, "To put it simply: we are facing a crisis on top of a crisis." ... "In economic terms, growth is *down* and inflation is *up*. In human terms, people's incomes are *down* and hardship is *up*."[133] (IMF)

Increasing global economic weakness and fragility during Industrialism3 – which are primarily attributable to increasing global deindustrialization – are manifested by diminishing industrial production.

Industrial production measures the total output – i.e., infrastructure, machines, products, and energy – produced by an economy's industrial sector during a specified time period. The industrial sector – which consists of mining, manufacturing, utilities, and construction – accounts for the NNR-derived real wealth created by an industrialized economy.

Accordingly, industrial production growth, which measures the change in total industrial sector output between two specified periods of time, serves as an excellent proxy for national or global economic strength.

The following long term industrial production growth data validate the permanent transition during the 1970s from global economic strength to global economic weakness – concurrent with the transition from our Old Normal (Nature's Stimulus) to our New Normal (Nature's Squeeze).

Table 7-13: Industrial Production Growth 1920-2007

Nation/Region	1920-1938	1950-1972	1973-1989	1990-2007
Industrial Leaders*	1.9%	5.2%	1.0%	2.1%
European Core	2.9%	4.0%	1.4%	2.0%
Scandinavia	3.9%	4.9%	1.1%	3.1%
European Periphery	4.7%	8.6%	3.5%	2.8%
Newly Settled	2.3%	5.2%	2.0%	2.3%
Asia	4.2%	8.1%	5.5%	4.2%
Latin America	2.8%	5.2%	2.9%	2.2%
Mid-East/N. Africa	4.9%	7.6%	6.4%	4.5%
Sub-Sahara Africa	4.6%	5.0%	3.5%	3.8%

Source: NBER,[134] *Industrial Leaders are the UK, US, and Germany.

With respect to each of the nine analyzed segments, industrial production growth peaked during the 1950-1972 post-WW2 rebuilding period, and decreased significantly during Industrialism3:

- "Since 1973, however, growth in the three post-war leaders [UK, US, and Germany] has only averaged slightly more than 2 per cent per annum. This leaders' slow down must have been due in part to the fact that war reconstruction forces were exhausted and to the poor macroeconomic conditions following the oil crises [Scarcity3]. But long-term deindustrialization forces were probably playing the bigger role, as suggested by the continued slow industrial growth between 1990 and 2007."[135] (NBER)
- Industrial production growth among the "periphery" nations – located in Latin America, the European periphery, the Middle East, Africa, Asia, and sub-Saharan Africa – peaked at the same time, "The high-point of peripheral industrial growth was the 1950-72 period..."[136] (NBER)

Global industrial production growth – and global humanity's economic circumstances – peaked at the end of Industrialism2, owing to the permanent transition from relative global NNR abundance to increasingly pervasive global NNR scarcity.

Increasing global economic weakness during Industrialism3 has caused increasing economic fragility – a precarious economic state in which our weakening global economy has become highly vulnerable to "large-scale crises caused by small, routine economic shocks".[137] (Lagunoff and Schreft)

Societal Volatility

Increasing societal volatility, attributable to phenomena such as increasing social fragmentation and wealth/income inequality, is becoming increasingly prevalent both globally and sub-globally.

Global Social Fragmentation During Industrialism3, the global societal landscape has evolved from "relatively integrated",

> Over the past three decades, flows of capital, goods, services, and people have transformed our world, helped by the spread of new technologies and ideas. These forces of integration have boosted productivity and living standards, tripling the size of the global economy and lifting 1.3 billion people out of extreme poverty...

...to "increasingly fragmented",

> Tensions over trade, technology standards, and security have been growing for many years, undermining growth—and trust in the current global economic system. Uncertainty around trade policies alone reduced global gross domestic product in 2019 by nearly 1 percent, according to IMF research.[138] (IMF)

Pierre-Olivier Gourinchas, chief economist at the IMF, sums up the destabilizing consequences associated with increasing societal fragmentation at the global level, "The danger is that these [geopolitical tectonic] plates will drift further apart, fragmenting the global economy into distinct economic blocs with different ideologies, political systems, technology standards, cross border payment and trade systems, and reserve currencies."

He concludes, "we must recognize that a fragmented world is a more volatile and vulnerable world, where access to safe assets is more restricted and the global financial safety net is less comprehensive."[139]

Sub-Global Social Fragmentation, "Inequalities of income, wealth, and opportunity have continued to worsen within too many countries for a long time—and across countries in recent years. People have been left behind as industries have changed amid global competition."[140] (IMF)

Among the victims of increasing sub-global societal fragmentation are industrialized Western nations, particularly America. Dr. Matthew Gentzkow from Stanford University describes increasing fragmentation within OECD nations, "Among the 12 OECD countries for which we were able to get data, the US has the largest increase in polarization. After 2000, all countries except Britain and Germany exhibit a positive [increasing polarization] linear trend."[141]

Dr. Gentzkow offers a specific example of increasing US social fragmentation, "In 1978, the average [US] partisan rated in-party members 27.4 points higher than out-party members on a "feeling thermometer" ranging from 0 to 100. In 2020, the difference was 56.3 points."[142]

A 2020 Pew Research Center study confirms Dr. Gentzkow's findings,

When the nonpartisan Pew Research Center recently surveyed people in 17 countries in Europe, Asia and North America, Americans were the most likely to say their society was split along partisan, racial and ethnic lines. The U.S. also reported more religious division than almost any other country surveyed.[143]

For example, "In 2012, fewer than half of Americans said they thought "very strong conflicts" existed between Democrats and Republicans. By 2020, that share had soared past 70%."[144]

The study concludes, "What makes the U.S. truly stand out, however — and threatens its democratic future — is that its political conflict combines with high levels of ethnic, racial and religious conflict."[145]

The trend toward increasing American social fragmentation had been well established by the dawn of the new millennium, with roots dating back to the beginning of Industrialism3,

> ...we propose that several key historical events during the 1970s and 1980s increased the salience of many social and moral issues while concomitantly redefining the terms conservative and liberal. These events led members of orthodox religious denominations to increasingly categorize themselves as conservative and members of progressive religious denominations to categorize themselves as liberal despite a lack of attitudinal changes. They further developed a more negative opinion of out-group members.[146] (Miller and Hoffmann)

Individual Social Fragmentation, which is manifested by the absence of family and/or community relationships or connections, is perhaps the least visible form of social fragmentation. Individual social fragmentation affects members of a society who become disconnected, disenfranchised, alienated, and disillusioned – cut off from the rest of society.

Limited available data indicate that individual social fragmentation is increasing. A University of Manchester study revealed an increase in social fragmentation – defined as "the numbers of private renters, single people, migrants and one person households in a community" – in England during the first decade of the 21st century, "Between 2001 and 2011, there was a 7.5% increase in single people and a 90% increase in the privately rented household statistic..."[147]

The study noted that, "Single people are also known to suffer from worse mental health outcomes."[148]

Wealth/Income Inequality According to the 2022 *World Inequality Report*, "The period from 1945 or 1950 till 1980, was a period of shrinking [wealth and income] inequality in many parts of the world (US, UK, France, but also India and China)."[149] However,

> Income and wealth inequalities have been on the rise nearly everywhere since the 1980s, following a series of deregulation and liberalization programs which took different forms in different countries. The rise has not been uniform: certain countries have experienced spectacular increases in inequality (including the US, Russia and India) while others (European countries and China) have experienced relatively smaller rises.[150]

Most recently, "…between 1995 and 2021, the top 1% captured 38% of the global increment in wealth, while the bottom 50% captured a frightening 2%. The share of wealth owned by the global top 0.1% rose from 7% to 11% over that period and global billionaire wealth soared."[151]

The Gini index, which is maintained by the World Bank, "often serves as a gauge of economic inequality, measuring income distribution or, less commonly, wealth distribution among a population."[152] A Gini index value of 0 indicates equal distribution of wealth or income across a human population, while a value of 100 indicates that all wealth or income is held by a single individual.

Notwithstanding a Gini index decrease from 67 to 62 between 2008 and 2013, owing primarily to extraordinary prosperity improvement among industrializing Eastern nations such as China and India, "Global inequality, as measured by the Gini index, has steadily increased over the past few centuries and spiked during the COVID-19 pandemic."[153] (Investopedia)

Commenting on the *2022 World Inequality Report*, the World Economic Forum concluded "that wealth and income inequality remain pronounced across the globe."[154] … "On average, an individual from the top 10% will earn $122,100, but an individual from the bottom half will earn just $3,920."[155]

In the aggregate, while the top 10% of the global population earn 52% of total global income, the bottom 50% earn just 8% of the total.

With respect to total global wealth, the differential between rich and poor is even more pronounced, "The poorest half of the global population owns just 2% of the global total, while the richest 10% own 76% of all wealth."[156] (WEF)

Regarding the long term trend in global wealth and income inequality, the *World Inequality Report 2022* found that despite recent decreases in inequality owing to Eastern industrialization,

> Global inequalities seem to be about as great today as they were at the peak of Western imperialism in the early 20th century. Indeed, the share of income presently captured by the poorest half of the world's people is about half what it was in 1820, before the great divergence between Western countries and their colonies.[157]

Industrialism3 Human Responses

> You can evade reality, but you can't evade the consequences of evading reality.[158] (Ayn Rand)

Since the inception of Industrialism3, Nature's Squeeze – increasingly pervasive global NNR scarcity – has caused faltering human prosperity – slowing economic growth and diminishing material living standard improvement – which has caused our deteriorating cultural circumstances – increasing political instability, economic fragility, and societal volatility.

Given our anthropocentric perspective, our responses have generally entailed:

- Increasingly desperate and futile attempts to "fix" our deteriorating cultural circumstances, and
- Increasingly desperate and dysfunctional attempts to cope with our deteriorating cultural circumstances.

Both response types are counterproductive – they exacerbate our already deteriorating cultural circumstances:

- Increasing coercion, oppression, warfare, and other forms of conflict, both within and among nations have exacerbated global political instability.
- Increasing fiscal imprudence at the individual, corporate, and government levels has exacerbated global economic fragility.
- Increasing individual-level dysfunction and societal-level dysfunction have exacerbated global societal volatility.

Responses to Increasing Political Instability

> Globally, the absolute number of war deaths has been declining since 1946. And yet, conflict and violence are currently on the rise, with many conflicts today waged between non-state actors such as political militias, criminal, and international terrorist groups. Unresolved regional tensions, a breakdown in the rule of law, absent or co-opted state institutions, illicit economic gain, and the scarcity of resources exacerbated by climate change, have become dominant drivers of conflict.[159] (UN)

Increasingly, responses to our deteriorating political circumstances during Industrialism3 have involved conflict; specifically:

- Conventional warfare – traditional modes of armed combat such wars, coups, and insurgencies; and
- Unconventional warfare – non-combative belligerent activities such as economic warfare, cyber warfare, and biological warfare – in which "battles" are waged through non-traditional means.

The goal in all cases has been to disrupt, weaken, or subdue an adversary, thereby providing the victor with increased control over the affairs and Earth resources – RNRs and NNRs – of the vanquished.

Conventional Warfare Between the Renaissance and Industrialism3, human conflict typically entailed wars among the "great powers" – France, Great Britain, the Netherlands, Spain, Italy, the Ottoman Empire, the Hapsburg Empire, Japan, China, and America. These wars, while relatively few in number, often spanned many years and produced enormous casualties.

Since WW2, and increasingly during Industrialism3, major wars have been displaced by an increasing number of regional conflicts – often involving smaller nations and non-state actors – which have typically produced fewer casualties, but have been more widespread and often more disruptive.

According to Our World in Data, "The absolute number of war deaths has been declining since 1946. In some years in the early post-war era, around half a million people died through direct violence in wars. In recent years, the annual death toll tends to be less than 100,000."[160]

However, "The increase in the number of wars is predominantly an increase of smaller conflicts. This follows from the previously shown declining number of war victims while the number of conflicts increased."[161]

Data from the Uppsala Conflict Data Program (UCDP) confirms the significant increase in the number of global conflicts during Industrialism3:[162]

- State-Based Violence increased by 80% between 1975 to 2021 – from 30 incidents to 54 incidents.
- Non-State Violence increased by 300% between 1988 and 2021 – from 19 incidents to 76 incidents.
- One-Sided Violence increased by 54% between 1988 and 2021 – from 26 incidents to 40 incidents.

Unconventional Warfare Various forms of unconventional warfare have supplemented or displaced conventional warfare during Industrialism3, as the means by which to de-stabilize, undermine, and ultimately destroy an adversary.

Economic Warfare The use of economic sanctions, which dates to ancient Athens (or before), has regained popularity during the past several decades,

> The average number of sanctions per decade has increased since the end of the Cold War in 1990. Economist Peter A. G. van Bergeijk suspects this isn't a coincidence—they're more palatable than an armed conflict, with less collateral damage than some other interventions. They also coincide with shifts in the openness of the world economy—the economy became more global after the collapse of the Soviet Union. Economic interdependence gave sanctions more teeth, so their use spiked.[163] (Quartz)

Because economic sanctions seek to undermine the economic viability of an adversary, and thereby cause or exacerbate political instability, such actions have generally been considered acts of war, "If you put on a financial embargo or an economic embargo on a state which really can't then attend to its basic needs, those can well be considered acts of war."[164] (Wigell)

The effectiveness associated with economic sanctions remains questionable however, "International relations since 1945 have provided many cases of economic sanctions aimed at forcing states to change their behaviour without bloodshed, most of them apparently un-successful."[165] (Harrison)

The primary reason, "In cases involving core national interests, economic pain rarely translates into political gain (Oegg and Elliott 2008; see also Jones 2015). Sanctions were likely to succeed only when stakes were low or when military disparities were very large."[165] (Harrison)

Interestingly, despite their apparent lack of effectiveness, and despite the "unintended consequences" often caused by their imposition – e.g., economic damage to the perpetrator, and diminished international prominence accorded to the perpetrator – the use of economic sanctions has continued unabated.

Cyber Warfare "…involves the actions by a nation-state or international organization to attack and attempt to damage another nation's computers or information networks through, for example, computer viruses or denial-of-service attacks."[166] (Rand Corporation)

"Cyber warfare began in 2010 with Stuxnet, which was the first cyber weapon meant to cause physical damage. Stuxnet is reported to have destroyed 20% of the centrifuges Iran used to create its nuclear arsenal."[167] (Fortinet)

Cyber warfare has proliferated globally from that point forward, "World cyber warfare statistics show an incredible increase in activity between 2009 and 2018, with cyber warfare attacks surging by 440%." (From the Business Information Industry Association) Specifically, "The past decade saw a huge expansion of cyber warfare, with thousands of politically motivated attacks on at least 56 countries."[168] (DataProt)

The incidence of corporate cyber-attacks has been equally alarming, "Cybercrime statistics reveal that as many as 64% of companies across the globe have experienced some sort of hacking attacks."[169] (DataProt)

In testifying before the US House of Representatives Committee on Armed Services in March of 2017, Peter Singer, Strategist and Senior Fellow at the New America Foundation, observed,

> These [cyber] attacks started years back, but it continued after the 2016 election. They have been reported as hitting clearly government sites, like the Pentagon's email system, as well as clearly private networks, like U.S. banks. They have also been reported as targeting a wide variety of American allies ranging from government, military, and civilian targets, and states that range from Norway to the United Kingdom, as well as now trying to influence upcoming elections in Germany, France, and the Netherlands.[170]

While nearly always covert, and nearly always difficult to prove, cyberattacks and other forms of cyber warfare (e.g., cyber espionage) have increased, as all major global powers, and many non-government actors, seek to gain advantages over adversarial nations and organizations.

Cyberwarfare and the threat of cyberwarfare therefore breed increasing distrust and suspicion among public and private entities, which further exacerbates global political instability.

Biological Warfare The disruptive – and destructive – potential associated with biological warfare is enormous,

Since the end of World War II, BW [biological warfare] science and technology has developed in ways that could make effectively disseminated biological weapons as deadly as thermonuclear weapons.[212] At the same time, globalization and the widespread adoption of so-called dual-use technologies—those with legitimate uses for commerce, science, or medicine—have made many of the underlying scientific and technical capabilities required for BW programs accessible even to small groups and individuals.[171] (Carus)

Fortunately, "The growth in BW's lethality was not matched by increased use. Indeed, there is no evidence of widespread use of biological agents since 1945 (through 2017)."[172] (Carus)

However, the SARS-CoV-2 virus and ensuing Covid-19 pandemic have provided a global wake-up call regarding the threats to political stability – and human existence more broadly – posed by both naturally-occurring and human-engineered biological pathogens, whether intentionally released or accidentally released.

The pandemic has also revealed how such pathogens might be "weaponized",

> The COVID-19 pandemic has shown us how effectively fears of infection can close down societies, sow mistrust among allies, and create political turmoil. Future biological wars may use the same dynamics to inflict shock and confusion upon the enemy by the mere threat of mass casualties, thereby circumventing several previous limitations of biological warfare.[173] (Gisselsson)

Moreover, the "…rapid developments in the field of synthetic biology may broaden the repertoire of bioweapons, enabling tactical versatility and more precise attacks."[174] (Gisselsson)

A "next generation" biowarfare strategy might involve a small, anonymous, fear-provoking attack, in which a "synthetic agent" maximizes disruption among a targeted population, and thereby enables an adversary to gain control during the ensuing confusion,

> It is becoming clear that a biological attack, however small, may still reach effects at the strategic level by shifting the target for biological weapons away from military contingents toward the whole of society.[175] (Gisselsson)

Importantly, such a strategy would require "fundamental changes in attitudes toward the use of disease as a weapon."[176] (Carus) That is, it would require a major global power, rogue state, or non-state actor to disregard the ultimate "deterrent against biological attacks: their moral reprehensibility, especially when directed against civilian targets."[177] (Gisselsson)

Regrettably, biological attacks and other previously inconceivable conventional and unconventional warfare methodologies will become increasingly pervasive as Nature's Squeeze further tightens, as our political circumstances further deteriorate, and as increasingly disenfranchised population segments become increasingly frustrated angry, and violent.

Responses to Increasing Economic Fragility

> So every time spending growth came to a halt, the central banks would step in and lower [interest] rates and consequently also debt servicing cost. With more money in consumers' pockets spending could resume. This process, which [David] Stockman refers to as dishonest market pricing, had even more perverted effects than just raising the overall debt level. It allowed the emergence of debt that consumed current resources without adding to future production. Unless paid for by prior production, through honest savings, debt funded consumption makes society poorer and less capable of meeting its future liabilities.[178] (Bohm-Bawerk)

By the 1970s, owing to Scarcity3, high cost nations such as America and most of Europe, could no longer create sufficient real wealth with which to discharge their increasingly onerous welfare state and warfare state obligations – and still achieve "acceptable" rates of prosperity improvement.

Increasingly desperate populations within these high cost nations have attempted to compensate for their "real wealth deficits" by resorting to unsustainable economic behavior – pseudo purchasing power (PPP):

- Incurring historically unprecedented debt at the individual, corporate, and government levels – debt that the borrowers have neither the capacity nor the intent to repay.
- Suppressing interest rates to sub-market levels through government debt monetization – expanding central bank balance sheets – thereby engendering suboptimal resource allocation and malinvestment.
- Creating enormous quantities of faith-based fiat currencies – money supply expansion – thereby causing asset inflation ("bubbles") and consumer price inflation.
- Underfunding investments in our future wellbeing – e.g., pension funds, retirement accounts, and "social entitlements" – thereby undermining our future financial solvency.

PPP has enabled us to increase our current consumption of NNR-derived infrastructure, machines, products, energy, and services – and thereby improve our current prosperity – at the expense of our future prosperity (and that of our descendants).

Unrepayable Debt "A large body of academic research shows that high debt is associated with slower GDP growth and higher risk of financial crises."[179] (McKinsey)

By supplementing current income (or current tax receipts) with debt, borrowers can live temporarily beyond their means. Debt becomes problematic, however, when interest rates increase, when lenders become unwilling or unable to extend additional credit, and/or when lenders demand partial or total repayment of their outstanding loans. Defaults and financial ruin result.

Total global debt has increased extraordinarily during Industrialism3 – particularly in response to Scarcity3 and Nixon's closing of the "gold window" in 1971, in response to Scarcity4 and the Great Recession in 2008/9, and in response to the Covid pandemic in 2020/1. (See Diagram 7-13)

According to the International Monetary Fund (IMF), global debt as a percent of global GDP stood at approximately 105% in 1950 – which was considered "excessive". Excessive debt at the time was considered "unavoidable", however, as debt that had been incurred to finance WW2 was deemed "necessary".

Diagram 7-13: Global Debt as a Percent of Global GDP 1950 to 2021

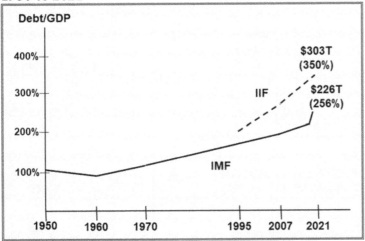

Sources: International Monetary Fund (IMF) = Solid Line;[180]
Institute of International Finance (IIF) = Dashed Line.[181]

Given that indebtedness was being reduced during the post-war period, global debt as a percent of global GDP had decreased to approximately 95% by 1960. From that point forward, however, the trend in global indebtedness has accelerated,

> The private sector's debt has tripled since 1950 (through 2017)." … "Global public debt, on the other hand, has experienced a reversal of sorts. After a steady decline up to the mid-1970s, public debt has gone up since, with advanced economies at the helm and, of late, followed by emerging and low-income developing countries.[182] (IMF)

Global debt as a percent of GDP reached approximately 115% by 1970 – only slightly greater than the 1950 level. But with the closing of the "gold window" in 1971, which essentially eliminated the externally-imposed constraint on central government borrowing and central bank money printing, our attitude toward borrowing became "whatever we can get away with".

Global debt as a percent of global GDP reached 195% in 2007, increased to 215% in 2019, and soared to an extraordinary 256% in 2020!

> In 2020, we observed the largest one-year debt surge since World War II, with global debt rising to $226 trillion as the world was hit by a global health crisis and a deep recession. Debt was already elevated going into the crisis, but now governments must navigate a world of record-high public and private debt levels, new virus mutations, and rising inflation.[183] (IMF)

Record debt has been incurred at all levels, "Borrowing by governments accounted for slightly more than half of the increase, as the global public debt ratio jumped to a record 99 percent of GDP. Private debt from non-financial corporations and households also reached new highs."[184] (IMF)

As the IMF accurately observed, recent global debt increases have exacerbated our previously existing over-indebtedness, "The debt surge amplifies vulnerabilities, especially as financing conditions tighten."[185]

The Institute of International Finance (IIF) presents an even more alarming assessment of recent global debt increases and current debt levels. IIF data show global debt as a percent of global GDP increasing from 200% in 1995 to 280% in 2007 – after which global debt-to-GDP increased to a "who cares anymore" 350% in 2021, or $303 trillion.

These numbers are staggering – $303,000,000,000,000,000 equates to over $38,000 of debt for every man, woman, and child on planet Earth![186]

The implications associated with global over-indebtedness are decidedly ominous, "That means emerging markets have started 2022 facing record high refinancing needs just as the Federal Reserve prepares to raise interest rates after years of record low borrowing costs."[187] (Reuters)

The IMF and IIF analyses lead to the same conclusion – in our increasingly desperate attempt to mitigate the debilitating effects resulting from our deteriorating economic circumstances, we have become addicted to debt.

Accordingly, we no longer reduce our enormous debt – much less repay it – because the negative impact on our material living standards would be "totally unacceptable". That is, we are unwilling to "live within our means", and refrain from incurring additional debt, much less to "live beneath our means" for the endless decades required to repay the mindboggling debt that we have already incurred.

Interest Rate Suppression and Balance Sheet Expansion "Stimulative" central bank responses to our deteriorating economic circumstances have consisted of:

- Interest rate suppression – maintaining artificially low interest rates, in order to stimulate incremental borrowing and economic activity; and
- Balance sheet expansion – "monetizing" central government debt – purchasing govern--ment debt with currency that is essentially conjured into existence – in situations where market lenders have been unwilling to purchase government debt at suppressed interest rates.

Interest Rate Suppression Between the inception of Industrialism1 in 1750 and the inception of Industrialism3 in 1973, global interest rates – both long term and short term – generally fluctuated between 4% and 6% annually.[188]

Following a spike to nearly 20% in 1981, which occurred in response to Scarcity3 and the "inflation of the 1970s", global interest rates have ratcheted down to their historically unprecedented post-GR low levels – almost exclusively as a result of central bank interest rate policies.

Diagram 7-14: Long Term Interest Rates 1981 to 2021

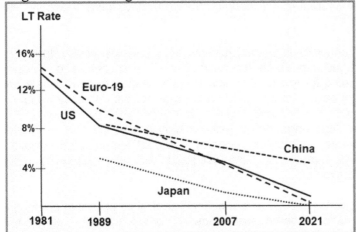

"Interestingly, rates aren't just low within the context of American history. They also happen to be at the lowest levels in the 5,000 years of civilization."[189] (*Business Insider*)

Sources: OECD long term interest rates 1981-2021;[190] China's long term interest rates 1991-2021.[191]

Between 1981 and 2021, the US long term interest rate decreased from 13.9% to 1.4%; the corresponding decrease among Euro-19 nations was 14.6% to 0.2%. Between 1989 and 2021, the Japanese long term interest rate decreased from 5.1% to 0.1%; and China's long term interest rate decreased (less significantly) from 8.6% to 4.4% between 1991 and 2021.

Global short term interest rates, while fluctuating due to central bank monetary policies, have trended downward since the mid-1990s – especially in response to the Great Recession – and have actually dipped into negative territory in some cases (e.g., Japan and the Euro-19).

Diagram 7-15: Short Term Interest Rates 1995 to 2021

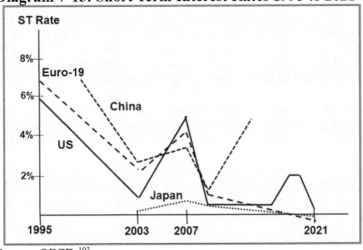

"By mid-2016, some 500 million people in a quarter of the world economy were living with [interest] rates in the red."[192] (Bloomberg)

Source: OECD.[193]

Between 1995 and 2021, the US short term interest rate decreased from 5.92% to 0.11%; the corresponding decrease among Euro-19 nations was 6.82% to -0.55%.

Between 2003 and 2021, the Japanese short term interest rate decreased from 0.09% to -0.07%; and China's short term interest rate decreased from 6.85% to 4.8% between 1998 and 2014.

The "stimulative effect" associated with historically low interest rates – especially during the post-GR period – has encouraged unprecedented malinvestment and speculation, by providing $trillions in low cost funding for low quality "investments" – in both hard assets and financial assets – that would not have occurred within a "normal interest rate environment".

Through 2021, "cheap money" has engendered extraordinary "asset inflation" – inflated stock, bond, and real estate prices – and untold levels of "bad debt" – unrepayable loans – the extent of which will not be revealed until interest rates "return to normal", and the "unproductive investments" are exposed.

[**Author's Note** As of the first quarter of 2023, major national central banks are attempting to "unwind" decades of artificially suppressed interest rates and balance sheet expansion, in their efforts to "fight price inflation". If history is any guide, the central bankers will persist with their "monetary tightening" policies until something in the economy "breaks" – malinvestments and resource misallocations are exposed – and national and/or global financial calamities occur.]

Balance Sheet Expansion National central banks were initially conceived as the "lenders of last resort" to their respective national banking systems. A central bank would "loan" money, which it essentially conjured into existence, to a member bank that was considered "illiquid" (temporarily short of cash), in order to prevent a bank run.

In the process of bailing out a temporarily illiquid member bank, the central bank would "expand its balance sheet" by the amount of the loan. When the loan was repaid, the central bank would "shrink its balance sheet" by the amount of the repaid loan.

Over time, especially since the Great Depression, the role of central banks has expanded to where these financial institutions have been mandated to "manage" their respective economies. Through various "policy tools", central banks are expected to maintain some combination of steady economic growth, price stability, and low unemployment.

One such policy tool empowers central banks to loan money, which they conjure into existence, to their respective central governments, ostensibly to "stimulate economic activity" during economic downturns, by purchasing government issued debt instruments – bills, notes, and bonds.

These "loans", which increase the size of central bank "balance sheets", are supposed to be repaid through government budget surpluses when economic conditions improve, thereby reducing the size of central bank balance sheets.

Since loans by central banks to central governments during Industrialism3 have typically not been repaid – and are instead "rolled over" – central bank balance sheets have ballooned during the period.

Historically, outstanding central bank balances fluctuated between 10% and 15% of global GDP – such balances were considered "acceptable". Exceptions to this rule included WW1, when global central bank balances amounted to 17% of global GDP, and WW2, when global central bank balances reached 38% of global GDP.[194]

In both cases, national central banks "cranked up the printing presses" in order to monetize central government debt – i.e., to purchase government issued bonds with money conjured into existence – that had been incurred to finance the world wars. Following each war, aggregate global central bank balances returned to 10%-15% of global GDP.

Central bank balance sheet expansion during Industrialism3 has differed fundamentally from the war-related episodes. Whereas world-war-related balance sheet expansion occurred during times of global conflict, recent balance sheet expansion has reflected increasingly desperate attempts by central banks to mitigate our deteriorating economic circumstances – i.e., to restore rapidly improving human prosperity through "monetary stimulus".

Prior to the Great Recession in 2007, the average central bank balance sheet stood at approximately 12% of national GDP. By 2014, as a result of the "quantitative easing" initiatives launched by major central banks in response to the Great Recession, the average central bank balance as a percent of national GDP had more than doubled to approximately 28%.[195]

From 2014 forward:[196]

- The US Federal Reserve's balance as a percent of US GDP actually decreased from 25% in 2014, to 20% in 2019 – before doubling to 40% of US GDP in 2021 – in response to Covid-19.
- The European Central Bank's balance as a percent of Eurozone GDP nearly doubled from 22% in 2014, to 40% in 2019, before nearly doubling again to 70% of Eurozone GDP in 2021 – in response to Covid-19.
- The Bank of Japan's balance as a percent of Japanese GDP nearly doubled from 55% in 2014, to 105% in 2019, from which it increased to 130% of Japanese GDP in 2021 – in response to Covid-19.

As is the case with interest rate suppression, the "stimulative effect" associated with central bank balance sheet expansion encourages malinvestment and misallocation of resources, by providing funding for government programs that taxpayers are unwilling to finance.

The extent of the economic "damage" caused by stimulative central bank balance sheet expansion will be revealed when (if) the central banks attempt to "withdraw significant amounts of liquidity from the system" – i.e., substantially reduce the size of their balance sheets by demanding that their respective central governments repay their outstanding loans.

Reducing bloated central bank balance sheets will prove to be a daunting task, however, given that, as Nature's Squeeze tightens, new "emergencies" (involving government spending programs) requiring additional central bank "stimulus" will become increasingly prevalent.

Money Supply Expansion

> I am coming round to the view that the external value of all major currencies is eroding and that this general erosion is able to substitute for at least a portion of the decline that one might expect in a particular currency versus its peers. Their objective is to deprive the independent observer of any reliable benchmark against which to measure the eroding value, not only of the US dollar, but of all fiat currencies. Central banks, and particularly the US Federal Reserve, are deploying their heavy artillery in the battle against a systemic collapse.[197] (Warburton)

A national central bank can expand its nation's money supply by:

- Expanding its balance sheet through the purchase of "high quality" government and corporate debt – which essentially "injects" newly created currency into the economy,
- Lowering member bank reserve requirements – which enables member banks to loan more money, and
- Lowering the rate at which a central bank lends money to its member banks – which encourages member banks to loan more money.

As is the case with central bank interest rate suppression and balance sheet expansion, money supply expansion is "stimulative" to an industrial economy – it provides additional "purchasing power", especially for the initial recipients of the newly created currency.

Historically, but especially since the closing of the "gold window" in 1971, money supply increases have exceeded – in some cases dramatically – economic growth in most national economies. (See Diagram 7-16)

Between the years 1960 and 2020, inflation-adjusted global economic output (GDP) increased by nearly 8 times. During the same period, the global M3 money supply (broad money) increased by 22.9 times.[198]

Accordingly, the global money supply, which amounted to approximately 50% of global GDP in 1960, expanded extraordinarily between 1960 and 2020, to over 143% of global GDP – 2.9 times the rate of global GDP expansion.

With respect to the US specifically (in 2021), "Our nation's current monetary policy is expansionary, which means artificially in-creasing the money supply and lowering interest rates to near zero. As a result, the growth rate of all the dollars in circulation ("M2 Money Supply") soared a historic record 27% in 2020-2021.

To put that in perspective, that is the biggest jump in the money supply in America's history. That is bigger than the Financial Crisis of 2007-2008 (10%), bigger than World War II (18%), and bigger than FDR's stimulus to fight the Great Depression (10%)."[200] (Moy)

Diagram 7-16: Global Money Supply (M3 – Broad Money) as a Percent of Global GDP

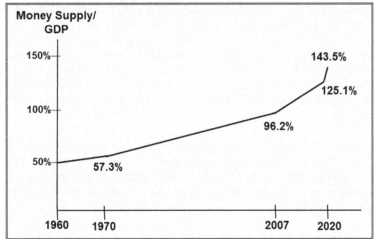

Sources: IMF, WB, OECD, and other.[199]

So while exorbitant money supply expansion has created the illusion of incremental purchasing power, the actual consequence has been price inflation – initially with respect to financial assets, and recently with respect to consumer products and services as well.

That is, the "real" (inflation adjusted) purchasing power associated with each currency unit – in terms of the NNRs and NNR-derived infrastructure, machines, products, energy and services that it will buy – has decreased significantly.

As an example, the purchasing power of a US dollar decreased by 83% between 1973 and 2021 – an item that cost 17 cents in 1973 would have cost one dollar in 2021. The British pound suffered an even greater loss in purchasing power between 1973 and 2021, decreasing by 92% during the period![201]

Thus, the monetary inflation created by excessive money supply expansion amounts to a "stealth tax" on the incomes of workers and on the accumulated wealth of savers, who experience continuous, but covert, devaluation of their currency units – and the simultaneous loss of real purchasing power.

Because inflation favors borrowers over savers, and because central governments are by far the largest borrowers in modern industrial economies, it is not surprising that central banks have typically pursued "accommodative monetary policies", which feature liberal (and typically underreported) doses of monetary inflation (currency devaluation).

The increasing frustration and anger being experienced by "ordinary people", as the real purchasing power of their wages and savings steadily erodes, exemplify the increasingly adverse consequences being inflicted by our increasingly desperate attempts to offset the increasingly debilitating effects of our NNR-scarcity-induced deteriorating economic circumstances with counterproductive economic expedients.

Unfunded Liabilities

Keep in mind different sources give us slightly different [US unfunded liability] balances but the one I refer to shows our current [2015] balance to be $115.8 trillion dollars. It breaks down like this. Let's start with Social Security. Some believe this is the largest of the three unfunded liabilities. Sorry, it actually comes in at number 3 with a balance of $15.2 trillion. Let's move on to Medicaid or as referred to, Prescription Drug Liability. That comes in at $20.2 trillion. Now on to Medicare. Clearly, it is the largest of the unfunded debts coming in at $80.4 trillion and rising.[202] (Engstrom)

Unfunded liabilities are the least visible – but by far the largest – form of unsustainable, PPP-based, economic profligacy. An unfunded liability is the difference – the "gap" – between the sum of projected annual cash outflows required to fulfill a future financial obligation, and the sum of annual cash inflows projected to be available to fulfill the obligation, expressed in current dollars (or other currencies).

Because we continue to incur new financial obligations – we promise ourselves additional future benefits – while failing to fully fund either our existing obligations or new obligations, our unfunded liabilities are enormous and ever-increasing.

Retirement Gap The retirement gap – the difference between projected future financial obligations regarding government, corporate, and private retirement funds and pension plans, and the sums of money projected to be available to discharge these obligations – is enormous, and ever-increasing.

According to a World Economic Forum (WEF) assessment of the retirement gap within Australia, Canada, China, India, Japan, the Netherlands, the UK, and the US,

The retirement savings gap in 2015 is estimated to be ~$70 trillion, with the largest shortfall being in the United States [$28 trillion]. In terms of GDP, this gap represents ~1.5 times the annual GDP across the countries studied. Based on our forward looking projections, the gap will grow by 5% each year to ~$400 trillion by 2050. This means an additional $28 billion of deficit each day.[203]

The cumulative 8-nation retirement gap represented an unfunded obligation of $9,600 for each of Earth's 7.3 billion human inhabitants in 2015. America's per capita retirement gap was more substantial by far – over $87,000 for each US citizen.

Closing or eliminating the retirement gap would require dramatic and continuous increases in contributions to retirement funds (at the expense of our current consumption levels), and/or dramatic and continuous decreases in retirement benefit payouts (at the expense of our future consumption levels) – neither of which is deemed "acceptable".

Fiscal Gap The fiscal gap is a broader measure of our unfunded liabilities, which includes unfunded future social entitlement and healthcare benefits in addition to unfunded future retirement benefits.

A June 2022 analysis by researchers at the University of Pennsylvania's Wharton School found that, "under current law, the U.S. federal government faces a permanent present-value fiscal imbalance of $244.8 trillion, or 10.2 percent of all future GDP."[204] Note that the $245 trillion US "fiscal imbalance" – the total US government unfunded liability – as calculated by the Wharton researchers, does not include the $28+ trillion US retirement gap.

As a point of reference, US household wealth as of the first quarter of 2022 totaled $149 trillion – nearly $125 trillion less than the $273 trillion US fiscal gap at the time. [Should America be considered financially insolvent?][205]

While estimates of the total global fiscal gap are unavailable, assuming the relationship between the US fiscal gap and US GDP also applies at the global level – the US fiscal gap exceeds 10 times US GDP – then given total global GDP of approximately $87 trillion (2021), the current global fiscal gap likely exceeds $900 trillion.[206]

Accordingly, the global fiscal gap of $900+ trillion exceeds total global wealth – $464 trillion[207] – by approximately a factor of two! [Should we *Homo sapiens* be considered financially insolvent?]

While it is difficult, if not impossible, to grasp the magnitude of our unfunded liabilities, it is easy to understand that we industrial *Homo sapiens* have made promises to ourselves and to our descendants that are economically – and geologically – impossible to fulfill.

The Illusion of PPP While unrepayable debt, unprecedented central bank interest rate suppression and balance sheet expansion, excessive money supply expansion, and underfunded investments in our future wellbeing have predicably failed to resolve our deteriorating economic circumstances, these PPP-based "expedients" have enabled us to "kick the can down the road" – to defer our inevitable economic day of reckoning.

More importantly, pseudo purchasing power, which has enabled industrial humanity to live increasingly beyond our means economically, has also enabled us to live increasingly beyond our means ecologically – temporarily.

Viewed from the ecological perspective, the PPP-based spending spree upon which we embarked during Industrialism3 enabled us to create NNR-based real wealth beyond that which would have existed in the absence of PPP-based "stimulus". In effect, pseudo purchasing power enabled us to "steal" NNRs from the future, and thereby "steal" prosperity from the future as well.

That is, the real wealth that enabled our recovery from Scarcity3 and our subsequent "last hurrah" during Industrialism3 was created by our accelerated depletion of Earth's already extensively depleted NNR reserves.

Ironically, but predictably, through our accelerated depletion of global NNR reserves during Industrialism3, we caused Scarcity4 and the Great Recession, we left insufficient globally available, economically viable NNR supplies to enable a post-GR recovery – and we accelerated our unraveling to collapse.

Responses to Increasing Societal Volatility

"Perceptions of stress, worry, and sadness have risen on average, as the world has become less peaceful."[208] (*Global Peace Index*)

"When you ain't got nothing, you got nothing to lose".[209] (Bob Dylan)

Responses to increasing societal volatility during Industrialism3 have been of two general types:

- Individual-level dysfunctional behavior, which includes stress, mental health disorders, and self-harm; and
- Societal-level dysfunctional behavior, which includes protests, civil unrest, crime and terrorism.

This counterproductive behavior – which is characterized by increasing frustration, anger, and violence – has exacerbated our already deteriorating societal circumstances during Industrialism3.

Individual-Level Dysfunctional Behavior

> Scientists have found biological evidence that stress and aggression feed off of each other, contributing to a 'cycle of violence' that can be tragic. When we are under stress, we are more likely to fly off the handle, and when we fly off the handle, that increases our level of stress.

> That vicious cycle 'would explain why aggressive behavior escalates so easily and is so difficult to stop once it has started...[210] (Dye)

Stress, mental health disorders, and self-harm are three increasingly prevalent forms of individual-level dysfunctional behavior that have exacerbated our deteriorating societal circumstances during Industrialism3.

Stress According to the American Psychological Association (APA), "Chronic stress comes when a person never sees a way out of a miserable situation. It's the stress of unrelenting demands and pressures for seemingly interminable periods of time. With no hope, the individual gives up searching for solutions."[211]

A 2022 Gallup poll covering 122 countries observed,

> As 2021 served up a steady diet of uncertainty, the world became a slightly sadder, more worried and more stressed-out place than it was the year before -- which helped push Gallup's Negative Experience Index to yet another new high of 33 in 2021.[212]

Gallup's Negative Experience Index decreased from 24 in 2006 to 23 in 2007, immediately prior to the Great Recession, before increasing steadily thereafter to 33 in 2021.

Key findings of the 2022 Gallup poll include:[213]

- "In 2021, four in 10 adults worldwide said they experienced a lot of worry (42%) or stress (41%), and slightly more than three in 10 experienced a lot of physical pain (31%).
- More than one in four experienced sadness (28%), and slightly fewer experienced anger (23%).
- Already at or near record highs in 2020, these experiences of stress, worry and sadness ticked upward in 2021 and set new records."

Gallup concluded,

> In the second year of the pandemic, people were living with even more uncertainty than the previous year -- with more people dying from COVID-19 despite the rollout of vaccines. Yet, the pandemic is not entirely to blame for the increase in negative emotions. Gallup's data show that the world has been on a negative trajectory for a decade.[214]

Mental Health Disorders While increasingly prevalent globally, mental health disorders often receive little attention, due either to the lack of therapeutic resources with which to treat them, or to negative perceptions regarding those who suffer from them.

According to the World Health Organization (WHO),

> For most of the world, the approach to mental health care remains very much business as usual. The result? Mental health conditions continue to exact a heavy toll on people's lives, while mental health systems and services remain ill-equipped to meet people's needs.
>
> In the meantime, global threats to mental health are ever present. Growing social and economic inequalities, protracted conflicts, violence and public health emergencies threaten progress towards improved well-being.[215]

The WHO notes that mental health disorders represent an enormous – and increasing – problem for our industrial societies, "Rates of already-common conditions such as depression and anxiety went up by more than 25% in the first year of the pandemic, adding to the nearly one billion people who were already living with a mental disorder."[216]

The "total burden of disease" on society, which is defined as total years of life lost plus total years of life lived with disabilities owing to disease, is measured in DALYs (Disability-Adjusted Life Years). According to the IHME (Institute for Health Metrics and Evaluation), the percent of the total global disease burden – total DALYs – attributable to mental health disorders increased by 58% between 1990 and 2019.[217]

Finally, according to Clubhouse International, a global organization that houses people suffering from mental health disorders:[218]

- One in four people globally suffers from some form of mental disorder – more than cancer, diabetes or heart disease.

- Mental and behavioral disorders account for the most time lost to disability (26%) – more than any other disease.
- The global cost of mental illness, direct and indirect, is approximately $2.5 trillion annually.

Self-Harm Increasingly, our attempts to cope with societal volatility have involved self-harm – particularly substance use/abuse and suicide. With respect to the former, both substance use and deaths related to substance use have increased considerably during Industrialism3,

> According to the [UDOC *World Drug Report 2022*] report, around 284 million people aged 15-64 used drugs worldwide in 2020, a 26 per cent increase over the previous decade. Young people are using more drugs, with use levels today in many countries higher than with the previous generation.

The relationship between our deteriorating societal circumstances and increasing substance use/abuse is clear, "UNODC Executive Director Ghada Waly stated: "Numbers for the manufacturing and seizures of many illicit drugs are hitting record highs, even as global emergencies are deepening vulnerabilities."[219]

Statista reports that the number of illegal drug users worldwide increased from 180 million in 1990 to 275 million in 2019, while the number of addicts increased from 25 million in 2003 to 36.3 million in 2019.[220]

Deaths and premature deaths attributable to substance use/abuse are also enormous and increasing. Between 1990 and 2019:[221]

- Premature deaths in which tobacco use was a factor increased by 29% – from 6.77 million to 8.71 million.
- Premature deaths in which alcohol use was a factor increased by 59% – from 1.64 million to 2.44 million.
- Premature deaths in which illicit drug use was a factor more than doubled – from 236,000 to 494,000.

Deaths directly attributable to:[222]

- Alcohol use disorders increased by 45% – from 116,000 in 1990, to 168,000 in 2019.
- Illicit drug use disorders more than doubled from 56,000 in 1990, to 128,000 in 2019.

Moreover, "In some countries drug overdoses rank highly on the leading causes of death: in the USA in 2017, for example, more people died from overdoses than in road accidents."[223] (Our World in Data)

With respect to suicide, the good news, "In 1990, the overall global suicide rate was 13.8 per 100,000 of the population, falling to 9.8/100,000 in 2019." The bad news, "The overall number of suicide deaths rose by 19,897 from 738,799 in 1990 to 758,696 in 2019..."[224] (BMJ)

Suicide – and other individual-level dysfunctional responses to increasing societal volatility – are often highly correlated with social fragmentation, which has increased significantly during

Industrialism3, "Higher levels of social fragmentation have long been linked with suicide, self-harm, mental disorders, and psychiatric health service use."[225] (Kontopantelis)

Specific research into the causes of suicide, which was conducted among 633 British parliamentary constituencies between 1981 and 1991, found social fragmentation to be a significant causative factor,

> Our analyses suggest that areas characterised by high social fragmentation have higher rates of suicide and that this association is independent of deprivation. Furthermore, the areas with the greatest absolute increase in social fragmentation between 1981 and 1991 also had greater increases in suicide, again independent of deprivation.[226] (University of Manchester)

Finally, the financial cost to society associated with suicide is enormous, "The economic impact of suicide was $757.1 billion in 2021, or 4.6 per cent of the global impact of violence, increasing by 4.7 per cent from the previous year."[227] (*Global Peace Index*)

Societal-Level Dysfunctional Behavior

Protests, civil unrest, and crime/terrorism are three increasingly prevalent forms of societal-level dysfunctional behavior that have exacerbated our deteriorating societal circumstances during Industrialism3.

Protests The increasing incidence of global protests between the years 1979 and 2013 is presented by a time series map, using data from the GDELT (*Global Database of Events, Language, and Tone*) database. The map from January 1979, the first month in the series, shows 7 instances of global protest. The map from October 2013, the last month in the series, shows over 200 instances of global protest.[228]

Additional evidence regarding the increasing incidence of global protests abounds.

In a March, 2020 report, The Center for Strategic and International Studies (CSIS) concluded, "Mass protests increased annually by an average of 11.5 percent from 2009 to 2019 across all regions of the world, with the largest concentration of activity in the Middle East and North Africa and the fastest rate of growth in sub-Saharan Africa."[229]

With reference to the CSIS study, The *Economist* noted, "…the world has experienced more political uprisings in the past few years than ever before. In 2019 alone there were protests on every continent and across 114 countries—from Hong Kong to Haiti, Bolivia to Britain."[230]

The Friedrich-Ebert-Stiftung (FES) Foundation in conjunction with the Initiative for Policy Dialogue (IPD) analyzed over 900 protest movements in 101 countries between 2006 and 2020. The FES/IPD, "found that the number of protest movements around the world had more than tripled in less than 15 years."[231] (*Washington Post*)

The *Washington Post* commented, "Their [FES/IPD] research found that a majority of the protest events they recorded — 54 percent — were prompted by a perceived failure of political systems or representation."[232]

More recently,

> After a pause in popular protest during the first year of the pandemic, people are returning to the streets. This year [2021], large and long-running anti-government demonstrations have occurred in some advanced economies where unrest is relatively rare, such as Canada and New Zealand.[233] (IMF)

Reflecting on the factors that are likely to impact future protest trends, the CSIS observed,

> Three potential catalyzing factors, which could intensify the trend or make it more manageable, warrant particular attention: (1) the use of technology by protestors and governments alike, (2) the tension between shifting democratic and authoritarian government types, and (3) the need for improved understanding and responsiveness between governments and their citizens.[234]

Civil Unrest In their *Global Peace Index 2020* report, the Institute for Economics & Peace (IEP) concluded, "The number of both protests and riots roughly doubled, while the number of general strikes quadrupled, from 33 events in 2011 to 135 in 2018."[235]

While specific metrics and methodologies vary among the three leading civil unrest trend trackers – the IMF Reported Social Unrest Index (RSUI), the Cross-National Time-Series Data (CNTSD), and the Armed Conflict Location and Event Database (ACLED) – all three sources indicate significantly increasing global civil unrest during the past 30-40 years, particularly during the 2010s.

According to the RSUI, which identified 679 specific social unrest events in 130 countries between 1985 and 2020, the percent of countries experiencing social unrest generally fluctuated between 0% and 1% between 1985 and 2010, before increasing to almost 3% during the Arab spring in 2011, and further increasing to nearly 4% in 2019.[236]

The RSUI and ACLED indices generally agree regarding global civil unrest trends,

> Despite measuring different phenomena using different methodologies, there is broad agreement between the two measures. Both are relatively low in the first decade of the 2000s and then exhibit a substantial and persistent increase starting in 2011. Within this, both series also show broad qualitative agreement in the last few years, with a rise in unrest around 2015, a subsequent decline during 2016-2017 and a pick-up since.[237] (IMF)

Interestingly, when compared with the RSUI and ACLED, the CNTSD indicates more persistently and dramatically increasing civil unrest since 2010, "The CNTS seems to show an almost monotonic increase in unrest events from around 2009 onward with very little variation prior."[238] (IMF)

The Institute for Economics and Peace confirms the recent trend toward increasing civil unrest, "A long-term data analysis of global protests, riots and strikes indicates a 102% increase from 2011-2018 according to the 2020 *Global Peace Index*..."[239]

Moreover, between 2011 and 2018, "More than 4,700 nonviolent demonstrations were recorded, compared to nearly 2,200 riots."[240] (Institute for Economics and Peace)

As is the case with all dysfunctional responses to our deteriorating societal circumstances, the economic costs associated with global civil unrest are staggering,

> ...unrest can have a negative economic impact as consumers become spooked by uncertainty and output is lost in manufacturing and services. As a result, 18 months after the most serious unrest events, gross domestic product is typically about 1 percentage point lower than it would have been otherwise.[241] (IMF)

Crime/Terrorism "Over 60% of people globally are worried about sustaining serious harm from violent crime."[242] (Institute for Economics and Peace)

Statistics from Our World in Data reveal a fluctuating increase in global homicides, from 373,000 in 1990, to 415,000 in 2019 – and a steady increase in terrorism related deaths, from 7,100 in 1990, to 26,400 in 2017, notwithstanding a spike to over 44,000 in 2014.[243]

"Events like 9/11 made terrorism global..." ... "Suddenly, people of all financial and social status were now susceptible and we realized how vulnerable all of society was. That kind of awareness brought the concept of stress to the forefront for people of all races and socio-economic status."[244] (Amaral)

As political instability, economic fragility, and societal volatility have intensified globally during Industrialism3, and as we have become increasingly frustrated, angry, and violent as a result, our responses to our deteriorating cultural circumstances have become increasingly counter-productive – and desperate.

Chapter 8:
Nature's Squeeze Tightens

Global rates of growth in both population and GDP have slowed over time with highest average growth rates experienced in the 1970s and lowest growth rates since 2000.[1] (UNEP)

The unfavorable trends that emerged during the early years of Industrialism3 – increasingly pervasive global NNR scarcity, diminishing industrial productivity growth, faltering global human prosperity, deteriorating human cultural circumstances, and counterproductive responses to our deteriorating cultural circumstances – accelerated during the first two decades of the new millennium.

Nature's Squeeze tightened – which accelerated our unraveling toward collapse.

Accelerating Global NNR Scarcity

...many of the traditional search terrains are now relatively mature. Most of the exposed deposits were found by the first waves of prospectors, or by the first application of systematic modern exploration surveys. Orebodies are becoming harder to find; they are certainly becoming harder to find cost-effectively.[2] (Blain)

By the dawn of the new millennium, most of Earth's economically viable NNR deposits had become extensively depleted or were in the process of becoming extensively depleted. Moreover, no major untapped NNR frontiers remained to be exploited.

Diagram 8-1: Accelerating Global NNR Scarcity

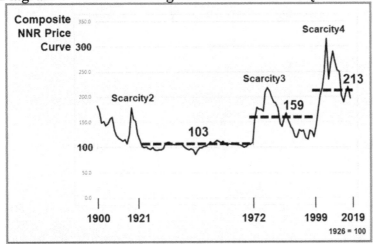

As a result, increasingly pervasive global NNR scarcity accelerated during the new millennium, as evidenced by unprecedented NNR price trend increases since the year 2000.

Sources: USGS, BP Statistical Review, US EIA, and other.[3]

- During the aftermath of Scarcity2, between 1921 and 1972, the Composite NNR Price Curve averaged 103. This historically low average NNR price level indicated relative global NNR abundance during the middle/end of Industrialism2.
- During Scarcity3 and its aftermath, between 1973 and 1999, the Composite NNR Price Curve averaged 159, a 54% increase from the 1921-1972 period. The substantial increase in the average NNR price level indicated increasingly pervasive global NNR scarcity during the early years of Industrialism3.
- During Scarcity4 and the ensuing "non-recovery", between 2000 and 2019, the Composite NNR Price Curve averaged 213, a 34% increase from the 1973-1999 period (and a staggering 107% increase from the 1921-1972 period). The significant incremental increase in the average NNR price level during the first two decades of the new millennium indicated accelerating global NNR scarcity.

"It should be no surprise to anyone, though, that current declining mineral discovery trends will likely continue, that ever-growing mineral commodity consumption will become harder to sustain, and that mineral and metal prices will increase."[4] (Beaty)

Rapidly Diminishing Industrial Productivity Growth

The drops in productivity growth have struck some as paradoxical, given the seemingly brisk pace of technological progress and plethora of new products that have been introduced and diffused throughout the world during the slowdown period.[5] (Brookings)

The absence of new NNR "building blocks" combined with rapidly increasing NNR price trends during the first two decades of the new millennium, further discouraged the development and deployment of highly-impactful, productivity-increasing innovations and efficiency improvements.

The result was trend acceleration – from diminishing global growth to rapidly diminishing global growth – with respect to both mining sector productivity and overall industrial productivity.

Mining Sector Productivity

Since around the year 2000, productivity in mining across the globe appears to have declined, and declined significantly.[6] (Humphreys)

In their 2020 report, *Has Global Mining Productivity Reversed Course*, McKinsey and Company observed,

After a significant decline in mining productivity between 2004 and 2009, the trend was relatively flat for about four years. In recent years, however, several indicators of global mining-sector performance have shown an upward trend. ... Yet, despite recent improvements, productivity is still [2018] some 25 percent lower than the starting point in the mid-2000s.[7]

Note that McKinsey was NOT referring to decreasing mining sector "productivity growth", BUT to decreasing mining sector "productivity", which decreased in absolute terms between 2004 and 2010, then increased anemically between 2010 and 2018 – and remained, as of 2018, 25% below the 2004 level.

Accordingly, global mining sector productivity decreased during the first two decades of the 21st century – mining sector "productivity growth" was negative.

Overall Industrial Productivity

> The paper poses the paradox that inventive activity as measured by patents issued has been accelerating while productivity growth has slumped to the slowest growth rates of the industrial era.[8] (Gordon)

Both industrialized and industrializing nations experienced rapidly diminishing – and in many cases negative – industrial productivity growth during the first two decades of the new millennium:

- "The global growth rate of total factor productivity (TFP), which measures the efficiency gains of labor and capital together, has come to a near standstill in the aftermath of the 2008-2009 financial crisis. It grew on average 1.2 percent a year from 1999 to 2008, slowed to 0.3 percent from 2009 to 2012, and has fallen to near zero since then". Moreover, "Most advanced economies, including the United States, Japan, and the Euro Area, are experiencing zero or negative productivity TFP growth."[9] (IFC)
- "The recent declines in both labor productivity growth—and TFP growth in particular— have been global phenomena, suggesting that United States-specific factors are less likely to be responsible for the productivity slowdown."[10] (Brookings Institution)
- "The latest estimates extend the downward trend in global labor productivity growth from an average annual rate of 2.6 percent between 2000-2007 to 1.7 percent between 2011-2019."[11] (The Conference Board)

Predictably, accelerating unfavorable trends with respect to the enablers of human industrialism – accelerating global NNR scarcity and rapidly diminishing industrial productivity growth – caused accelerating unfavorable trends with respect to the outcomes of human industrialism – rapidly faltering human prosperity and rapidly deteriorating human cultural circumstances – during the new millennium.

Rapidly Faltering Human Prosperity

> We argue that potential output growth in developed economies has been on a declining path since the 1980s and that the crisis [Great Recession] has caused a further, permanent decline in both the level and growth rate of output. Moreover, we observe that output growth has been slowing since 2008 also in emerging markets, most prominently China.[12] (International Center for Monetary and Banking Studies)

"For the first time in the 32 years that UNDP have been calculating it, the Human Development Index, which measures a nation's health, education, and standard of living, has declined globally for two years in a row."[13] (UNDP)

That global human prosperity has faltered since Scarcity3 and the inception of Industrialism3 is obvious. That global human prosperity has faltered even more rapidly since Scarcity4 and the Great Recession is equally obvious.

Diagram 8-2: Global Human Prosperity Improvement 1945-2019
Economic Output (GDP)   Material Living Standard (pc GDP)

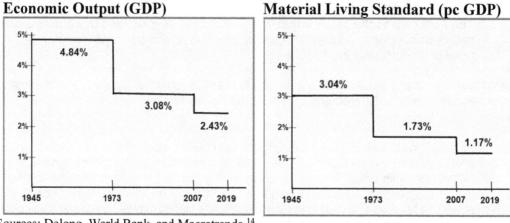

Sources: Delong, World Bank, and Macrotrends.[14]

- During the post-WW2 rebuilding period, between 1945 and 1973, global GDP (economic output) increased at an unprecedented 4.84% compounded annually, while global pc GDP (the average material living standard) increased at a remarkable 3.04% compounded annually.
- During the pre-GR years of Industrialism3, between 1973 and 2007, the compound annual growth rate in global GDP (economic output) decreased significantly to 3.08%, and the compound annual growth rate in pc GDP (the average material living standard) also decreased significantly, to 1.73%.
- From the Great Recession forward, between 2007 and 2019, the compound annual growth rate in global GDP (economic output) further decreased to a lackluster 2.43%, while the compound annual growth rate in global pc GDP (the average material living standard) further decreased to an anemic 1.17%.

From the ecological perspective, remaining globally available, economically viable NNRs are insufficient to enable industrial humanity to "grow our way out" of the Great Recession – much less to resurrect the "good old days" that were characteristic of our Old Normal.

Rapidly faltering global human prosperity has become industrial humanity's new reality – the Great Recession marked the beginning of industrial humanity's Final Recession.

Rapidly Deteriorating Human Cultural Circumstances

> There is a nagging sense that whatever control we have over our lives is slipping away, that the norms and institutions we used to rely on for stability and prosperity are not up to the task of today's uncertainty complex.[15] (UNDP)

> Much of the energy of western democracies is being diverted into prosperity-destroying divisionist politics and fads. It is in the interest of those who would see prosperous nations fall to drive the divisions within them, fragmenting and dividing society, and pitting group against group to undermine prosperity.[16] (Legatum Prosperity Index)

The inevitable consequence associated with rapidly faltering global human prosperity during the first two decades of the new millennium was rapidly deteriorating global human cultural circumstances – rapidly increasing political instability, economic fragility, and societal volatility.

Rapidly Increasing Political Instability

> Global freedom faces a dire threat. Around the world, the enemies of liberal democracy—a form of self-government in which human rights are recognized and every individual is entitled to equal treatment under law—are accelerating their attacks.[17] (Freedom House)

The BTI Project – a collaboration of nearly 300 country and regional experts from leading universities and think tanks worldwide – publishes the Bertelsmann Stiftung's Transformation Index (BTI), a series of analyses that monitor the transformation of nations toward democracy and market economies. The following findings were contained in their 2022 report.[18]

"Democracy is losing ground: For the first time since 2004, the Bertelsmann Stiftung's Transformation Index (BTI) counts more autocratically governed states than democracies. Among the 137 countries surveyed [2021], only 67 are still democracies, while the number of autocracies has risen to 70."

Moreover, "A creeping autocratization has long been evident: Over the past 10 years, the quality of democracy has declined in nearly one in five democracies, including in regionally important and once-stable democracies."

Notably, government responses to Covid-19 exacerbated the situation, "Politically, autocracies in particular used the pandemic to further limit fundamental rights and suppress critical voices."

The cause, according to the BTI Project, underlying our deteriorating political circumstances, "The decline in the quality of democracy has most often been driven by political elites focusing on securing their own political and economic power at the expense of societal develop-ment."

The *Freedom In the World 2022 Report, Global Expansion of Authoritarian Rule*, published by Freedom House, highlights the global deterioration in freedom and democracy that occurred during the new millennium:[19]

- The percentage of the global population living in a "free" country declined from 46% in 2005 to 20.3% in 2021,
- The percentage of the global population living in a "not free" country increased from 36.1% in 2005 to 38.4% in 2021, and
- The percentage of the global population living in a "partially free" country increased from 17.9% in 2005 to 41.3% in 2021.

Summing up,

> The present threat to democracy is the product of 16 consecutive years of decline in global freedom.[20]

Rapidly Increasing Economic Fragility

"The system of global economic governance appears increasingly bewildered and hamstrung by the challenges of the 21st century."[21] (UNCTAD)

"The Great Recession created an unusually large and long-lasting gap between actual and potential GDP. That 'output gap' was manifested in substantial excess unemployment and underemployment and idle productive capacity among businesses."[22] (Center on Budget and Policy Priorities)

"In all the countries affected by the Great Recession, recovery was slow and uneven, and the broader social consequences of the downturn—including, in the United States, lower fertility rates, historically high levels of student debt, and diminished job prospects among young adults—were expected to linger for many years."[23] (Duignan)

Compounding the "bewildering" economic challenges imposed by the Great Recession, are those engendered by the Covid-19 pandemic,

> The global economy, already marked by uncertainty and sluggish growth, has been severely damaged by the pandemic. Measures implemented in almost all countries, such as contact restrictions and lockdowns, significantly weakened global economic momentum and led to reduced demand for certain goods and raw materials. In many countries, this triggered significant declines in economic growth while also boosting unemployment and poverty rates. As significant spending increases were needed to bolster national health sectors, stimulate economies and cushion social hardships, there was also a rise in fiscal deficits and overall debt levels.[24] (BTI)

And those engendered by the war in Ukraine,

> ...the impact of the war will contribute to [GDP growth] forecast downgrades for 143 economies this year [2022]—accounting for 86 percent of global GDP.[25] (IMF)

Rapidly Increasing Societal Volatility

> A growing body of research suggests that social media is accelerating the trend [toward societal polarization], and many political scientists worry it's tearing our country apart. It isn't clear how to solve the problem. And new research suggests that one often-proposed solution—exposing users on the platforms to more content from the other side—might actually be making things worse, because of how social media amplifies extreme opinions.[26] (*WSJ*)

As with political instability and economic fragility, global societal volatility accelerated during the first two decades of the new millennium, owing to the incessant barrage of "emergencies" – Scarcity4 and the Great Recession, the Covid-19 pandemic, and the war in Ukraine – that confronted industrial humanity during the period.

The *Global Peace Index (GPI)*, which is compiled by the Institute for Economics and Peace, ranks 163 independent states and territories (99.7% of the global population) according to their level of peacefulness. The key findings in their 2020 report:[27]

- "The results this year show that the level of global peacefulness deteriorated, with the average country score falling by 0.34 per cent. This is the ninth deterioration in peacefulness in the last twelve years,
- Only two of the nine regions in the world became more peaceful over the past year,
- Peacefulness has declined 2.5 percent since 2008,
- Fifteen of the 23 GPI indicators are less peaceful on average in 2020 when compared to 2008,
- From 2011 to 2019, the number of riots rose by 282 per cent and general strikes rose by 821 per cent, and
- The economic impact of violence on the global economy in 2019 was $14.5 trillion in purchasing power parity (PPP) terms. This figure is equivalent to 10.6 per cent of the world's economic activity (gross world product) or $1,909 per person."

A 2021 Pew Research Center survey revealed that the Covid-19 pandemic has caused increasingly acute societal divisions both within and among nations,

> As the coronavirus outbreak enters its second year disrupting life around the globe, most people believe their society is now more divided than before the pandemic, according to a new Pew Research Center survey in 17 advanced economies. While a median of 34% feel more united, about six-in-ten report that national divisions have worsened since the outbreak began. In 12 of 13 countries surveyed in both 2020 and 2021, feelings of division have increased significantly, in some cases by more than 30 percentage points.[28]

"The resulting global divergence [in Covid-19 responses between developed and developing nations] will create tensions—within and across borders—that risk worsening the pandemic's cascading impacts and complicating the coordination needed to tackle common challenges..."[29] (WEF)

Finally, the war in Ukraine has exacerbated the already heightened level of global societal volatility during the new millennium,

> The current conflict has severely strained U.S.-Russia relations and increased the risk of a wider European conflict. Tensions are likely to increase between Russia and neighboring NATO member countries that would likely involve the United States, due to alliance security commitments. The conflict will also have broader ramifications for future cooperation on critical issues like arms control; cybersecurity; nuclear nonproliferation; global economic stability; energy security; counterterrorism; and political solutions in Syria, Libya, and elsewhere.[30] (CFR)

Increasingly Counterproductive Human Responses

> The rise of technonationalism. Diverging regulatory regimes. The spread of 'walled gardens.' Polarization like nothing we've seen before. The confluence of several trends is poised to completely fragment our real and digital worlds.[31] (MIT)

The incessant barrage of "emergencies" with which we have been confronted during the early years of the 21st century has accelerated our already deteriorating political, economic, and societal circumstances. Increasingly counterproductive responses to our rapidly deteriorating circumstances have predictably exacerbated the situation.

Responses to Rapidly Increasing Political Instability

> Violent conflict has increased after decades of relative decline. Direct deaths in war, numbers of displaced populations, military spending, and terrorist incidents, among others, have all surged since the beginning of the century.[32] (World Bank)

Global conflict – destabilizing acts of human aggression, which exemplify our waning capacity to resolve disputes through peaceful means – increased significantly during the first two decades of the new millennium.

According to the Uppsala Conflict Data Program, the incidence of global conflict, which remained relatively subdued during the late 20th century, increased dramatically between 2005 and 2021:[33]

- State-Based Violence increased by 64% – from 33 incidents in 2005, to 54 incidents in 2021.
- Non-State Violence increased by 162% – from 29 incidents in 2005, to 76 incidents in 2021.
- One-Sided Violence increased by 43% – from 28 incidents in 2005, to 40 incidents in 2021.

Factional conflict within nations also increased significantly during the new millennium, "In another sign that international deterrents against antidemocratic behavior are losing force, coups were more common in 2021 than in any of the previous 10 years."[34] (Freedom House)

Responses to Rapidly Increasing Economic Fragility

> Indeed, focusing on inflation through February 2022 which does not capture many disruptions associated with the war in Ukraine, we show that countries with large fiscal stimulus, or with high exposure to foreign stimulus through international trade, experienced stronger inflation outbursts.[35] (US Federal Reserve)

The industrialized and industrializing nations of the world attempted to recover from the incessant barrage of "emergencies" during the new millennium by employing an endless barrage of historically unprecedented PPP-based central government and central bank economic stimulus initiatives – increasingly desperate expedients that generally exacerbated our already fragile economic circumstances.

Increasing Debt

> After the 2008 financial crisis and the longest and deepest global recession since World War II, it was widely expected that the world's economies would deleverage. It has not happened. Instead, debt continues to grow in nearly all countries, in both absolute terms and relative to GDP. This creates fresh risks in some countries and limits growth prospects in many.[36] (McKinsey)

Diagram 8-3: Global Debt as a Percent of Global GDP 1995 to 2021

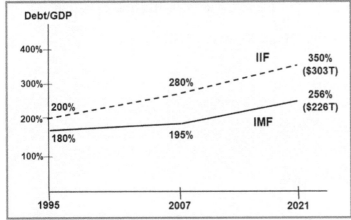

Our already enormous global debt at the end of the 20th century became even more enormous during the first two decades of the 21st century, primarily in response to the Great Recession and the Covid-19 pandemic.

Sources: International Monetary Fund (IMF) = Solid Line;[37]
Institute of International Finance (IIF) = Dashed Line.[38]

According to the International Monetary Fund (IMF), global debt as a percent of global GDP increased from an already elevated 180% in 1995, to 256% in 2020.

The International Institute of Finance (IIF) contends that global debt-to-GDP increased from 200% in 1995, to an astounding 350% in 2021. By either account, global debt in 2021 was historically unprecedented.

The inevitable consequence,

> The attempt to solve what was essentially a global debt crisis with mountains of more debt means we will have another global financial crisis – the question is when rather than if.[39] (O'Byrne)

Interest Rate Suppression In attempting to restore rapidly improving prosperity following the Great Recession, global central banks resorted to previously inconceivable measures – such as "negative" interest rates,

> Unthinkable before the 2008 financial crisis, the idea [of negative interest rates] is to jolt lending, spur inflation and reinvigorate the economy after other options have been exhausted. It's an unorthodox move that has distorted financial markets and triggered complaints that the strategy is backfiring. Negative rates will either mark the start of a new era for the world's central banks, or finally expose the limit of their powers.[40] (Bloomberg)

It became obvious in the aftermath of the Great Recession that borrowers across the global economy had become addicted to "cheap money". Accordingly, any attempt to "normalize" interest rates would displace the "wealth effect", which was intentionally created by "loose monetary policy", with the "poverty effect", which would inevitably result from "tight monetary policy" – and crash the global economy.

Balance Sheet Expansion Central bank balance sheet expansion during the new millennium was equally as unprecedented – and alarming – as interest rate suppression.

Diagram 8-4: Four Major Central Bank Balances 2002 to 2021

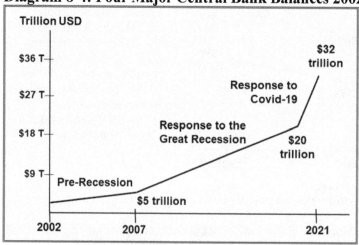

Sources: Yardini and Marsh.[41]

The combined balance sheets of the US Federal Reserve, the European Central Bank, the Bank of Japan, and the People's Bank of China:

- Increased from approximately $3 trillion in 2002 to $5 trillion in 2007 – prior to the Great Recession,
- Increased extraordinarily (by a factor of four) to approximately $20 trillion in 2019 – in response the Great Recession, and
- Increased meteorically to $32 trillion in 2021 – in response to the Covid-19 pandemic.

Money Supply Expansion In attempting to stimulate persistently anemic economic growth following the Great Recession, the global banking community expanded the global money supply significantly. They then expanded the global money supply spectacularly in response to plummeting economic growth during the Covid-19 pandemic.

Diagram 8-5: Global Money Supply (M3 – Broad Money) as a Percent of Global GDP

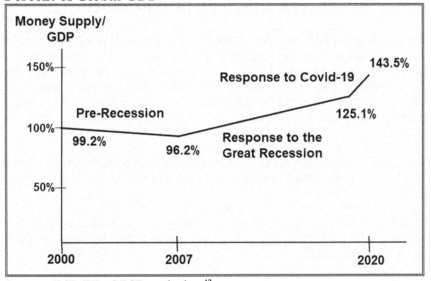

Sources: IMF, WB, OECD, and other.[42]

During the new millennium, global money supply as a percent of global GDP:

- Decreased slightly from 99.2% to 96.2% between 2000 and 2007 – prior to the Great Recession,
- Increased significantly from 96.2% to 125.1% between 2007 and 2019 – in response to the Great Recession, and
- Increased spectacularly from 125.1% to 143.5% in a single year (2019 to 2020) – in response to the Covid-19 pandemic.

Unsurprisingly, unprecedented global central bank money supply expansion failed to offset the adverse economic effects imposed by the Great Recession and the Covid-19 pandemic.

Pieces of paper and entries on digital ledgers are not real wealth, and cannot produce or restore human prosperity.

The global banking community did, however, create trillions of additional currency units, which reinflated asset bubbles that existed prior to the Great Recession, and produced rampant global price inflation during the early 2020s.

Viewed from the ecological perspective, the Great Recession was not simply another temporary economic downturn, from which we in the industrialized world would recover by "stimulating" our national economies with borrowed money, printed money, and artificially suppressed interest rates.

By the end of the second decade of the 21st century, it had become obvious that dwindling globally available, economically viable NNRs are insufficient to "fix" our increasingly fragile global economy.

Responses to Rapidly Increasing Societal Volatility

> Each country has different histories and realities on the ground... But they all faced a perfect storm of preexisting social, economic, and political hardships, which fallout from the COVID-19 pandemic only inflamed further. And they are merely a foreshadowing of the post-coronavirus global tinderbox that's looming as existing tensions in countries across the world morph into broader civil unrest and uprisings against economic hardships and inequality deepened by the pandemic.[43] (Foreign Policy)

Increasingly counterproductive responses to rapidly increasing global societal volatility during the early years of the 21st century amplified already heightened tensions at both the individual level and the societal level.

Accordingly, the incidence of stress, mental health disorders, and self-harm accelerated during the new millennium. In their 2022 report, *Stress in America 2021*, the American Psychological Association (APA) noted that,

> ...all sources of stress remain somewhat higher than pre-pandemic levels, with the economy, housing costs, personal safety and discrimination representing more dramatic spikes.[44]

In 2021:[45]

- 66% of survey respondents noted work-related stress,
- 61% of survey respondents noted money-related stress,
- 59% of survey respondents noted stress related to the economy,
- 51% of survey respondents noted stress related to personal health, and
- 44% of survey respondents noted stress related to personal safety, a significant increase from 35% in 2019.

Globally,[46]

- 1.3% of all deaths in 2019 resulted from suicide,
- Approximately twice as many people die from suicide as from homicide, and
- Depression and other mood disorders are widely recognized among the most important risk factors for suicide.

The incidence of protest and civil unrest also accelerated during the new millennium:

- "There were 14,871 violent demonstrations, protests and riots recorded globally in 2020."[47] (Institute for Economics and Peace)
- "Violent demonstrations recorded the largest deterioration of any indicator, deteriorating by almost 50 per cent since 2008. This indicator worsened in 126 countries of the 163 nations assessed in the [2021] GPI [*Global Peace Index*]."[48] (Institute for Economics and Peace)
- "The *violent demonstrations* score is now the highest since the inception of the index, with the largest deteriorations occurring in Belarus, Myanmar, Russia, the United States, and the Kyrgyz Republic."[49] (Institute for Economics and Peace)

Going forward,

> Incidences of social unrest are unlikely to abate any time soon, given the aftershocks of Covid-19, the cost-of-living crisis, and the ideological shifts that continue to divide societies around the world.[50] (Todorovic)

Chapter 9:
Humanity Will Crack – and
Industrialism Will Collapse!

In nature, the over-extension of a population upon a resource which diminishes is well known, and the results tend to be disastrous.[1] (Youngquist)

No Happy Ending

The point of this talk is simply that reliance on non-renewable natural resources (NNRs), which enabled us to do more things than we did before we began that reliance, has made us vulnerable. *Such reliance is a commitment to impermanence.*[2] (Catton)

The evolution of human industrialism has been governed by the evolving relationship between Nature (NNRs) and human ingenuity (industrial productivity). This evolving relationship has, in turn, governed the evolution of human prosperity and human cultural circumstances.

During Our Old Normal (Nature's Stimulus), between the mid-18th century and the 1970s, the relationship between Nature and human ingenuity became increasingly favorable to industrial development. Nature's increasingly-reinforcing "geological tailwind" – relative global NNR abundance – amplified human ingenuity efficacy, and fostered rapid industrial productivity growth.

Relative global NNR abundance combined with rapid industrial productivity growth enabled rapidly improving global human prosperity and rapidly improving human cultural circumstances during the period.

During Our New Normal (Nature's Squeeze), from the 1970s forward, the relationship between Nature and human ingenuity has become increasingly unfavorable to industrial development. Nature's increasingly-debilitating "geological headwind" – increasingly pervasive global NNR scarcity – has attenuated human ingenuity efficacy, and caused diminishing industrial productivity growth.

Increasingly pervasive global NNR scarcity combined with diminishing industrial productivity growth have caused faltering global human prosperity and deteriorating human cultural circumstances – increasing political instability, economic fragility, and societal volatility – during the period.

During the New Millennium, the increasingly unfavorable relationship between Nature and human ingenuity has intensified. Nature's severely-debilitating "geological headwind" – accelerating global NNR scarcity – has further attenuated human ingenuity efficacy, and caused rapidly diminishing industrial productivity growth.

Accelerating global NNR scarcity combined with rapidly diminishing industrial productivity growth have caused rapidly faltering global human prosperity and rapidly deteriorating human cultural circumstances during the new millennium.

Viewed from the ecological perspective, by predicating our existence upon finite, non-replenishing, and increasingly scarce fossil fuels, metals, and nonmetallic minerals, we uniquely ingenious industrial *Homo sapiens* have unwittingly committed our species to impermanence. That is, we have enmeshed ourselves in a predicament from which a positive outcome is geologically impossible.

Our Predicament

William Catton, in his seminal classic, *Overshoot – The Ecological Basis of Revolutionary Change...* described the basis for humanity's predicament as follows,

> ...organisms using their habitat unavoidably reduce its capacity to support their kind by what they necessarily do to it in the process of living.[3]

Notably, however, a critical – and inevitably fatal – distinction exists between *Homo sapiens* and all non-human species in this regard.

The existence of all non-human species populations is enabled exclusively by renewable natural resources (RNRs) – water, soil, and naturally-occurring biota – which replenish periodically through naturally-occurring biological, geological, chemical, and physical processes. The Earth resource utilization behavior that undermines non-human species populations is therefore "reversible"; it is offset by Nature.

We industrial *Homo sapiens* are unique among Earth species because our existence is enabled – and undermined – through our utilization of NNRs. NNRs do not replenish on a time scale that is relevant from the perspective of "human time", in the event that they replenish at all. The Earth resource utilization behavior that undermines industrial *Homo sapiens* is therefore "irreversible"; it is NOT offset by Nature.

Accordingly, both our industrial existence and the NNR utilization behavior by which it is enabled are terminally unsustainable. And therein lies our predicament...

If we discontinue our unsustainable NNR utilization behavior – refrain from further NNR utilization – we will perish from the lack of NNR-derived infrastructure, machines, products, energy, and services that perpetuate our industrial existence.

Alternatively, if we continue our unsustainable NNR utilization behavior, we will perish as our persistent depletion inevitably renders Earth's NNR reserves insufficient to support our species.

We are therefore doomed if we attempt to perpetuate our industrial existence, and we are doomed if we do not. There is no solution – and certainly no positive resolution – to our predicament.

The Tightening Vice – a Metaphor for Our Predicament

Picture a vise tightening around the collective skulls of humankind in a relentless, remorseless "squeeze". The handle of the vise turns at only 1/1000th of a revolution per day, which causes almost imperceptible incremental pain on a day-to-day basis.

Over a 10-year period, however, the vise handle makes 3+ complete revolutions; over 20 years, 7+ revolutions; and over 30 years, 10+ revolutions.

While the precise timing associated with the culmination of this scenario cannot be known with certainty, the outcome is certain – humanity will crack.

Applying the "vice metaphor" to human industrialism – ironically, it is we *Homo sapiens* who are turning the vise handle. In the process of perpetuating our industrial existence – by extracting and utilizing enormous and ever-increasing quantities of finite and non-replenishing NNRs – we are causing Nature's Squeeze.

More ironically, we must continue to turn the vice handle. In order to perpetuate our unsustainable industrial existence, we must persist in our unsustainable NNR utilization behavior. Failure to do so will cause our instantaneous demise.

Most ironically, our demise is inevitable in either case. Because the unsustainable NNR utilization behavior that enables our existence is simultaneously and irreversibly undermining our existence, we are doomed if we continue to turn the vise handle (persist in our unsustainable behavior), and we are doomed if we do not.

The Case for Collapse

> Maintenance of Earth's human population is now totally dependent on continuing supplies of natural resources: fertilizers to increase crop yields, water to drink and to irrigate crops, metals to build machines, fuels to energize them and a myriad other materials. Without continuing supplies civilized society must collapse and the population wither.[4] (Skinner)

Accelerating global NNR scarcity (Nature) is in the process of completely overwhelming industrial productivity (human ingenuity), which is causing our rapidly faltering and inevitably decreasing prosperity.

These accelerating trends are causing our rapidly deteriorating and inevitably disintegrating cultural circumstances, to which we are responding with increasingly counterproductive and inevitably self-terminating behavior.

This degenerative evolutionary process – devolution – will inevitably cause industrial humanity to "crack" and human industrialism to "collapse".

Terminal Global NNR Scarcity

> Future supply-demand inequality for strategic resources will cause a variety of global problems including inaccessibility, price increases, instability, and environmental and humanitarian disregard.[5] (MIT)

Future NNR Requirements Industrial humanity's already enormous NNR requirements will increase unabated in the future. Fewer than two billion of Earth's eight billion human inhabitants currently occupy nations that are fully industrialized, which leaves over six billion people who occupy nations that are either in the process of industrialization or who remain pre-industrial.

Based on UN projections,

> Assuming that the world will implement similar systems of production and systems of provision for major services – housing, mobility, food, energy and water supply – nine billion people will require 180 billion tonnes of materials by 2050, almost three times today's [2010] amounts.[6] (UNEP)

Moreover, despite exceptional productivity growth during our industrial era, we have become less efficient with respect to NNR utilization during the new millennium, thereby further increasing our NNR requirements, "The material intensity of the world economy has been increasing for the past decade, driven by the great acceleration that has occurred since the year 2000. Globally, more material per unit of GDP is now required."[7] (UNEP)

Future NNR Supplies Extensively depleted global NNR reserves will constrain future NNR supplies,

> Exploration of new locations and technological innovation in mining and extraction has kept the available and known material reserves on par with the increase in demand. Will this continue in the 21st century as well? It is difficult to predict a century ahead, but looking at a number of developments, we are afraid the answer is: no.[8] (Materials Innovation Institute)

Additionally, NNR "trade has grown faster than domestic extraction and direct trade in materials has expanded fourfold since 1970."[9] (UNEP) Increasing NNR import reliance, particularly among NNR-deficient major global powers such as the EU, the US, and China, will cause increasing competition for increasingly scarce NNR imports, which will become a source of increasing global tension – and conflict.

Finally, remaining reserves of critical NNRs are often highly concentrated geographically, thereby further jeopardizing future supplies,

> A key challenge for strategic elements is the concentration of many of the world's largest deposits and reserve bases in a small number of countries. As the global economy grows more dependent on individual nations for mineral supplies, political, environmental, or economic problems within these producing nations could quickly and negatively influence world strategic mineral prices.[10] (MIT)

The inescapable conclusion to be drawn from these increasingly unfavorable global NNR demand/supply dynamics is that continuously accelerating global NNR scarcity will devolve into terminal NNR scarcity,

> …we also believe [NNR] production costs are likely to continue rising on a structural basis. The additional supply required to meet higher trend demand growth will be higher cost. Margins are expected to remain constant, and prices will be driven higher.[11] (Heap)

Diagram 9-1: Continuously Accelerating Global NNR Scarcity

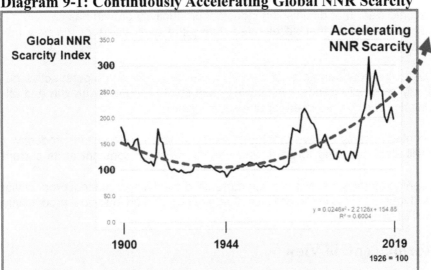

"It should always be borne in mind that the past was a much more expensive place and the future promises to likely be the same."[12] (Jacks)

Decreasing Industrial Productivity

> Synchronized declines in productivity growth have become steeper and recoveries shallower since 1980, pointing to risks ahead of what is expected to be the largest contraction in global output since World War II due to COVID-19.[13] (World Bank)

At issue is,

> …whether the succeeding waves of technological change represented by the four industrial revolutions have similar relevance to this particular economic sector [mining]. My conclusion is that they probably do not and that the more recent revolutions, while they will be supportive of productivity developments, may struggle to deliver the same quantum improvements that the industry was able to extract from the earlier ones.[14] (Humphreys)

Since the appearance of genus *Homo* approximately three million years ago, human ingenuity has been our only recourse against the inexorable "forces of Nature".

In our pre-industrial incarnation, human beings became sufficiently ingenious to "harness" Nature, and thereby to create complex political, economic, and societal systems.

As an industrialized species, we *Homo sapiens* have employed our unparalleled ingenuity to exploit fossil fuels, metals, and nonmetallic minerals on an industrial scale – and, through industrial productivity, to employ NNRs in ways that have afforded our species previously inconceivable prosperity.

During our Old Normal, we believed that perpetually rapid industrial productivity growth would enable us to achieve perpetually rapid prosperity improvement. During our New Normal, however, it has become clear that diminishing industrial productivity growth has caused faltering human prosperity – trends that accelerated during the early years of the new millennium.

Unsurprisingly, those who view human existence from the anthropocentric perspective believe that prevailing unfavorable trends – diminishing industrial productivity growth and faltering human prosperity – will be reversed, or at least mitigated:

- The anthropocentric minority believe that the currently diminishing industrial productivity growth trend will stabilize going forward, and remain relatively constant at its current anemic rate.
- The anthropocentric majority believe that the currently diminishing industrial productivity growth trend will reverse (or is in the process of reversing), and an industrial productivity renaissance will occur.

Minority Anthropocentric View

According to the anthropocentric minority, advancing the industrial state-of-the-art with productivity-increasing innovations and efficiency improvements has become increasingly difficult during the past half century. As industrial societies have become increasingly advanced, the "bar" for developing highly-impactful innovations has been raised significantly, and future innovations will fail increasingly to clear the bar,

> If reaching the frontiers of knowledge requires standing on the shoulders of giants, "one must first climb up their backs, and the greater the body of knowledge, the harder this climb becomes."[15] (Wladawsky-Berger)

The anthropocentric minority contend that perpetually anemic future industrial productivity growth is simply another manifestation of "diminishing returns" – in this case diminishing returns on investments in productivity-increasing innovations and efficiency improvements,

> Innovation may be hitting a wall of diminishing returns. There was little growth before 1800, and there might conceivable be little growth in the future." ... "...in many contexts and at various levels of disaggregation, research effort is rising substantially, while research productivity is declining sharply.[16] (Wladawsky-Berger)

Accordingly, rapid industrial productivity growth is no longer achievable, "They [economists such as Robert J. Gordon and John G. Fernald] claim that productivity growth cannot be expected to sustainably continue on the same high-growth trend that previously had been seen as of the mid-20th century."[17] (US Bureau of Labor Statistics)

Future global industrial productivity growth will remain perpetually anemic as a result.

Majority Anthropocentric View

The anthropocentric majority perceive the diminishing industrial productivity growth trend as temporary – we are simply experiencing a time lag between innovation and impact,

> We're still in a long *in-between* period, where multiple, overlapping technologies are continuing to emerge from R&D labs into the marketplace, but because of their profound transformative nature, their full deployment is still ahead of us.[18] (Wladawsky-Berger)

The currently unfavorable industrial productivity growth trend will soon reverse, and rapid industrial productivity growth will restore rapidly improving human prosperity for the indefinite future, "…productivity is expected to be the main driver of economic growth and well-being over the next 50 years, via investment in innovation and knowledge-based capital."[19] (OECD)

The prophesied enabler of our industrial productivity renaissance will be "disruptive", productivity-increasing innovations and efficiency improvements engendered by Industry 4.0.

Industry 4.0 "…builds on the third [industrial] revolution and is characterised by technologies which integrate the physical, digital and biological spheres. Features of the new revolution are robotics, artificial intelligence, blockchain, nanotechnology, quantum computing, biotechnology, the Internet of Things (IoTs), 3D printing and autonomous vehicles."[20] (Humphreys)

Diagram 9-2: Global Industrial Productivity Growth – Anthropocentric Majority

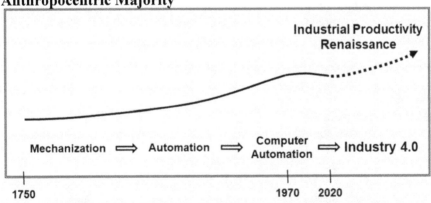

"Technologies of the Fourth Industrial Revolution will generate inclusive growth and bring benefits beyond the factory's four walls. They will potentially deliver up to $3.7 trillion in value[3] for the global economy, offering new products and services to society and supporting the environment by optimizing resource consumption."[21] (WEF, McKinsey)

173

Industry 4.0 and Mining Sector Productivity

4IR [fourth industrial revolution] technologies have many highly attractive applications within the mining sector. ... It is no surprise, then, that expectations are high for these transformative technologies.[22] (S-RM)

Potentially-transformative Industry 4.0 mining sector applications include:[23]

- High precision satellite/drones/laser survey/imaging
- Big data/predictive analytics
- High powered computing/cloud
- Internet of Things/connectivity
- Operating technologies-IT integration
- High precision guidance/control
- Remote/tele-remote control
- Automation/robotics
- Ore sorting/pre-concentration
- Gaming type visualization/software

"Mining research and development can not only lead to new technologies that reduce production costs. It can also enhance the quality of existing mineral commodities while reducing the environmental impacts of mining them and create entirely new mineral commodities."[24] (National Research Council)

Industry 4.0 and Overall Industrial Productivity

Industry 4.0 will make it possible to gather and analyze data across machines, enabling faster, more flexible, and more efficient processes to produce higher-quality goods at reduced costs. This in turn will increase manufacturing productivity, shift economics, foster industrial growth, and modify the profile of the workforce—ultimately changing the competitiveness of companies and regions.[25] (Boston Consulting Group)

Potentially-transformative Industry 4.0 general industrial applications include:

- Fully automated manufacturing (lights out)
- Smart factories/buildings/machines
- Automated industrial process control (numerical control, computer numerical control)
- Artificial intelligence and expert systems
- Computer Aided <fill in the blank>; e.g., Design, Manufacturing
- Predictive analytics
- High speed digital communication networks, primarily Internet-based (cloud)
- Internet of things (IoT)
- M2M (machine to machine) communications
- Increasingly functional wireless communication networks
- Robotics (autonomous robots, cobots, machine learning, machine vision)
- Autonomous vehicles

- Nanotechnology
- 3D printing (additive manufacturing)
- Virtual/augmented reality (e.g., 3D simulations)
- Wearable technology (e.g., exoskeletons, gloves)

To date, however, the universally transformative benefits anticipated from Industry 4.0 – and the emergence of an Industry 4.0-based industrial productivity renaissance – have failed to materialize. According to McKinsey,

> In the past five years, a select group of companies have started pulling ahead in their efforts to implement Industry 4.0 across their manufacturing networks. Leading manufacturers are now realizing significant value from data and analytics, AI, and machine learning (ML). However, a large majority remain stuck in pilot purgatory, struggling to capture the full potential of their transformation efforts or deliver a satisfactory return on investment.[26]

With respect to the mining sector specifically,

> ...while there is much discussion in the industry around the arrival of a fourth industrial revolution and how this might 'disrupt' the sector and deliver a new boost to productivity through the promotion of intelligent mining" ... "thus far there is little evidence of such a boost. In its absence, the mining industry faces the prospect of rising costs as grades fall and waste volumes grow.[27] (Humphreys)

Ecological Reality

> Some will argue that new exploration techniques for penetrating the enormous covered areas of the earth will enable new discoveries, and new techniques for exploring deeper in the crust will open up massive unexplored regions for future discovery. I disagree—not with the potential for actual discovery but with the potential for economic extraction in these frontier exploration regions.[28] (Beaty)

Unsurprisingly, the anthropocentrists completely misperceive the fundamental cause underlying diminishing industrial productivity growth. We ARE NOT experiencing human ingenuity limits – temporary or permanent. Human ingenuity is as extraordinary as ever.

We ARE, however, experiencing geological limits – with respect to the new NNR "building blocks" and high quality/low cost NNRs that had historically enabled us to develop highly-impactful, productivity-increasing innovations and efficiency improvements.

Industrial Productivity During Our Old Normal During our Old Normal, Nature's increasingly-reinforcing "geological tailwind" – relative global NNR abundance – amplified human ingenuity efficacy, and fostered rapid industrial productivity growth.

That is, the NNR-related prerequisites for developing highly-impactful, productivity-increasing innovations and efficiency improvements existed during our Old Normal:

- Each of the 90+ NNRs that enable our industrial existence was initially exploited on an industrial scale during our Old Normal – some during the 18th century (e.g., coal, iron, and the basic industrial metals), others during the late 19th century (e.g., oil, steel, steel alloys, and industrial chemicals), and still others during the early/mid-20th century (e.g., aluminum, uranium, inorganic fertilizers, super alloys, and high-tech metals).

  As these NNR "building blocks" were brought into industrial use, each made its unique contribution, both individually and in combination with other NNRs, as constituent elements of new productivity-increasing innovations and efficiency improvements. With respect to each NNR, however, the most impactful of these innovations and efficiency improvements were typically developed during the early years of its industrial use.

- Increasing NNR quality during our Old Normal caused generally decreasing NNR exploitation costs and price trends, which caused decreasing development and deployment costs with respect to productivity-increasing innovations and efficiency improvements – thereby creating a cultural environment that nurtured human ingenuity.

Being unaware of the fundamental role played by relative global NNR abundance in enabling rapid industrial productivity growth during our Old Normal, we misattributed our industrial success exclusively to human ingenuity.

Industrial Productivity During Our New Normal During our New Normal, Nature's increasingly-debilitating "geological headwind" – increasingly pervasive global NNR scarcity – has attenuated human ingenuity efficacy, and caused diminishing industrial productivity growth.

That is, the NNR-related prerequisites for developing highly-impactful, productivity-increasing innovations and efficiency improvements no longer exist during our New Normal:

- The expanding array of new NNR "building blocks", which had been the primary source of productivity-increasing innovations and efficiency improvements during our Old Normal, was exhausted prior to our New Normal, and cannot be replicated.

  Because no new NNR "building blocks" have been brought into industrial use during our New Normal, productivity-increasing innovations and efficiency improvements developed during the period have employed previously available NNRs – with which the most highly-impactful innovations and efficiency improvements were developed during our Old Normal.

- Decreasing NNR quality during our New Normal has caused increasing NNR exploitation costs and price trends, which have caused increasing development and deployment costs with respect to productivity-increasing innovations and efficiency improvements – thereby creating a cultural environment that has repressed human ingenuity.

We remain understandably perplexed by diminishing industrial productivity growth during our New Normal – and by our diminishing industrial success more broadly – which has called into question the viability of our unparalleled ingenuity.

NO Industrial Productivity Renaissance

> While the scale of the challenge will vary amongst commodities, pressures from depletion are unlikely to abate and may well intensify. …there is some evidence that depletion may be non-linear and that the challenges faced by productivity in offsetting depletion are set to get materially harder (Mitra 2018).[29] (Humphreys)

Because the prerequisites for developing highly-impactful, productivity-increasing innovations and efficiency improvements no longer exist, an industrial productivity renaissance will not occur.

Accordingly, future productivity-increasing innovations and efficiency improvements, including those pertaining to Industry 4.0, will fail to forestall – much less reverse – rapidly diminishing global industrial productivity growth.

Diagram 9-3: Global Industrial Productivity Growth – Ecological Perspective

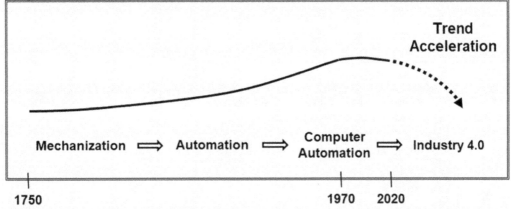

Going forward, Nature's inevitably devastating "geological headwind" – terminal global NNR scarcity – will completely overwhelm human ingenuity efficacy, and cause decreasing industrial productivity (negative industrial productivity growth).

We will be dumbfounded, as our highly anticipated industrial productivity renaissance fails to materialize – despite our unparalleled ingenuity.

Those who view human existence from the ecological perspective understand that the increasngly unfavorable trends that emerged half a century ago – increasingly pervasive global NNR scarcity and diminishing global industrial productivity growth – are permanent, and accelerating.

An industrial productivity renaissance is, therefore, geologically impossible.

Declining Global Human Prosperity

> The world is lurching from crisis to crisis, trapped in a cycle of firefighting and unable to tackle the roots of the troubles that confront us.[30] (UNDP)

Diagram 9-4: Devolving Global Human Prosperity

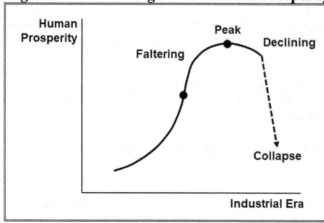

During the coming decades, global human prosperity will devolve from faltering, to peak, to declining, to collapse – a scenario that will be characterized by accelerating global economic contraction and rapidly declining human material living standards.

And while the precise trajectory associated with devolving global human prosperity is unknown, the linear trendline (dotted line) derived from the 1961-2019 global pc GDP growth curve (solid line) provides a possible scenario.

Diagram 9-5: Linear Devolution of Global Human Prosperity

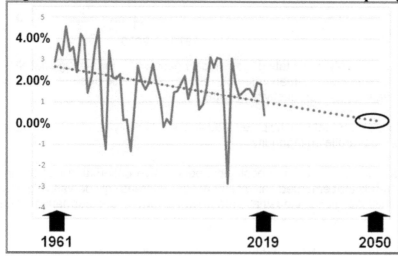

Extrapolating the linear trendline beyond 2019 indicates 0% global pc GDP growth – "peak human prosperity" – by 2050.

Source: World Bank.[31]

Diagram 9-6: Accelerating Devolution of Global Human Prosperity

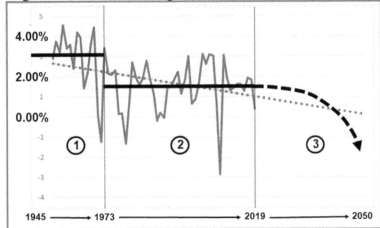

It is almost certain, however, that the accelerating unfavorable trends with respect to global NNR scarcity and industrial productivity growth will produce an accelerating unfavorable trend with respect to global human prosperity as well.

Source: World Bank through 2019.[32]

1 During the post WW2 rebuilding period, between 1945 and 1973 – industrial humanity's "heyday" – the annual growth rate in global pc GDP averaged an extraordinary 3.04%.

2 During Industrialism3, between 1973 and 2019, the average annual growth rate in global pc GDP halved, to an anemic 1.4%.

3 Going forward, between 2020 and 2050, trend acceleration will almost certainly bring about "peak human prosperity" sooner than linear trendline extrapolation predicts. The combined effects of terminal global NNR scarcity and decreasing industrial productivity will "bend" the declining trajectory of our prosperity improvement trendline from "downward linear" (dotted line) to "downward accelerating" (dashed line).

Notably, vast segments of our global population – including millions of people occupying the industrialized West – are already experiencing declining prosperity. This phenomenon accounts for our rapidly deteriorating cultural circumstances – rapidly increasing political instability, economic fragility, and societal volatility – and for our increasingly counterproductive behavior – characterized by rapidly increasing frustration, anger, and violence.

Accordingly, as we approach "peak human prosperity", Nature's ever-tightening "Squeeze" will almost certainly cause industrial humanity to "crack", and thereby induce our self-inflicted global societal collapse by mid-century.

Unraveling to Collapse

The 'developed' nations have been widely regarded as previews of the future condition of the 'underdeveloped' countries. It would have been more accurate to reverse the picture...[33] (Catton)

179

Human cultural circumstances are deteriorating rapidly, both globally and within most industrialized nations – a phenomenon that has become almost universally acknowledged. Predictably, however, the vast majority of humankind believes, unquestioningly, that our deteriorating circumstances can and will be "fixed".

Anthropocentric Perspective – Our System is "Broken" Viewed from the anthropocentric perspective, our deteriorating cultural circumstances are attributable to our increasingly dysfunctional national and global cultural environments.

That is, owing to some combination of malice, greed, corruption, incompetence, negligence, apathy, and ignorance, we have adopted increasingly imprudent political, economic, and societal behavior, which is causing increasing political instability, economic fragility, and societal volatility. Our system is "broken".

Fortunately, say the anthropocentrists, because the "systemic flaws" within our dysfunctional cultural environments are human-related, the situation can be "fixed".

Proposed solutions involve "prudent" political, economic, and societal reforms, which will bring about a global cultural renaissance – i.e., a global cultural environment characterized by political stability, economic resilience, and societal cohesion.

Our reformed cultural environment will then facilitate the development of myriad transformative, productivity-increasing innovations and efficiency improvements – such as those envisioned by Industry 4.0 – which will revitalize human industrialism, and enable humankind to achieve our goal of universal prosperity through global industrialism.

From the anthropocentric perspective, an "aura of permanence" – contingent upon the continued application of our unparalleled ingenuity and initiative – surrounds human industrialism.

Ecological Reality – Our System is "Terminally Unsustainable" Viewed from the ecological perspective, our deteriorating cultural circumstances are the product of our increasingly unfavorable natural environment – specifically, accelerating global NNR scarcity – which is "squeezing", relentlessly and remorselessly, our rapidly deteriorating cultural environments.

Accordingly, because the fundamental cause underlying our rapidly deteriorating cultural circumstances is Nature-related – lower quality, higher cost, and higher priced NNRs – our deteriorating circumstances cannot be "fixed" by "cultural reforms", or by any means. Our "system" – human industrialism – is not broken, it is terminally unsustainable; it is inevitably and irreversibly self-eradicating.

NO Cultural Environment Renaissance Viewed from the anthropocentric perspective, it is inconceivable that we industrial *Homo sapiens* are terminally vulnerable to naturally-imposed phenomena that are beyond our capacity to resolve. It is ingrained in our cultural DNA that "for every problem there is a solution"; human ingenuity and human initiative have always prevailed, and they always will.

This misperception was established and reinforced during the first 200+ years of our industrial era, when our "fixes" appeared to "work".

During our Old Normal, we came to believe that our periodically deteriorating cultural circumstances were remedied through the application of our unparalleled ingenuity – i.e., political, economic, and societal expedients that, we believed, restored our rapidly improving prosperity and cultural circumstances.

In truth, our expedients only "worked" – or appeared to "work"[34] – within the context of relative global NNR abundance. Abundant economically viable NNRs enabled us to create sufficient surplus real wealth to restore our improving cultural circumstances – and inflate our collective self-perception as extraordinarily ingenious problem solvers!

During our New Normal – owing to Nature's Squeeze – we can no longer create sufficient NNR-based real wealth to perpetuate the illusion that our expedients "work". Within the context of increasingly pervasive global NNR scarcity, our cultural environments – and human industrialism more broadly – are "dying of starvation" for lack of sufficient economically viable NNRs. This geological reality cannot be "fixed".

A cultural environment renaissance is, therefore, geologically impossible.

Global Societal Collapse

> Nature provides many examples where organisms have exceeded the long term carrying capacity of the land. A population increases for a time based on an abundant but depletable resource. When the resource is exhausted, the species in some instances has been reduced by up to 90 percent[35] (Youngquist)

Political, economic, and societal collapses have occurred throughout human history at the tribal, city-state, nation-state, and empire levels.[36] In each case, humanity recovered and created new political, economic, and societal systems – often superior to those that existed previously.

Such recoveries were made possible by sufficiently favorable natural environments – suitable climate and geography, and sufficiently abundant Earth resources – to enable them.

In contrast to our limited and temporary historical collapses, our impending collapse will be a complete and permanent global societal collapse – species collapse. Our industrial mosaic – and the constituent NNR-based and NNR-derived societal support systems that perpetuate our industrialized way of life – will cease to function permanently, at the local, national, and global levels.

Table 9-1: Societal Support Systems

• Water storage, treatment, and distribution	• Transportation
• Food production, processing, and distribution	• Communications
• Energy generation and distribution	• Governance
• Industrial production and distribution	• Finance/Banking
• NNR exploration, extraction, refinement, and provisioning	• Education
• Sanitation and waste disposal	• Defense
• Healthcare	• Law enforcement

And although the precise timing associated with our impending global societal collapse cannot be known with certainty, collapse is inevitable, imminent, and irreversible.

Collapse is Inevitable

> ...we hardly wish to deny that *Homo sapiens* is an 'exceptional' species. What we do deny is the belief that sociologists can still afford to suppose that the exceptional characteristics of our species *exempt* us from ecological principles and from environmental influences and constraints.[37] (Catton and Dunlap)

As one of the millions of species that occupy planet Earth, *Homo sapiens* is subject to the same ecological laws of Nature that govern all other species. With respect to our industrial existence and the Earth resource utilization behavior by which it is enabled, one natural law is paramount: **"Net Depletion" of Earth Resource Reserves is Unsustainable**.

That is, the rate at which an Earth resource reserve is depleted must not exceed the rate at which the reserve is replenished. Persistent "net depletion" will inevitably render the Earth resource reserve insufficient to support dependent species populations.

Given that all depletion of non-replenishing NNR reserves constitutes "net depletion", our persistent NNR depletion – especially depletion on an industrial scale – will inevitably render Earth's NNR reserves insufficient to support our NNR-dependent species.

The unavoidable consequence imposed by this ecological reality is our inevitable transition to a sustainable lifestyle paradigm – a non-industrial way of life in which a drastically reduced human population will subsist exclusively on RNRs (think hunter-gatherers).

At issue is HOW we effect our transition to sustainability:

• We could voluntarily cease NNR utilization instantaneously – go "cold turkey" – and experience instantaneous global societal collapse, as our industrial mosaic ceases to function. All or nearly all of humankind would perish in the resulting die-off.

• We could voluntarily wean ourselves completely from NNRs during the coming decades, and reduce our global population and material living standards to sustainable, RNR-enabled levels during our transition.

In the process, we would utilize Earth's remaining accessible NNRs to orchestrate a relatively gradual – albeit horrifically painful – transition, and thereby optimize our population level and material living standards both during our transition and at sustainability. Our best-case outcome in this scenario would be subsistence level existence for a few million people.

- Or, we could persist in our current NNR utilization behavior, deplete Earth's remaining NNR reserves to levels at which they fail to enable our industrial existence, exacerbate our deteriorating circumstances in the process, and transition to sustainability through global societal collapse.

Given our anthropocentric perspective – which does not even permit us to recognize our predicament, much less to decide as a species how best to address it – we will not transition voluntarily. We have, therefore, already made our choice – by default.

We will pull out all the stops in an increasingly desperate attempt to perpetuate our industrial existence, until Nature's Squeeze causes industrial humanity to crack – and human industrialism to collapse.

Collapse is Imminent Owing to Earth's enormous NNR reserves, we have been able to "get away with" our unsustainable Earth resource utilization behavior for well over 250 years.

However, given that we have extensively depleted most NNR reserves during this time – as evidenced by rapidly decreasing global NNR quality, rapidly increasing NNR exploitation costs, and rapidly increasing NNR price trends – our good fortune is "running out" – as evidenced by rapidly faltering global human prosperity.

As demonstrated previously, "peak human prosperity" will almost certainly occur by the middle of this century. Accordingly, it is highly probable that global humanity will crack as "peak human prosperity" approaches – and induce our self-inflicted global societal collapse by 2050.

Collapse Will Be Irreversible Earth's once-abundant NNR reserves have been extensively depleted during our industrial era – most economically viable NNRs have been discovered and extracted – and WILL NOT be replenished.

Moreover, as increasingly intense international and intranational competition for remaining NNRs devolves into increasingly destructive resource wars, an increasing number of currently-productive NNR deposits will become irreparably damaged and permanently unproductive.

Accordingly, Earth's extensively depleted and irreparably damaged NNR reserves will be unable to yield sufficient economically viable NNRs to enable a post-collapse "industrial renaissance". There will be nothing left with which to restore human industrialism.

The Limiting Factor Justus von Liebig, a 19th century German scientist, postulated "Liebig's Law of the Minimum". Liebig's Law states that the maximum output attainable from any process is determined by the least available input – the "limiting factor".

If, for example, a car manufacturer has sufficient parts to build 1,000 cars – EXCEPT, it has only 500 steering wheels – it can build only 500 cars. The steering wheel is the limiting factor.

Our global industrial mosaic is comprised of innumerable local, national, and global societal support systems, each of which is comprised of innumerable NNR-based and NNR-derived components.

A supply disruption associated with any NNR – even the seemingly least critical – can therefore functionally impair a system component, which can functionally impair an entire societal support system, which can functionally impair our entire global industrial mosaic.

Liebig's Law of the Minimum will become increasingly relevant going forward, as an increasing number of NNRs become increasingly scarce globally.

Devolution to Collapse

> 'Oh, we'll muddle through,' is a very western view, because you're not killing each other yet, and oil prices haven't risen to $1,000 a barrel. If you live in a poor country, where you have to walk miles for water, or you have to fight for water or resources, it is already happening.[38] (Moyo)

Notwithstanding a species-terminating nuclear (or other) apocalypse, as Nature's Squeeze tightens – global NNR scarcity accelerates unabated – and global human prosperity peaks and enters terminal decline, human industrialism will devolve toward collapse.

Given, however, that our industrial existence is perpetuated by billions of people and physical entities engaged in trillions of independent interactions, our devolution is impossible to script – but it can be sketched.

Diagram 9-7: Industrial Humanity's Unraveling Timeline

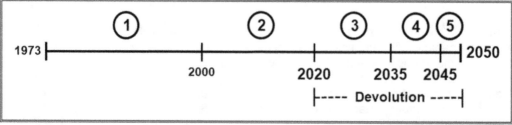

1 Between 1973 and 2000 – major unfavorable evolutionary trends emerged:

- Increasingly pervasive global NNR scarcity,
- Diminishing industrial productivity growth,
- Faltering global human prosperity, and
- Deteriorating human cultural circumstances.

2 Between 2000 and 2020 – previously established unfavorable trends accelerated.

3 Between 2020 and 2035 (Early-Stage Devolution) – accelerating unfavorable trends will further accelerate.

4 Between 2035 and 2045 (Middle-Stage Devolution) – further accelerating unfavorable trends will hyper-accelerate.

5 Between 2045 and 2050 (Late-Stage Devolution) – industrial humanity will crack and human industrialism will collapse.

Industrial humanity's devolution will be imposed by a series of increasingly severe and protracted impairments to our industrial mosaic and its constituent societal support systems. Like a snowball rolling downhill, our devolution will gain momentum as negative feedback loops induced by local, national, and global systemic impairments exacerbate our already deteriorating circumstances.

Early-Stage Devolution (2020-2035)

> The central driver of risk will be fading legitimacy of governments and intensifying civil unrest, as those in power struggle to engineer economic recoveries, answer for the human toll of the pandemic, or fall victim to internal political divisions.[39] (Verisk Maplecroft)

During the early stage of our devolution, increasingly frequent temporary impairments to our societal support systems – and to our industrial mosaic more broadly – will cause further accelerating political instability, economic fragility, and societal volatility – to which we will respond with further accelerating counterproductive behavior.

Temporary Industrial Mosaic Impairments Increasingly severe, widespread, and protracted impairments to our global industrial mosaic – owing to increasingly severe, widespread, and protracted impairments to one or more constituent local, national, or global societal support systems – will render increasing portions of our industrial mosaic unstable and unreliable.

Initially, impairments will involve societal support systems featuring:

- International system footprints, supply chains, networks, and infrastructure;
- Single-stranded (non-redundant) system architectures;
- Few (e.g., single source) system component suppliers;
- Tightly-controlled (e.g., by governments, monopolies, or cartels) system component supplies; and
- Complex, technology-based system components.

Initial societal support system impairments will be caused primarily by temporary resource constraints – e.g., labor, equipment, and system component shortages – and will be completely remedied in nearly all cases.

Increasingly, simultaneous impairments will occur across multiple local, national, and global societal support systems, thereby further impairing the operation of our industrial mosaic.

These system impairments will be caused by permanently deferred investments in maintenance and operational support, and by economic warfare, conventional warfare, sabotage, and new forms of high-tech warfare (e.g., cyberwarfare and biowarfare).

Further Accelerating Human Cultural Circumstances Deterioration As increasing portions of our industrial mosaic become increasingly unstable and unreliable:

* Political instability will further accelerate, owing to increasingly severe, widespread, and protracted breakdowns in government institutions – established government systems, organizations, norms, and rules – and their authority.

  Initially, the remnants of rule-of-law and individual rights, democratic governance and meritocracy, and government ethics, transparency, and accountability will give way to corruption, wealth confiscation, authoritarianism, and totalitarianism.

  Increasingly, international order and unstable nation-states will break down; coups, regime changes, and resource wars will become increasingly frequent; and local, regional, and national demagogues will emerge.

* Economic fragility will further accelerate, owing to increasingly severe, widespread, and protracted breakdowns in economic institutions – established economic systems, organizations, norms, and rules – and their credibility.

  Initially, economic weakness and wealth/income disparities will become increasingly pronounced; business ethics and sound corporate governance will continue to erode; and real wealth creation will diminish.

  Increasingly, deindustrialization will proliferate and real wealth creation will become sporadic; financial and banking systems, commercial markets and trade networks, and currency and credit systems will break down; welfare state promises and warfare state commitments will be repudiated; individual and corporate bankruptcies and failures will become common; and economic crises, recessions, and depressions will become unrelenting. Global GDP will peak, and enter terminal decline.

* Societal volatility will further accelerate, owing to increasingly severe, widespread, and protracted breakdowns in social institutions – established social systems, organizations, norms, and rules – and their effectiveness.

  Initially, fragmentation, divisiveness, sociopathy, crime, and civil unrest will become increasingly prevalent, as family-based and community-based stabilizing influences become increasingly marginalized and ineffective.

Increasingly, compassion, tolerance, and common decency, borne of abundance, will give way to cruelty, intolerance, and animosity, borne of scarcity. Homelessness, refugee migrations, disease, and starvation will become common; and Earth's human population will peak and enter terminal decline.

Further Accelerating Counterproductive Human Behavior Industrial humanity will respond to the further acceleration of our deteriorating cultural circumstances with the further acceleration of our counterproductive behavior. We will resort to "us versus them" behavior – whereby competing factions will pursue antithetical agendas at each other's expense.

Initially, our political, economic, and societal "leaders" will blame their adversaries – foreign and domestic – for our deteriorating circumstances. They will resort to increasingly desperate and extreme measures – e.g., extraordinary PPP-based fiscal imprudence, cold wars, and hot wars – in their attempts to perpetuate "our" industrialized way of life, at "their" expense. A moral vacuum will ensue.

Increasingly, tensions and hostility among warring factions will degenerate into uncivilized (previously unacceptable) behavior – extralegal governance and extrajudicial punishments (executions) will occur with increasing frequency.

A perpetual state of martial law will exist within a perpetual state of emergency; and government propaganda, surveillance, control, censorship, and oppression will increase at all levels – until failing societal support systems preclude such behavior.

"Enemies" will be consigned to forced labor camps reminiscent of the Stalinist and Maoist eras – or killed. The unproductive – e.g., the elderly, infirm, and infants – will be perceived as unaffordable "resource competitors" within the "negative sum game" of "continuously less and less" – and will be treated as such.

Our social fabric will fray at the local, national, and global levels, and social cohesion will come under increasing pressure. And while the vast majority of humankind will remain unaware of the geological cause and inevitable consequences associated with our predicament, they will understand that our "broken system" cannot be "fixed".

Mid-Stage Devolution (2035-2045)

During the middle stage of our devolution, increasingly frequent permanent impairments to our societal support systems and overarching industrial mosaic will cause hyper-accelerating political instability, economic fragility, and societal volatility – to which we will respond with hyper-accelerating counterproductive behavior.

Permanent Industrial Mosaic Impairments Increasingly widespread permanent impairments to our global industrial mosaic – owing to increasingly widespread permanent impairments to one or more constituent local, national, or global societal support systems – will render increasing portions of our industrial mosaic permanently inoperable.

Our global industrial mosaic will devolve into shrinking "islands of operability".

Hyper-accelerating Human Cultural Circumstances Deterioration As increasing portions of our industrial mosaic become permanently inoperable:

- Political instability will hyper-accelerate, owing to increasingly widespread and permanent breakdowns in local, national, and global government institutions.

  Formal political systems and law enforcement agencies will break down completely, and governance, to the extent that it exists, will be conducted in an ad hoc manner by localized, warring factions.

- Economic fragility will hyper-accelerate, owing to increasingly widespread and permanent breakdowns in local, national, and global economic institutions.

  Formal economic systems and industrial facilities will cease to function, and trade among individuals and groups, to the extent that it occurs, will be conducted in an ad hoc manner, primarily through barter. Increasingly, economic exchanges will be conducted through assault and robbery.

- Societal volatility will hyper-accelerate, owing to increasingly widespread and permanent breakdowns in local, national, and global social institutions.

  Our extensively impaired, bankrupt, and war-ravaged global industrial mosaic will fail to provide societal essentials – clean water, food, energy, infrastructure, products, and services – to expanding segments of our panicking global population.

  Industrialized nations – irrespective of their political ideologies, economic systems, and societal orientations – will collapse, taking the aid-dependent, non-industrialized nations with them.

Hyper-accelerating Counterproductive Human Behavior Industrial humanity will respond to the hyper-accelerating deterioration in our cultural circumstances with hyper-accelerating counterproductive behavior. We will resort to "us OR them" behavior – we will seek to eliminate "resource competitors", before they eliminate us.

In the process of eliminating each other, we will further reduce the capacity of our natural environment and cultural environments to enable our industrial existence. NNR scarcity (and RNR scarcity) will become debilitating, both through persistent depletion, and, increasingly, through war-related destruction.

As the capacity of ruling elites to appease, control, and suppress the general population ceases to exist, local warlords will fill the power vacuums left by dissolving formal governments. Perpetual resource wars will ensue, and inhumane (previously inconceivable) behavior will become commonplace. Rampant genocides, ethnic cleansings, and massacres will occur.

Social cohesion will be displaced by social entropy, as the global human population becomes decimated by war, starvation, and disease. Self-preservation will become the primary human objective, as the veneer of civilization completely disappears.

As our social fabric shreds and human panic devolves into chaos, it is possible, if not probable, that one or more desperate nuclear powers will initiate a global nuclear war – or other species-terminating disaster – thereby relieving humankind from experiencing our late-stage devolution.

Late-Stage Devolution (2045-2050)

During the late stage of our devolution, the total breakdown of our societal support systems and industrial mosaic will cause disintegrating political, economic, and societal circumstances, to which humankind will respond with self-terminating behavior.

Total Industrial Mosaic Breakdown Permanent impairments to our global industrial mosaic – owing to permanent impairments to all remaining constituent local, national, and global societal support systems – will render our industrial mosaic completely inoperable. Human industrialism will cease to exist.

Human Cultural Circumstances Disintegration As our industrial mosaic becomes completely inoperable, the remnants of our industrialized political, economic, and societal circumstances will disintegrate. The absence of newly created NNR-based and NNR-derived real wealth, combined with completely depleted, previously created real wealth stocks, will cause a barbarous free-for-all for the remnants of our industrial existence.

Self-Terminating Human Behavior As governance, real wealth creation, and social cohesion cease to exist, it will become universally understood that continued existence depends on the elimination of all "resource competitors". Within this "you OR me" environment, *Homo sapiens* will resort to inhuman behavior.

As extensively depleted and irreparably damaged Earth resource reserves become permanently unproductive, industrial humanity will crack – engage in a culminating war of all-against-all – and human industrialism will collapse – completely and permanently – almost certainly by the year 2050.

Diagram 9-8: Global Societal Collapse

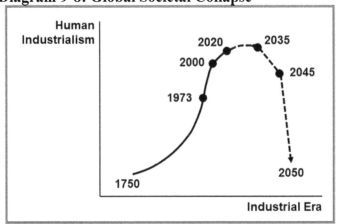

Viewed from the ecological perspective, industrialism represents a mere 300-year "blip" along the three-million year-timeline of human history. Industrialism is, by natural law, transitory.

Our global societal collapse will culminate when small, isolated, non-competing groups of humans find themselves in areas containing sufficient RNRs to support them sustainably – or when humankind goes extinct.

"Even writers deeply concerned with ecological aspects of the human predicament have remained strongly fettered by time-honored cornucopian thoughtways; many books have tried to persuade readers that if we will all become ecologically concerned in the nick of time, we may still avert the natural sequel to our excessive success. **We *didn't* become enlightened in time for that...**"[40] (Catton)

The significance of Catton's words cannot be overstated. Our window of opportunity to "become enlightened" closed during the mid-18th century when we embarked upon indus-trialization – and thereby predicated our existence on Earth's finite and non-replenishing fossil fuels, metals, and nonmetallic minerals. At that moment, we made our commitment to impermanence, and collapse became inevitable.

Appendixes

Appendix A:
NNRs and NNR Applications

The following table contains major applications (uses) associated with each of the 87 NNRs that enable humanity's industrial existence.

Table A-1: NNRs and NNR Applications

NNR	Major Applications
Abrasives	Finishing agent used to shape, finish, or polish a work-piece through rubbing; strategically significant (DOD).
Aluminum	Most widely used non-ferrous metal in the world; application areas include transportation, packaging, building & electrical; gallium & vanadium are byproducts; strategically significant (DOD).
Antimony	Flame retardant (aircraft & clothing); transportation (hardness alloy in lead batteries); semiconductor (ultra-high conductivity); strategically significant (DOD).
Arsenic	Wood preservative; pesticide; herbicide; insecticide; alloy; medicine; pigment; high performance semiconductor (solar cell, telecommunication, optical & infrared) applications.
Asbestos	Chloralkali industry applications (electrolysis of sodium chloride to produce chlorine and caustic soda); roofing products; flame retardants (brake pads).
Barite	Weighting agent (gas & oil well drilling fluids, paints, plastics & rubber); filler (paper), extender; radiation shield (barium).
Bauxite	By far the superior price/performance source of alumina & aluminum; production of abrasives, chemicals & refractories; strategically significant (DOD).
Beryllium	Aerospace (satellites, space vehicles, space optical system components); defense (inertial guidance systems, military aircraft brakes, nuclear weaponry); computers & communications; strategically significant (DOD).
Bismuth	Nontoxic replacement for lead in solder; alloy; pharmaceuticals; electronics; superconductor (bismuth-tellurium oxide alloy); strategically significant (DOD).
Boron	Fiberglass; detergents; glass (Pyrex); ceramics; insecticides; preservatives; neodymium magnet component (wind turbines); jet engine fuel ignition material, superconductor, fertilizer micronutrient.
Bromine	Fire retardant; oil/gas well drilling fluid; dye; pharmaceuticals, pesticide; removes mercury from coal power plants.
Cadmium	Nickel cadmium batteries; cadmium telluride solar panels; pigment; plastic stabilizer; corrosion-resistant plating; strategically significant (DOD).
Cement	Ubiquitous building material – binder in mortar and concrete.
Cesium	Oil/gas well drilling fluid; atomic clocks (GPS); photoelectric cells; cancer treatment.
Chromium	Stainless steel alloy; electroplating; anodizing; pigment; dye; wood preservative; catalyst; superalloy (jet engines & gas turbines); strategically significant (DOD).

Table A-1: NNRs and NNR Applications (continued)

Clays	Tile; ceramics; pottery; bricks; pipes (drainage, sewer); paper; rubber; fiberglass; oil/gas well drilling mud; refractory agent; sealant.
Coal	Primary energy source (electricity generation, heating & cooking); coking coal used in iron & steel processing.
Cobalt	Alloy; pigment; cancer treatment agent; super-alloy in gas turbine blades & jet aircraft engines; lithium-ion, nickel-cadmium & nickel-metal-hydride batteries; catalyst; super magnet applications; strategically significant (DOD).
Copper	Thermal conductor; electrical conductor; building material; metal alloy (brass & bronze); super-conductor; antibacterial; fertilizer micronutrient; arsenic, antimony, cobalt, gold, molybdenum, PGMs, rhenium, selenium, silver, tellurium & thallium are byproducts; strategically significant (DOD).
Diamond	Industrial cutting, grinding & polishing applications; niche semiconductor applications.
Diatomite	Mild abrasive; filtration aid; cement additive; filler; insecticide; absorbent; component of dynamite.
Feldspar	Container glass; ceramics (flux); geopolymers; filler; insulator (fiberglass); abrasive; solar cells; mica is a byproduct.
Fluorspar	Steel & aluminum production (flux); petroleum refining; opalescent glass manufacture, feedstock for hydrofluoric acid & fluorine bearing chemicals; water fluoridation; strategically significant (DOD).
Gallium	Fuel cells; solar cells (CIGS); high-temperature thermometric applications; alloy; electronic components (microwave, infrared, LEDs); high performance semiconductors; strategically significant (DOD).
Garnet	Abrasive (sand blasting, water jet cutting & polishing); water filtration medium.
Germanium	Catalyst (satellite based solar cells); infrared optics; optical fiber cores; thermal imaging, semiconductor (memory & wireless communication applications); nanowires (emerging application); strategically significant (DOD).
Gold	Coinage; dentistry; alloy; semiconductors; corrosion resistance applications; mercury & silver are byproducts; strategically significant (DOD).
Graphite	Fuel cells; "lead" pencils; refractory; brake linings; semiconductors; zinc-carbon batteries; lubricant; composites (carbon fibers); strategically significant (DOD).
Gypsum	Wallboard & plaster; (Portland) cement; soil conditioner.
Hafnium	Cladding material for nuclear fuel rods; strategically significant (DOD).
Helium	Cryogenics (very low temperature); superconducting magnets (MRI scanners); superconductivity (electronics); arc welding; strategically significant (DOD).
Indium	LCDs; computer touch screens (ITO); thin-film solar cells; semiconductor component; lubricant: alloy: lead-free solders; control rods (nuclear reactors); strategically significant (DOD).
Iodine	Biocides; iodized salts; LCDs; synthetic fabric treatments; x-ray contrast media.
Iron Ore	Primary feedstock for pig iron, which is used to make steel; niobium, REMs, scandium & vanadium are byproducts.
Iron and Steel	Iron & steel account for approximately 95% of all metals used globally; strategically significant (DOD).
Kyanite	Refractory (iron & steel production); ceramics (plumbing fixtures & dishware); electronics (insulator).

Table A-1: NNRs and NNR Applications (continued)

Lead	Automotive batteries (Starting-Lights-Ignition, lead-acid); ammunition; solder; pewter; alloy; radiation shielding; arsenic, bismuth, cadmium, cobalt, gallium, germanium, indium, silver, thallium & vanadium are byproducts; strategically significant (DOD).
Lime	Building mortar, plaster & concrete; chemical feedstock (steelmaking); flue gas desulfurization; water & soil treatment; pulp & paper production.
Lithium	Heat-resistant glass & ceramics; high strength alloy (aircraft parts); coolant; batteries (lithium-ion); rocket propellant manufacture; production of H-bombs; cesium & rubidium are byproducts; strategically significant (DOD).
Magnesium Compounds	Refractories (furnace linings); fertilizer macronutrient; carbon dioxide sequestration.
Magnesium Metal	Third most commonly used structural metal; alloy (cars, aerospace equipment, electronic devices, beverage cans); iron & steel desulphurization; reducing agent for uranium & titanium production.
Manganese	Aluminum, iron & (stainless) steel alloy; gasoline additive; pigment; batteries; fertilizer micronutrient; strategically significant (DOD).
Mercury	Chlorine & caustic soda production; meters, valves & switches; compact florescent light bulbs; gold & aluminum amalgams; strategically significant (DOD).
Mica	Electronics & electrical equipment (insulator); joint (drywall) compound; oil-well drilling additive; paint, plastics, roofing & rubber products additive.
Molybdenum	High temperature iron & steel alloy (aircraft parts, electrical contacts, industrial motors, automotive, solar cells, wind turbines, tool steels & filaments); superalloy; catalyst; fertilizer micronutrient; rhenium is a byproduct; strategically significant (DOD).
Natural Gas	Primary energy source (cooking, central heating, electricity generation, industrial); fertilizer feedstock; hydrogen fuel cells.
Nickel	Batteries (rechargeable); alloy (stainless steel & cast iron); nonferrous alloy & superalloy; catalyst; plating; magnets (wind turbines); alkaline fuel cells; cobalt, PGMs, selenium & tellurium are byproducts; strategically significant (DOD).
Niobium	Alloy (steel strengthening); superalloy (jet & rocket engines & gas turbines); superconducting magnets (MRI); electronics (capacitors); strategically significant (DOD).
Nitrogen (Fixed)	Ammonia (anhydrous ammonium sulfate, urea); inorganic (NPK) fertilizers; pharmaceuticals; explosives; cleaning products.
Oil (All Liquids)	Motor fuels (gasoline, diesel, jet fuel); plastics; pharmaceuticals; pesticides; solvents & thousands of industrial & consumer products.
Peat	Limited use primary energy source (cooking and heating); soil conditioner; oil absorbent; filtration medium.
Perlite	Plaster, mortar, ceiling tiles & insulation; filler; horticultural aggregate; filtration applications.
Phosphate Rock	Primary NPK (nitrogen, phosphorous, potassium) fertilizer component (macronutrient); animal feed supplements; industrial chemicals.
Platinum Group Metals (PGMs)	Catalysts (chemicals); catalytic converters; fuel cells; computer & communication devices; glass fibers; nuclear reactors; rhodium & ruthenium are byproducts of platinum & palladium; iridium & osmium are byproducts of platinum; strategically significant (DOD).
Potash	Primary NPK (nitrogen, phosphorous & potassium) fertilizer component (macronutrient); soap; glass; ceramics; chemical dyes; medicines; synthetic rubber; explosives.

Table A-1: NNRs and NNR Applications (continued)

Pumice	Light-weight concrete & cinder blocks; soil conditioner; abrasive; absorbent.
Quartz Crystal	Electronics (frequency controls, timers & gauges); optical (lenses); oscillators & filters (computer circuits); communication equipment; strategically significant (DOD).
Rare Earth Minerals (REMs)	Renewable energy (wind turbines, solar cells); electric vehicles; batteries, lasers, & magnets; motors; superconductors; alloy; catalyst (petroleum cracking); strategically significant (DOD).
Rhenium	Alloy & superalloy; superconductor; chemical industry catalyst (petroleum reforming); jet engine (F-15, F-16, F-22 & F-35) & gas turbine engine blades; strategically significant (DOD).
Rubidium	Chemical & electronic R&D applications; medical research; GPS frequency standard; atomic clocks; potential superconductor.
Salt	Food seasoning; food preservation; highway deicing; chemical industry feedstock (chlorine & caustic soda); water treatment.
Sand & Gravel (Construction)	Brick making; road base; road coverings (asphalt); concrete production.
Sand & Gravel (Industrial)	Glassmaking; hydraulic fracturing (shales); well packing; foundries (casting); abrasive (sandblasting); icy highway treatment; water filtration.
Selenium	Glass; chemicals (catalyst); manganese refinement; pigment; photocells; solar cells; strategically significant (DOD).
Silicon	Alloy (aluminum & steel); natural stone component (construction); semiconductor (electronics, solar cells & wind turbines); glass; plastics; ceramics; cement; abrasive; sealant; bonding agent; strategically significant (DOD).
Silver	Electrical conductor; coinage; chemical catalyst; dental amalgam; germicide; optical coating; photographic films; solar cells; mercury is a byproduct; strategically significant (DOD).
Soda Ash	Fiber glass; specialty glass; flat glass; chemical industry (acidity regulator); water acidity neutralizer; medicine; electrolyte; water softener.
Stone (Crushed)	Macadam road construction; cement manufacture; riprap; railroad track ballast; filter stone; soil conditioner.
Stone (Dimension)	Building, construction & refurbishment applications (masonry, counter tops, tile).
Strontium	Pyrotechnics & flares; ceramic ferrite magnets; drilling fluid; alloy (aluminum & magnesium); pigment; filler; CRT glass.
Sulfur	Sulfuric acid feedstock; fertilizer macronutrient, fertilizer production (phosphate extraction); rubber (car tires); black gunpowder; insecticide & fungicide.
Talc	Lubricant; astringent; filler (paper, plastic & paint); coating; pharmaceuticals; ceramics (automotive & construction industries).
Tantalum	Electronics (capacitors); alloys (carbide tools, jet engine components, nuclear reactor components, missile parts, surgical instruments); superconductors; catalyst (optical glass); refractory metal; strategically significant (DOD).
Tellurium	Electronics (CDs, DVDs, far-infrared detectors & optical fibers); alloy (iron, steel, copper & lead); vulcanizing agent (rubber); thermal imaging; solar cells; catalyst (synthetic fibers); strategically significant (DOD).
Thallium	Electronics; medical imaging; pharmaceutical; glass manufacturing; infrared detectors; pesticide & insecticide; high temperature superconductor.
Thorium	Nuclear fuel (breeder reactors); alloy (magnesium); heat resistant ceramics; glass additive; catalyst.

Table A-1: NNRs and NNR Applications (continued)

Tin	Alloy (bronze, pewter, solder); metal coating; food packaging; window glass; superconducting magnets; LCD monitors; circuit boards; indium, niobium & tantalum are byproducts; strategically significant (DOD).
Titanium Mineral Concentrates	Titanium dioxide (TiO_2) pigments (paints, paper, toothpaste & plastics); metal feedstock; photocatalyst.
Titanium Metal	Alloy (iron, molybdenum, vanadium & aluminum) in aerospace (jet engines, missiles, airframes & spacecraft) applications; chemicals & petrochemicals; pulp & paper; orthopedic implants; thorium is a byproduct; strategically significant (DOD).
Tungsten	Cutting & wear-resistant materials (construction, mining & metal working); x-ray tubes; high temperature alloy & superalloy (rocket engine nozzles & turbine blades); catalyst; incandescent light bulb filament; bismuth is a byproduct; strategically significant (DOD).
Uranium	Primary energy source (20% of US electricity); weapons; scandium is a byproduct.
Vanadium	Iron & steel alloy (aerospace & automotive applications); catalyst (sulfuric acid); superconducting magnets; surgical instruments; lithium batteries (anode).
Vermiculite	Insulator (refractories & buildings); soil conditioner; packing material; fireproofing agent; absorbent; lightweight concrete/plaster aggregate.
Wollastonite	Plastics; rubber products; ceramics (additive).
Zeolites	Animal feed; pet litter; cement (drilling industry); water purification; odor control; wastewater cleanup; gas absorbent; fertilizer carrier; catalyst.
Zinc	Galvanizing; die casting; batteries; alloy (brass); dietary supplement; fertilizer micronutrient; consumer products (deodorant & shampoo); arsenic, bismuth, cadmium, cobalt, gallium, germanium, indium, silver & thallium are byproducts; strategically significant (DOD).
Zirconium	Alloy (nuclear power plants, space vehicles, jet engines & gas turbine blades); refractory & foundry material; abrasive; ceramics; armaments; hafnium & thorium are byproducts; strategically significant (DOD).

Sources: USGS, BP, EIA **Bold = Core-20 NNR.**

Appendix B:
Analytical Data and Dataset Derivation

Most of the analyses in *Industrialism* employ some combination of economic data and NNR data. (Note that all economic and financial data are adjusted for inflation unless otherwise indicated.)

Specific analytical metrics pertain to human population, GDP (economic output), pc GDP (average material living standard), NNR extraction, production, and utilization, and NNR prices – dating to 3,000,000 BP in some cases – at both the sub-global (national and regional) and global levels.

Because no single source provides comprehensive timeseries data with respect to any of these metrics, dataset combinations from various sources were inevitable, as were estimates, approximations, and derivations in cases where reliable data were unavailable.

Following are the data sources and underlying assumptions employed in *Industrialism*.

Industrialized and Industrializing Population Data

Pre-2019 Population Data – Lahmeyer, J., "Population Statistics", Populstat, 2006 – http://www.populstat.info/.

2019 Population Data – Cairn Info, International Edition – from Pison, G., "The Population of the World (2019)", *Population & Societies*, Volume 569, Issue, 2019, pages 1-8 – https://www.cairn-int.info/article-E_POPSOC_569_0001--the-population-of-the-world-2019.htm.

Gross Domestic Product (GDP) and Per Capita Gross Domestic Product (pc GDP) Data

1,000,000 BP-1960 AD Global GDP and Global pc GDP Data– DeLong, J., "Estimates of World GDP, One Million B.C. – Present" (expanded from Maddison), U.C. Berkeley, 1998, GDP data on pages 7, 8 [GDP], and 5,6 [pc GDP] (*Industrialism* used the "preferred" data set, which is denominated in 1990 International $.) – http://delong.typepad.com/print/20061012_LRWGDP.pdf.

Post 1960 AD Global GDP and Global pc GDP Data – derived from "World Development Indicators", World Bank, 2022. WDI annual global GDP percentage growth rates were applied to the 1960 DeLong GDP figure, thereby preserving the 1990 International $ as the inflation adjusted metric – GDP growth (annual %) | Data (worldbank.org).

British GDP and pc GDP Data from 1750 to 2019 – Johnston, L. and Williamson, S., "What Was the U.S. GDP Then?" Measuring Worth, 2022 – https://www.measuringworth.com/datasets/ukgdp/result.php.

US GDP and pc GDP Data from 1790 to 2019 – Johnston, L. and Williamson, S., "What Was the U.S. GDP Then?" Measuring Worth, 2022 – https://www.measuringworth.com/datasets/usgdp/result.php.

Japanese and Chinese GDP and pc GDP Data – "National GDP, 1950-2019", Our World in Data, 2022 (previously available dataset went back to 1945) – https://ourworldindata.org/grapher/national-gdp?country=CHN~JPN~USA~GBR; and "GDP per capita, 730 to 2018", Our World in Data, 2022 – https://ourworldindata.org/grapher/maddison-data-gdp-per-capita-in-2011us-single-benchmark?country=GBR~USA~CHN~JPN.

NNR Extraction/Production and Pricing Data

Global metal and nonmetallic mineral extraction/production data and price data from 1900 to between 2015 and 2018 (varied per NNR) – "Historical Statistics for Mineral and Material Commodities in the United States" (Data Series 140), USGS – https://www.usgs.gov/centers/nmic/historical-statistics-mineral-and-material-commodities-united-states.

Global energy (coal, natural gas, and oil) extraction/production data and price data by primary energy source – "BP Statistical Review of World Energy" (every June) – https://www.bp.com/content/dam/bp/business-sites/en/global/corporate/pdfs/energy-economics/statistical-review/bp-stats-review-2018-full-report.pdf.

US (proxy for global) **natural gas price data** from 1922 to 2015 (inflation adjusted by US CPI) – "U.S. Natural Gas Wellhead Price (Dollars per Thousand Cubic Feet", US Energy Information Administration, 2016; EIA file name: n9190us3a.xls, EIA webpage: http://tonto.eia.gov/dnav/ng/hist/n9190us3a.htm

US (proxy for global) **coal price data** from 1926-2019 – Saint Louis Federal Reserve, https://fred.stlouisfed.org

Pre-1900 NNR extraction estimates derived from Hewett, Lovering, The Mineral Education Coalition, and various NNR industry trade publications, investment research publications, and independent research publications.

Appendix C:
Global NNR Scarcity Status NNRs

Global NNR scarcity status was determined by the trajectory of the long term NNR price curve trendline (as of 2019), which was derived by conducting a regression analysis with respect to the underlying long term, inflation-adjusted NNR price data.

Linear regression analyses were employed in situations where the NNR price trendline trajectory increased (or decreased) during the entire analysis period. Quadratic (second degree polynomial) regression analyses were employed in situations where the NNR price trendline trajectory reversed from decreasing to increasing during the analysis period.

Table C-1: Global NNR Scarcity Status NNRs

Abrasives (Manufactured)	Mica (Scrap)
Aluminum	Molybdenum
Antimony	Natural Gas
Arsenic	Nickel
Asbestos	Nitrogen (Ammonia)
Barite	Oil
Bauxite	Peat
Beryllium	*Perlite*
Bismuth	Phosphate Rock
Boron	Platinum Group Metals (PGMs)
Bromine	Potash
Cadmium	Pumice
Cement	*REMs*
Cesium	Rhenium
Chromium	Salt
Clays	Sand and Gravel (Construction)
Coal	Sand and Gravel (Industrial)
Cobalt	*Selenium*
Copper	Silicon
Diamond (Industrial)	Silver
Diatomite	Soda Ash
Feldspar	Sodium Sulfate
Fluorspar	*Stone (Crushed)*
Gallium	Stone (Dimension)
Garnet (Industrial)	Strontium
Germanium	*Sulfur*
Gold	Talc
Graphite	Tantalum
Gypsum	Tellurium
Hafnium	Thallium

Table C-1: Global NNR Scarcity Status NNRs (continued)

Helium	**Thorium**
Indium	**Tin**
Iron Ore	**Titanium Dioxide Pigments**
Kyanite	**Titanium Metal**
Lead	**Tungsten**
Lime	*Vanadium*
Lithium	**Vermiculite**
Magnesium Compounds	**Wollastonite**
Magnesium Metal	**Zinc**
Manganese	**Zirconium**
Mercury	

Bold (scarce), *bold italics (transition),* plain (abundant).

Global NNR scarcity status as of 2019 was based on the following classification scheme:

- **Relatively Abundant** – decreasing long term NNR price curve trendline trajectory.
- **Transitioning from Relatively Abundant to Increasingly Scarce** – apparent in-process scarcity transition, defined as:
  o Post-2000 price curve trendline trajectory reversal from decreasing to increasing,
  o Post-2000 price curve trend reversal, despite decreasing price curve trendline trajectory, and
  o Post-1990 visually obvious flattening price curve, despite decreasing price curve trendline trajectory.
- **Increasingly Scarce** – increasing long term NNR price curve trendline trajectory.

Appendix D:
High-Tech NNRs

Table D-1: High-Tech NNRs

NNR	High Technology Application Area(s)				
	Solar	Wind	EV/Storage	Super Alloy	Industry 4.0
Aluminum	X	X	X	X	X
Arsenic					X
Barite					X
Bismuth					X
Boron				X	X
Cadmium	X				X
Chromium		X		X	X
Cobalt		X	X	X	X
Copper	X	X	X		X
Fluorspar					X
Gallium	X				X
Germanium	X				X
Gold					X
Graphite			X		X
Hafnium				X	
Indium	X			X	X
Iron	X	X	X	X	X
Lead	X	X	X		X
Lithium			X		X
Magnesium					X
Manganese		X	X		X
Mercury					X
Molybdenum		X		X	X
Nickel	X		X		X
PGMs*					X
Phosphate Rock					X
Potash					X
*REMs**￼*		X	X	X	X
Rhenium				X	
Selenium	X				X
Silicon	X		X	X	X
Silver	X				X
Sulfur					X
Talc					X
Tantalum				X	X
Tellurium	X				X
Tin	X				X

Table D-1: High-Tech NNRs (continued)

Titanium			X	X	X
Tungsten				X	X
Vanadium				X	X
Zinc	X	X			X
Zirconium				X	X

Bold (scarce), *bold italics (transition),* plain (abundant).

*Applicable PGMs: platinum, palladium, iridium, ruthenium, and osmium (specific PGMs vary per application).

**Applicable REMs: neodymium, praseodymium, dysprosium, terbium, lanthanum, europium, gadolinium, cerium, and yttrium (specific REMs vary per application).

Appendix E:
Conflict NNRs

Table E-1: Conflict NNRs

Aluminum	**Fluorspar**	**Potash**
Antimony	*Gallium*	*REMs*
Arsenic	**Germanium**	**Rhenium**
Barite	**Graphite**	**Silicon**
Bauxite	**Indium**	**Silver**
Beryllium	**Iron Ore**	**Tantalum**
Bismuth	*Lithium*	**Tin**
Boron	**Magnesium Compounds**	**Titanium Metal**
Chromium	**Manganese**	*Vanadium*
Cobalt	Oil	**Zinc**
Copper	**Platinum Group Metals (PGMs)**	**Zirconium**

Bold (scarce), *bold italics (transition),* plain (abundant).[1]

Appendix F:
Practically Inexhaustible NNRs

Table F-1: Practically Inexhaustible NNRs

Asbestos	Garnet (Industrial)	**Salt**
Bauxite	*Gypsum*	**Sand and Gravel (Construction)**
Bromine	Kyanite	**Sand and Gravel (Industrial)**
Cement	Lime	**Silicon**
Clays	**Magnesium Compounds**	*Stone (Crushed)*
Diatomite	**Magnesium Metal**	*Sulfur*
Feldspar	**Mica (Scrap)**	**Talc**
	Pumice	**Wollastonite**

Bold (scarce), *bold italics (transition),* plain (abundant).

Endnotes

Preface

1. Catton, W., "The Future Won't Be What It Used to Be", Conference on Michigan's Future: Energy, Economy & Environment", November 2013.
2. Catton, W., *Overshoot – The Ecological Basis of Revolutionary Change*, University of Illinois Press, 1982, page 96.
3. Skinner, B. J., *earth resources*, Prentice-Hall, Inc., New Jersey, 1976, page 1.
4. De Long, B., "Estimates of World GDP, One Million B.C. – Present", U.C. Berkeley, 1988.
5. De Long, B., "Estimates of World GDP, One Million B.C. – Present".
6. De Long, B., "Estimates of World GDP, One Million B.C. – Present"; and Kremer, M., "Population Growth and Technological Change: One Million B.C. to 1990", *The Quarterly Journal of Economics*, Vol. 108, No.3, August 1993, pages 681-716 (data on page 683), and World Bank, "World Development Indicators".
7. "Historical Statistics for Mineral and Material Commodities in the United States" (Data Series 140), USGS and "Coal Information 2019 – Analysis", IEA for 2019 data; unique source per NNR for 1750 data (available upon request).
8. Ericsson and Hodge, "Trends in the mining and metals industry", International Council on Mining and Metals, 2012, page 1.
9. "Global Material Flows and Resource Productivity", United Nations Environment Programme, 2016, page 17.
10. See Appendix B for details.
11. De Long, B., "Estimates of World GDP, One Million B.C. – Present", World Bank, "World Development Indicators", and Macrotrends, "World GDP Growth Rate" (2019 data).
12. See Appendix B for details.
13. De Long, B., "Estimates of World GDP, One Million B.C. – Present", World Bank, "World Development Indicators", and Macrotrends, "World GDP Growth Rate" (2019 data).
14. World Bank, "World Development Indicators", and Macrotrends, "World GDP Growth Rate" (2019 data).

Part One

1. Diederen, A., et al., "Scarcity of Minerals – A strategic security issue", The Hague Centre for Strategic Studies, The Netherlands, 2010, page 17.

Chapter 1

1. Brobst, D. and Pratt, W., "United States Mineral Resources (US Geological Survey Professional Paper 820)", US Government Printing Office, 1973, page 1.
2. Lovering, T. S., *Minerals in World Affairs*, Prentice-Hall, Inc. New York, 1943, page 5.
3. "BP Statistical Review of World Energy June 2021", London, UK, June 2021, page 11.
4. Skinner, B. J., *earth resources*, page 2.
5. Kesler, S., "Mineral Supply and Demand into the 21st Century", USGS, 2007, page 55.
6. Diederen, A., et al., "Scarcity of Minerals – A strategic security issue", page 17.
7. "Products Made from Oil and Natural Gas", US Department of Energy, 2019.
8. "BP Statistical Review of World Energy June 2021", London, UK, June 2021, page 11.
9. "Mineral Commodities Summary 2019", USGS; Wikipedia, "Metal".

10. "Mineral Commodities Summary 2019", USGS; Wikipedia, "Industrial Mineral".

11. Skinner, B. J., *earth resources*, page 4.

12. Wagner, Sullivan, Sznopek, "Economic Drivers of Mineral Supply (USGS Open-File Report 02-335)", USGS, 2002, pages 21 and 23.

13. 3.18 million tons of US NNR utilization in 1800 derived from 1200 lbs./year per US citizen (MII 1776 number - PowerPoint Presentation (mineralseducationcoalition.org)) times 5.3 million US inhabitants in 1800; 6,639 million tons of US NNR utilization in 2019 derived from 3,190,000 lbs./lifetime [78.8 year US lifetime] per US citizen (MII 2019 number - Mineral Baby 2019.jpg (mineralseducationcoalition.org)) times 328 million US citizens in 2019; $8.4 billion (1800) and $19.1 trillion (2019) US GDP numbers from Measuring Worth - Measuring Worth - GDP result.

14. Smith, V. Kerry, *Scarcity and Growth Reconsidered*, Taylor and Smith, 1979 (first published), page 166.

15. "Global Material Flows and Resource Productivity", UNEP, page 33 (see Figure 7).

16. "Global Material Flows and Resource Productivity", UNEP, page 24.

17. Diamond, J. *Collapse: How Societies Choose to Fail or Succeed*; Penguin Books, NY, NY, 2005.

18. "Origin of the Elements", *Guide to the Nuclear Wall Chart*, August 2000; Choi, C., "Our Expanding Universe: Age, History & Other Facts", *Space.com*, June 2017; "How elements are formed", *Science Learning Lab*, October 2009.

19. "Universal Element Formation", *Science Learning*, University of Waikato, September 2009.

20. Lovering, *Minerals in World Affairs*, page 5.

21. Wikipedia, "Continental Crust".

22. Wikipedia, "Abundance of Elements in Earth's Crust" contains estimates from five sources.

23. Luyendyk, B., "Oceanic Crust", *Encyclopedia Britannica*.

24. Skinner, *earth resources*, page 15.

25. Peterson, B.T. and Depaolo, D. J., "Mass and Composition of the Continental Crust Estimated Using the CRUST2.0 Model", AGU Fall Meeting Abstracts, 2007.

26. "Mineral Commodities Summary 2009", USGS, page 192.

27. My calculations; data available upon request.

28. Youngquist, W., "*Geodestinies – The inevitable control of Earth resources over nations and individuals*", National Book Company, Portland, OR, 1997, page 25.

29. The NNR depletion cycle, as described at length by Hewett, Lovering, and Skinner – Hewett, D. F. "Cycles in Metal Production", The American Institute of Mining and Metallurgical Engineers (Technical Publication No. 183), published by the USGS, Washington, DC, 1929, pages 27 and 28; Lovering, T. S., *Minerals in World Affairs*, Prentice-Hall, Inc. New York, 1943, pages 18 and 19; and Skinner, B. J., "Earth resources (minerals/metals/uses/geochemistry/mining)", National Academy of Sciences Annual Meeting, USA, September 1979, page 4213.

30. Youngquist, W., "*Geodestinies – The inevitable control of Earth resources over nations and individuals*", page 38.

31. Brobst, D. and Pratt, W., "United States Mineral Resources (US Geological Survey Professional Paper 820)", page 1.

32. Sass, S., *The Substance of Civilization*, Arcade Publishing, NY, NY, 1998, page 123.

33. "Global Material Flows and Resource Productivity", UNEP, page 5.

Chapter 2

1. Tilton, J. et al., "Public policy and future mineral supplies", *Resources Policy*, page 56, February 2018.

2. The critical difference between an "NNR tree" and a real tree is that fruit on a real tree replenishes, while NNRs on an NNR tree do not – there is only one harvest from an NNR tree.

3. Skinner, "Earth resources", National Academy of Sciences, page 4212.

4. Humphreys, D., "Mining productivity and the fourth industrial revolution", *Miner Econ* 33, 115–125 (2020), page 116.

5. Wagner, Sullivan, Sznopek, "Economic Drivers of Mineral Supply", USGS, page 98.

6. Relative global NNR scarcity is determined by the trajectory of the NNR price curve trendline, which is derived by conducting a regression analysis on long term, inflation-adjusted NNR price data. Linear regression analyses are employed in situations where the secular NNR price trend increases (or decreases) during the entire data interval. Quadratic (second degree polynomial) regression analyses are employed in situations where the trajectory of the NNR price trend reverses from decreasing to increasing during the analysis period.

7. Skinner, "Earth resources", National Academy of Sciences, page 4212.

Chapter 3

1. *Evolutionary and Revolutionary Technologies for Mining*, The National Academies Press, National Research Council, Washington, DC, 2002, page 17 (Chapter 2).

2. Calcagnini, G. et al., "The Productivity Gap Among Major European Countries, USA and Japan", Italian Economic Journal (2021) 7:59–78, October, 2020, page 59.

3. "Multifactor Productivity", OECD Data, OECD Compendium of Productivity Indicators, 2020.

4. Krüger, J., *Long-run productivity trends: A global update with a global index*, "Review of Development Economics", Wiley Online Library, 2020.

5. Youngquist, W., "*Geodestinies – The inevitable control of Earth resources over nations and individuals*", page xv.

Chapter 4

1. "Global Material Flows and Resource Productivity", UNEP, page 84.

2. Lovering, *Minerals in World Affairs*, page 57.

3. Some human prosperity definitions consider intangible, qualitative, and/or subjective prosperity-related factors such as general happiness, good health, rewarding social relationships, and spiritual fulfillment. *Industrialism* considers only tangible, quantitative [measurable], and objective prosperity-related factors.

4. Lovering, *Minerals in World Affairs*, page 17.

Part Two

1. Youngquist, W., "*Geodestinies – The inevitable control of Earth resources over nations and individuals*", page x.

2. Lovering, *Minerals in World Affairs*, page 56.

3. Lovering, *Minerals in World Affairs*, pages 15, 16.

4. Lovering (from Hewett), *Minerals in World Affairs*, page 18.

5. Lovering, *Minerals in World Affairs*, page 18.

6. Lovering, *Minerals in World Affairs*, page 75.

7. With the exception of Scarcity1, which predated the Global NNR Scarcity Index (and reliable global NNR extraction/production data), NNR scarcity episodes are defined by "trough to peak" intervals on the Composite NNR Price Curve – from the low price level year to the high price level year – although most NNR scarcity episodes persisted (NNR price levels remained elevated) beyond the high price level year.

8. Benetrix, A. S., O'Rourke, K. H., and Williamson, J. G., "The Spread of Manufacturing to the Periphery 18870-2007: Eight Stylized Facts", NBER Working Paper 18221, July, 2012, page 2.

9. Maddison, A., *The World Economy: A Millennial Perspective*, OECD, Paris, France, 2001, page 17.

10. Moyo, "The world will be drawn into a war for resources".

Chapter 5

1. Lovering, *Minerals in World Affairs*, page 53.
2. Lovering, *Minerals in World Affairs*, page 61.
3. Sass, "The Substance of Civilization", page 154.
4. Clark, G., and Jacks, D., "Coal and the Industrial Revolution, 1700-1869", University of California at Davis, page 2; also graph on page 54.
5. Lovering, *Minerals in World Affairs*, page 61.
6. See Appendix B for details.
7. Lovering, *Minerals in World Affairs*, page 61.
8. Hewett, "Cycles in Metal Production", page 22.
9. See Appendix B for details.
10. Lovering, *Minerals in World Affairs*, page 61.
11. Hewett, "Cycles in Metal Production", pages 26-28; "History of zinc mining", *Minerals and mines*, British Geological Survey, 2011; Wikipedia, "Peak Coal".
12. Wallace, A., "Early Industrialization – Historical Trends", *Encyclopedia Britannica*.
13. Jébrak, M., "Innovations in mineral exploration: Targets, methods, and organization since the first globalization period", University of Quebec, Montreal, June 2012, pages 19, 20.
14. Jébrak, "Innovations in mineral exploration: Targets, methods, and organization since the first globalization period", page 17.
15. Wallace, "Early Industrialization – Historical Trends", *Encyclopedia Britannica*.
16. Crafts, N., "Productivity Growth in the Industrial Revolution: A New Growth Accounting Perspective", London School of Economics, January, 2002, page 21.
17. Crafts, "Productivity Growth in the Industrial Revolution: A New Growth Accounting Perspective", page 4.
18. Crafts, "Productivity Growth in the Industrial Revolution: A New Growth Accounting Perspective", page 2.
19. Crafts, "Productivity Growth in the Industrial Revolution: A New Growth Accounting Perspective", pages 16,17.
20. Crafts, "Productivity Growth in the Industrial Revolution: A New Growth Accounting Perspective", page 3.
21. "List of English Inventions and Discoveries", Wikipedia.
22. Williamson, G., "Why Was British Growth So Slow During the Industrial Revolution?" *The Journal of Economic History*, Vol. 44, No. 3, Cambridge University Press, September 1984, page 688.
23. Williamson, G., "Why Was British Growth So Slow During the Industrial Revolution?", pages 688 and 689.
24. Lovering, *Minerals in World Affairs*, page 67.
25. Nicholas Crafts, N., and Mills, T. C. "Six centuries of British economic growth: a time-series perspective", *European Review of Economic History*, Volume 21, Issue 2, May 2017, Pages 141–158, Introduction.
26. Lovering, *Minerals in World Affairs*, page 61.
27. See Appendix B for details.
28. See Appendix B for details.
29. See Appendix B for details.
30. "Economic Growth is Exponential and Accelerating, v2.0", *The Futurist*, July 2007.
31. See Appendix B for details.
32. Benetrix, A. S., O'Rourke, K. H., and Williamson, J. G., "The Spread of Manufacturing to the Periphery 18870-2007: Eight Stylized Facts", page 2.
33. Lovering, *Minerals in World Affairs*, pages 62 and 73.
34. Williamson, G., "Why Was British Growth So Slow During the Industrial Revolution?", page 689.
35. Lovering, *Minerals in World Affairs*, page 63.
36. Williamson, "Why Was British Growth So Slow During the Industrial Revolution?" page 688.

37. "Industrial Revolution", Graph: "Relative Share of World Manufacturing Output, 1750-1900", Wikipedia.
38. "Cornucopianism", Wikipedia.

Chapter 6

1. Mokyr, J., "The Second Industrial Revolution, 1870-1914, Northwestern University, August, 1998.
2. Lovering, *Minerals in World Affairs*, page 67.
3. "Long Depression", Wikipedia.
4. Lovering, *Minerals in World Affairs*, page 72.
5. Lovering, *Minerals in World Affairs*, page 32.
6. Youngquist, W., "*Geodestinies – The inevitable control of Earth resources over nations and individuals*", page 51.
7. Lovering, *Minerals in World Affairs*, page 28.
8. See Appendix B for details.
9. Jébrak, "Innovations in mineral exploration: Targets, methods, and organization since the first globalization period", page 19.
10. Lovering, *Minerals in World Affairs*, page 69.
11. Jébrak, "Innovations in mineral exploration: Targets, methods, and organization since the first globalization period", pages 14 and 15.
12. "Historical Statistics for Mineral and Material Commodities in the United States" (Data Series 140), US Geological Survey, 2017.
13. Jébrak, "Innovations in mineral exploration: Targets, methods, and organization since the first globalization period", page 26.
14. Jébrak, "Innovations in mineral exploration: Targets, methods, and organization since the first globalization period", page 24 (specifics on page 25).
15. See Appendix B for details.
16. De Long, B., "Estimates of World GDP, One Million B.C. – Present", World Bank, "World Development Indicators", and Macrotrends, "World GDP Growth Rate" (2019 data).
17. Jébrak, "Innovations in mineral exploration: Targets, methods, and organization since the first globalization period", page 23.
18. Lovering, *Minerals in World Affairs*, page 52.
19. "List of regions by past GDP (PPP)" – from "Contours of the World Economy, 1-2030", Wikipedia; Madison, A.; page 379, Table A4. Link – Contours of the World Economy 1-2030 AD - Google Books
20. See Appendix B for details.
21. Hewett, "Cycles in Metal Production", page 22.
22. Lovering, *Minerals in World Affairs*, page 64.
23. Hewett, "Cycles in Metal Production", page 11; Lovering, *Minerals in World Affairs*, page 69.
24. Lovering, *Minerals in World Affairs*, page 19.
25. Hewett, "Cycles in Metal Production", pages 29, 30.
26. Skinner, "Earth resources", National Academy of Sciences, page 4212.
27. See Appendix B for details.
28. "List of regions by past GDP (PPP)" – from "Contours of the World Economy, 1-2030", Wikipedia; Madison, A.; page 379, Table A4.
29. Hewett, "Cycles in Metal Production", page 30.
30. "Historical Statistics for Mineral and Material Commodities in the United States" (Data Series 140), US Geological Survey; "Oil Production by Country", *Peak-Oil.org*, ASPO USA, 2010.
31. Lovering, *Minerals in World Affairs*, page 19.
32. Jébrak, "Innovations in mineral exploration: Targets, methods, and organization since the first globalization period", page 29.

33. Cooper, R., and Lawrence, R., "The 1972-1975 Commodity Boom", *Brookings Papers on Economic Activity*, Brookings Institution and Yale University, 1975, page 671, and graph on page 674 (The Economist commodity price indexes for 1860-1975 used in this section appear in Economist, vol. 248 (July 7, 1973), pp. 70-71; vol. 250 (March 2, 1974), pp. 86, 87; and vol. 256 (September 6, 1975), pp. 80-81.).
34. Radetzki, M., "The anatomy of three commodity booms", *ScienceDirect*, Lulea University of Technology, June 2006, page 60.
35. Radetzki, "The anatomy of three commodity booms", page 60.
36. Cooper and Lawrence, "The 1972-1975 Commodity Boom", page 707.
37. Hewett, "Cycles in Metal Production", page 6.
38. Jacks, D., "From Boom to Bust: A Typology of Real Commodity Prices in the Long Run", NBER Working Paper No. 18874, March 2013 (revised in 2018), Abstract from the 2013 version.
39. Krueger, A. "The World Economy at the Start of the 21st Century, Remarks by Anne O. Krueger, First Deputy Managing Director, IMF", Rochester University, April 2006.
40. Humphreys, D., "Mining productivity and the fourth industrial revolution", page 116.
41. Jébrak, "Innovations in mineral exploration: Targets, methods, and organization since the first globalization period", page 23.
42. Jébrak, "Innovations in mineral exploration: Targets, methods, and organization since the first globalization period", page 21.
43. Ericsson, "Global mining towards 2030!" slide 5.
44. Jébrak, "Innovations in mineral exploration: Targets, methods, and organization since the first globalization period", page 23.
45. Sass, "The Substance of Civilization", page 191.
46. Humphreys, D., "Mining productivity and the fourth industrial revolution", page 119.
47. Humphreys, D., "Mining productivity and the fourth industrial revolution", page 121.
48. Wallace, "Early Industrialization – Historical Trends", *Encyclopedia Britannica*.
49. Wallace, "Early Industrialization – Historical Trends", *Encyclopedia Britannica*.
50. Wallace, "Early Industrialization – Historical Trends", *Encyclopedia Britannica*.
51. Wallace, "Early Industrialization – Historical Trends", *Encyclopedia Britannica*.
52. Wallace, "Early Industrialization – Historical Trends", *Encyclopedia Britannica*.
53. "William Stanley Jevons", Wikipedia.
54. George, H., *Progress and Poverty, Volumes I and II: An Inquiry into the Cause of Industrial Depressions and of Increase of Want with Increase of Wealth*, Doubleday and McClure Company, 1898.
55. Lovering, *Minerals in World Affairs*, page 75.
56. Smith, V. Kerry, *Scarcity and Growth Reconsidered*, Taylor and Smith, 1979 (first published), page 166.
57. See Appendix B for details.
58. Krueger, "The World Economy at the Start of the 21st Century, Remarks by Anne O. Krueger, First Deputy Managing Director, IMF".
59. See Appendix B for details.
60. Youngquist, W., "*Geodestinies – The inevitable control of Earth resources over nations and individuals*", page 158.
61. See Appendix B for details.
62. Patton, M., "U.S. Role in Global Economy Declines Nearly 50%", Forbes, February 2016 (shows US GDP as 40% of the global total as of 1960, the first year in the series).
63. See Appendix B for details.
64. See Appendix B for details.
65. "List of regions by past GDP (PPP)" – from "Contours of the World Economy, 1-2030", Wikipedia; Madison, A.; page 379, Table A4.
66. "Second Industrial Revolution", Wikipedia.
67. "List of regions by past GDP (PPP)" – from "Contours of the World Economy, 1-2030", Wikipedia; Madison, A.; page 379, Table A4.
68. See Appendix B for details.

Chapter 7

1. "Global Material Flows and Resource Productivity", UNEP, page 24.
2. Sarel, M., "Growth in East Asia – What We Can and Cannot Infer", International Monetary Fund, September 1996; "GDP per capita growth" – East Asia & Pacific and World (comparison graph: 1960-2017), World Development Indicators, 2019.
3. Soilen, K., "The Service Economy Fallacy – A Materialist Perspective", 2012 Cambridge Business & Economics Conference, June 2012, page 4.
4. Soilen, "The Service Economy Fallacy – A Materialist Perspective", page 4.
5. Skuflic, L., & Druzic, M., "Deindustrialization and productivity in the EU", *Economic Research Journal*, December 2016.
6. Ericsson and Hodge, "Trends in the mining and metals industry", page 3.
7. Grant, A., et al., "Mining and commodity exports", Australian Government – The Treasury, Spring 2005 (see also Chart 3).
8. Humphreys, D., "Mining investment trends and implications for minerals availability", Polinares (EU Policy on Natural Resources), March 2012, page 9.
9. Jébrak, "Innovations in mineral exploration: Targets, methods, and organization since the first globalization period", page 32.
10. Given an average 2010 per capita Material Footprint of 10.1 metric tonnes (7.4 metric tonnes of NNRs), and a 2010 North American MF of 26 tonnes (21 metric tonnes of NNRs), the world would have had to utilize approximately 180 billion metric tonnes of materials (145 billion metric tonnes of NNRs) – 2.57 times (2.84 times) the 70 billion metric tonnes (51 billion metric tonnes of NNRs) of "materials" (NNRs) actually used – to enable Earth's entire human population to "consume" at the North American rate; "Global Material Flows and Resource Productivity", UNEP, data from page 70.
11. Jébrak, "Innovations in mineral exploration: Targets, methods, and organization since the first globalization period", pages 38, 39.
12. See Appendix B for details.
13. Nassar, N., et al., "By-product metals are technologically essential but have problematic supply", *Science Advances*, April 2015, last page.
14. Nassar, N., et al., "By-product metals are technologically essential but have problematic supply", from "The wheel of metal companionality (Figure 2)".
15. Nassar, "By-product metals are technologically essential but have problematic supply", Abstract.
16. Mills, R., "A Paradigm Shift, Exiting Easy And Cheap", *Ahead of the Herd*, quotation at the end of the article.
17. "Global Material Flows and Resource Productivity", UNEP, page 50.
18. "Global Material Flows and Resource Productivity", UNEP, page 51.
19. Jébrak, "Innovations in mineral exploration: Targets, methods, and organization since the first globalization period", page 42.
20. Jébrak, "Innovations in mineral exploration: Targets, methods, and organization since the first globalization period", page 30.
21. Jébrak, "Innovations in mineral exploration: Targets, methods, and organization since the first globalization period", page 30.
22. "Global Material Flows and Resource Productivity", UNEP, page 33.
23. "Global Material Flows and Resource Productivity", UNEP, graph (Figure 7) on page 33.
24. "Global Material Flows and Resource Productivity", UNEP, page 33.
25. West, "Resource Efficiency: Economics and Outlook for China", page 6 (data).
26. See Appendix B for details.
27. Beaty, R., "The Declining Discovery Trend: People, Science or Scarcity?" *Society of Economic Geologists Newsletter*, April 2010, page 2.
28. Erten and Ocampo, "Super-cycles of commodity prices since the mid-nineteenth century", page 18.

29. For detailed information regarding sub-global – regional and national – NNR scarcity, see *Blip*, pages 213-215 and pages 259-282 – Clugston, C., "Blip – Humanity's 300 year self-terminating experiment with industrialism", Booklocker, St. Petersburg, FL, 2019.

30. Wagner, Sullivan, Sznopek, "Economic Drivers of Mineral Supply", pages 21 and 23.

31. For additional information regarding NNR price trend dynamics, see *Blip*, pages 283-286.

32. "U.S. Crude Oil First Purchase Price Annual", US Energy Information Administration (https://www.eia.gov/opendata/qb.cfm?sdid=PET.F000000__3.A).

33. NNR Scarcity Index selection was based on:
- Perceived NNR criticality to the perpetuation of human industrialism – including factors such as relative importance, economically viable substitutes, and application depth and breadth, and
- The availability of reliable and consistent long-term price data. See Excel for the weighting scheme and annual NNR price data.

A representative NNR sample was selected to minimize Index bias, while keeping the total NNR count at a manageable number.

34. See Appendix B for details.

35. Pre-1900 NNR price data from Jacks ("From Boom to Bust: A Typology of Real Commodity Prices in the Long Run", Working Paper 18874, National Bureau of Economic Research, March 2013) and Credit Suisse ("Long Run Commodity Prices: Where Do We Stand?", July 2011) support the contention that prices associated with most NNRs that were exploited on an industrial scale prior to 1900 trended lower as they approached 1900 – indicating relative global abundance during the 19th century.

35. "Do We Take Minerals for Granted?" USGS Mineral Resources Program, 2009, page 4.

36. "Report on Critical Raw Materials for the EU", European Commission, May 2014, pages 7, 8.

37. Gulley, A., et al., "China, the United States, and competition for resources that enable emerging technologies", Proceedings of the National Academy of Sciences, April 2018, Abstract.

38. Doggett, M., "Global Mineral Exploration and Production – The Impact of Technology", Workshop on Deposit Modeling, Mineral Resource Assessment, and Sustainable Development, 2000, page 63.

39. Erten and Ocampo, "Super-cycles of commodity prices since the mid-nineteenth century", page 14.

40. For additional information regarding Scarcity4 price trend dynamics, see *Blip*, pages 216-219 [Scarcity4 was called Scarcity3 in *Blip*].

41. Skinner, "Earth resources", National Academy of Sciences, page 4216.

42. NNR discoveries in response to Scarcity3 came onstream during the 1980s and 1990s. These incremental NNRs exacerbated the NNR oversupply condition that had been caused by NNR demand destruction owing to inordinately high NNR prices during Scarcity3.

43. Somasundaran, P. and Patra, P. "Challenges in the Beneficiation of Complex Problematic Ores – Case Studies: Phosphates, Sulphides, and Coal", *Separation Technologies for Minerals, Coal, and Earth Resources, Society for Mining, Metallurgy, and Exploration*, 2012, page 617.

44. Stifel Nicolaus from Weisenthal, "A 216-Year Look at Commodities Suggests the Current Super-Cycle is Coming to an End". The commodities index used in the graph includes agricultural commodity prices as well as NNR prices. The net effect is to understate NNR price increases. The diagram is in the following article – "The Anti-Grantham" by Joe Weisenthal, April 26, 2011. https://www.businessinsider.com/the-anti-grantham-2011-4

45. Kota, H. and Smart, R., "Advances in Mineral Processing – Special Issue Information", *MDPI Minerals*, 2013.

46. Nyden, M., and Skinner, B., "New thinking needed on costly mining as ores get less rich", *The Conversation*, January 2014.

47. Sprague, S., "The U.S. productivity slowdown: an economy-wide and industry-level analysis," *Monthly Labor Review*, U.S. Bureau of Labor Statistics, April 2021.

48. "The Productivity Puzzle: A Closer Look at the United States", McKinsey and Company, 2017, preface.

49. Sprague, S., "The U.S. productivity slowdown: an economy-wide and industry-level analysis," *Monthly Labor Review*, U.S. Bureau of Labor Statistics, April 2021.

50. Moss, E., Nunn, R., and Shambaugh, J. "The Slowdown in Productivity Growth and Policies That Can Restore It", The Hamilton Project (Brookings Institution), June 2020, page 6.

51. The significance of an expanding mix of NNR "building blocks": productivity-increasing innovations and efficiency improvements that were impossible during the 18th and 19th centuries – e.g., computers, rockets, and nuclear reactors – became possible during the 20th century because NNR "building blocks" that were unavailable during the 18th and 19th century came into industrial use during the 20th century. Computers, rockets, and nuclear reactors could not have been constructed and operated using pre-20th century NNR "building blocks". Note too that this logic is consistent with the notion that "we have run out of good ideas" or that "industrial productivity is experiencing diminishing returns" – such explanations are synonymous with "there are NO NEW NNR building blocks".

52. The significance of relative global NNR abundance: continuously decreasing NNR prices during our Old Normal created an environment of affordable experimentation, in which an increasing array of highly-impactful productivity-increasing innovations and efficiency improvements were developed and deployed. No new NNR "building blocks" in combination with increasing NNR price trends during Industrialism3 have constrained both the quantity and the quality of productivity-increasing innovations and efficiency improvements developed during the period. Consequently, highly-impactful productivity-increasing innovations and efficiency improvements have become increasingly rare.

53. Hanlon, M., "The Golden Quarter", *Aeon*, December, 2014.

54. Humphreys, D., "Mining investment trends and implications for minerals availability", page 9.

55. Jébrak, "Innovations in mineral exploration: Targets, methods, and organization since the first globalization period", page 40.

56. Schodde, R., "The Challenges and Opportunities for Geophysics for Making Discoveries Under Cover", KEGS, PDAC Breakfast Meeting, March 2020, Slide 9.

57. Schodde, R., "The Challenges and Opportunities for Geophysics for Making Discoveries Under Cover", KEGS, PDAC Breakfast Meeting, March 2020, Slide 10.

58. Schodde, R., "Trends in Exploration", International Mining and Resource Conference (IMARC), October, 2019, Slide 25. Note that data from the Minex Consulting analysis include estimates of unreported recent NNR discoveries – discoveries that had yet to be officially reported due to reporting lags. This number will likely be revised as actual NNR discovery data become available. However, even if the value of NNR discoveries between 2009 and 2018 doubles from its currently reported $109 billion, it would only slightly exceed the $198 billion expended to make those discoveries.

59. Schodde, R., "The Challenges and Opportunities for Geophysics for Making Discoveries Under Cover", KEGS, PDAC Breakfast Meeting, March 2020, Slide 9.

60. "World Exploration Trends 2008", Metals Economics Group, 2009, page 4.

61. Humphreys, D., "Mining productivity and the fourth industrial revolution", page 124.

62. *The Rise and Fall of American Growth*, by Robert Gordon, explores American innovations and efficiency improvements in detail.

63. Gordon, R., "Why Has Economic Growth Slowed When Innovation Appears to be Accelerating?", NBER, April, 2018, Table 1 on page 4.

64. Gordon, R., "Why Has Economic Growth Slowed When Innovation Appears to be Accelerating?", page 3.

65. Gordon, R., "Why Has Economic Growth Slowed When Innovation Appears to be Accelerating?", page 4.

66. Moss, E., Nunn, R., and Shambaugh, J., "The Slowdown in Productivity Growth and Policies That Can Restore It", The Hamilton Project (Brookings Institution), June 2020, page 2 (See diagrams on pages 3 and 26).

67. Voytek, K., "The Importance of Productivity", NIST, November 2019.

68. Bloom, N., Jones, C., Van Reenen, J., and Webb, M., "Are Ideas Getting Harder to Find?", *American Economic Review* 2020, 110(4): 1104–1144, page 1105.

69. Bloom, N., Jones, C., Van Reenen, J., and Webb, M., "Are Ideas Getting Harder to Find?", page 1105.

70. Wladawsky-Berger, I., "Are Innovation and R&D Yielding Decreasing Returns?" irvingwb.com, July 2018; also appeared in the Wall Street Journal, "In an Era of Tech Innovation, Whispers of Declining Research Productivity, July 13, 2018.

71. Moss, E., Nunn, R., and Shambaugh, J. "The Slowdown in Productivity Growth and Policies That Can Restore It", The Hamilton Project (Brookings Institution), June 2020, page 2.

72. Wallace, "Early Industrialization – Historical Trends", *Encyclopedia Britannica*.

73. Calcagnini, G., Giombini, G. & Travaglini, G. "The Productivity Gap Among Major European Countries, USA and Japan", *Ital Econ J* 7, 59–78 (2021), page 61 (See Table 1 on page 67).

74. Calcagnini, G., Giombini, G. & Travaglini, G. "The Productivity Gap Among Major European Countries, USA and Japan", page 67.

75. Calcagnini, G., Giombini, G. & Travaglini, G. "The Productivity Gap Among Major European Countries, USA and Japan", page 66.

76. Gordon, R., "Why Has Economic Growth Slowed When Innovation Appears to be Accelerating?", page 15, Table 5.

77. Dieppe, Alistair, ed. 2021. Global Productivity: Trends, Drivers, and Policies. Washington, DC: World Bank. doi:10.1596/978-1-4648-1608-6. License: Creative Commons Attribution CC BY 3.0 IGO, page 52 (See Figure 1.1 on page 53).

78. Dieppe, Alistair, ed. 2021. Global Productivity: Trends, Drivers, and Policies. Washington, DC: World Bank. doi:10.1596/978-1-4648-1608-6. License: Creative Commons Attribution CC BY 3.0 IGO, page 53.

79. For information regarding the relationship between NNR utilization and human prosperity improvement at the sub-global level see *Blip*, pages 197-200.

80. Catton, W., *Overshoot – The Ecological Basis of Revolutionary Change*, page 131.

81. Schulmeister, S. (2021). "The Road from Prosperity into the Crisis: The Long Cycle of Post-War Economic, Social and Political Development". In: De Souza Guilherme, B., Ghymers, C., Griffith-Jones, S., Ribeiro Hoffmann, A. (eds) *Financial Crisis Management and Democracy*, page 11.

82. See Appendix B for details.

83. See Appendix B for details.

84. See Appendix B for details.

85. Banko, R., "Ending the Warfare/Welfare State", *Forbes*, February 2011.

86. See Appendix B for details.

87. For additional information regarding the relationship between British NNR utilization and British prosperity improvement see *Blip*, pages 207-208.

88. "Report on Critical Minerals for the EU", European Commission, May 2014, page 30.

89. "Report on Critical Minerals for the EU", European Commission, May 2014, page 8.

90. "National GDP, 1950-2019", Our World in Data, 2022 (previously available dataset went back to 1945).

90a. Gordon, R., "Why Has Economic Growth Slowed When Innovation Appears to be Accelerating?", page 2.

91. For additional information regarding the relationship between American NNR utilization and American prosperity improvement see *Blip*, pages 206-207.

92. Ericsson and Hodge, "Trends in the mining and metals industry", page 3.

93. Silberglitt, R., "Critical Materials and U.S. Import Reliance – Recent Developments and Recommended Actions", Rand Corporation, December 2017.

93. "Mineral Commodity Summaries 2020", USGS, page 7.

94. "National GDP, 1950-2019", Our World in Data, 2022 (previously available dataset went back to 1945).

95. Youngquist, W., "*Geodestinies – The inevitable control of Earth resources over nations and individuals*", page 27.

96. For additional information regarding the relationship between Japanese NNR utilization and Japanese prosperity improvement see *Blip*, pages 204-205.

97. "Global Material Flows and Resource Productivity", UNEP, page 55, and chart on page 60.

98. "Global Material Flows and Resource Productivity", UNEP, page 144.

99. "National GDP, 1950-2019", Our World in Data, 2022 (previously available dataset went back to 1945).

100. For additional information regarding the relationship between Chinese NNR utilization and Chinese prosperity improvement see *Blip*, pages 205-206.

101. "National GDP, 1950-2019", Our World in Data, 2022 (previously available dataset went back to 1945).

102. West, "Resource Efficiency: Economics and Outlook for China", page 1.

103. Basov, V. "The Chinese scramble to mine Africa", Mining.com, December 2015.
104. West, "Resource Efficiency: Economics and Outlook for China", page 9, and page 8 (chart).
105. West, "Resource Efficiency: Economics and Outlook for China", page 9.
106. "BP Statistical Review of World Energy, June 2022, pages 15, 19 and 29, 31.
107. Repucci, S. and Slipowitz, A., "Freedom in the World 2021: Democracy under Siege", Freedom House, 2021.
108. "Economy Report", BTI Transformation Index, 2022, Conclusion.
109. Gallagher, K. and Kozul-Wright, R., "The global economic system is in dire need of an overhaul", UNCTAD, February, 2022.
110. "Uncertain Times, Unsettled Lives – Shaping our Future in a Transforming World", Human Development Report 2021/2022 (Overview), UNDP, September 2022, Page 3.
111. "Global Peace Index 2020", Institute for Economics and Peace, 2022, page 4.
112. "Fragile States Index Annual Report 2022", The Fund for Peace, 2022, pages 10, 11.
113. "A New Era of Conflict and Violence", United Nations, 2020.
114. "Fragile States Index Annual Report 2019", The Fund for Peace, 2019.
115. "Fragile States Index Annual Report 2019", The Fund for Peace, 2019, page 9.
116. Fragile States Index Annual Report 2022", The Fund for Peace, 2022, page 11.
117. "Country Rankings – Quality of Governance", The GlobalEconomy.com, 2020.
118. Repucci, S. and Slipowitz, A., "Freedom in the World 2021: Democracy under Siege", Freedom House, 2021.
119. Repucci, S. and Slipowitz, A., "Freedom in the World 2021: Democracy under Siege", Freedom House, 2021. (See the graph – A Growing Democracy Gap: 15 Years of Decline)
120. "Freedom in the World 2022: The Global Expansion of Authoritarian Rule", Freedom House, 2022. (See the graph – 16 Years of Democratic Decline)
121. "Combating Corruption", World Bank.
122. "Government Accountability and Transparency", Freedom House.
123. "Governance, Corruption, and Conflict (A Study Guide Series on Peace and Conflict)", United States Institute of Peace, page 6.
124. Bennett, P., and Naim, M., "21-st Century Censorship", Columbia Journalism Review, January/February 2015.
125. Bennett, P., and Naim, M., "21-st Century Censorship", Columbia Journalism Review, January/February 2015.
126. Bennett, P., and Naim, M., "21-st Century Censorship", Columbia Journalism Review, January/February 2015.
127. Bitso, C., Fourie, I., Bothma, T., "Trends in transition from classical censorship to Internet censorship", IFLA, page 24.
128. Bitso, C., Fourie, I., Bothma, T., "Trends in transition from classical censorship to Internet censorship", page 25.
129. Bitso, C., Fourie, I., Bothma, T., "Trends in transition from classical censorship to Internet censorship", page 24.
130. Bitso, C., Fourie, I., Bothma, T., "Trends in transition from classical censorship to Internet censorship", page 26.
131. "UN/DESA Policy Brief #53: Reflection on development policy in the 1970s and 1980s", Department of Economic and Social Affairs, UN, November 2017.
132. Gallagher, K. and Kozul-Wright, R., "The global economic system is in dire need of an overhaul", UNCTAD.
133. Georgieva, K. "Facing Crisis Upon Crisis: How the World Can Respond", IMF, April 2022.
134. Benetrix, A. S., O'Rourke, K. H., and Williamson, J. G., "The Spread of Manufacturing to the Periphery 18870-2007: Eight Stylized Facts", NBER Working Paper 18221, from the table on page 12.
135. Benetrix, A. S., O'Rourke, K. H., and Williamson, J. G., "The Spread of Manufacturing to the Periphery 18870-2007: Eight Stylized Facts", NBER Working Paper 18221, page 16.
136. Benetrix, A. S., O'Rourke, K. H., and Williamson, J. G., "The Spread of Manufacturing to the Periphery 18870-2007: Eight Stylized Facts", page 16.

137. Lagunoff, R., and Schreft, S., "A Model of Financial Fragility". *Journal of Economic Theory* 99 (1–2): 220–264.].

138. Georgieva, K., Gopinath, G., and Pazarbasioglu, C., "Why We Must Resist Geoeconomic Fragmentation—And How", IMF Blog, May 2022.

139. Gourinchas, P., "Shifting Geopolitical Tectonic Plates", IMF Finance and Development, June 2022.

140. Georgieva, K., Gopinath, G., and Pazarbasioglu, C., "Why We Must Resist Geoeconomic Fragmentation—And How".

141. Gentzkow, M., "Which Countries Are the Most Divided?", TAP, November 2021. (See Figure 1)

142. Gentzkow, M., "Which Countries Are the Most Divided?", TAP, November 2021.

143. Devlin, K., Fagan, M., and Connaughton, A., "People in Advanced Economies Say Their Society Is More Divided Than Before Pandemic" (Press Release), Pew Research Center, June 2021.

144. Devlin, K., Fagan, M., and Connaughton, A., "People in Advanced Economies Say Their Society Is More Divided Than Before Pandemic" (Press Release), Pew Research Center, June 2021.

145. Devlin, K., Fagan, M., and Connaughton, A., "People in Advanced Economies Say Their Society Is More Divided Than Before Pandemic" (Press Release), Pew Research Center, June 2021.

146. Miller, A., and Hoffmann, J., "The Growing Divisiveness: Culture War or a War of the Worlds", Social Forces, Vol. 78, No. 2 (Dec. 1999), pp. 721-745, Abstract.

147. "Growing social fragmentation driven by rising single people and private renters" (Press Release), University of Manchester, January 2019.

148. "Growing social fragmentation driven by rising single people and private renters" (Press Release), University of Manchester.

149. Chancel, L., et al., "World Inequality Report 2022", in conjunction with the UNDP, 2022, page 3. (See Figure 7 on page 14)

150. Chancel, L., et al., "World Inequality Report 2022", in conjunction with the UNDP, 2022, page 11.

151. Chancel, L., et al., "World Inequality Report 2022", in conjunction with the UNDP, 2022, page 3.

152. Hayes, A., "Gini Index Explained and Gini Co-efficients Around the World", Investopedia, August 2022.

153. Hayes, A., "Gini Index Explained and Gini Co-efficients Around the World", Investopedia, August 2022. (See Figure 0.9)

154. Myers, J., "These charts show the growing income inequality between the world's richest and poorest", World Economic Forum, December 2021.

155. Myers, J., "These charts show the growing income inequality between the world's richest and poorest".

156. Myers, J., "These charts show the growing income inequality between the world's richest and poorest".

157. Chancel, L., et al., "World Inequality Report 2022", in conjunction with the UNDP, 2022, page 12. (See Figures 5 and 7 on pages 13 and 14)

158. Quote attributed to Ayn Rand.

159. "A New Era of Conflict and Violence" United Nations, 2018.

160. "War and Peace", Our World in Data (uses Uppsala data), 2022.

161. "War and Peace", Our World in Data (uses Uppsala data), 2022. (See The decline of wars between "Great Powers", Deaths in state-based conflicts, by world region, and Number of active State-based conflicts, World, 1946 to 2020.)

162. Uppsala Conflict Data Program, Department of Peace and Conflict Research, Uppsala Universitet, 2019. (See Number of Conflicts graph on the home page):
[1]A contested incompatibility that concerns government and/or territory where the use of armed force between two parties, of which at least one is the government of a state, results in at least 25 battle-related deaths in one calendar year.
[2]The use of armed force between two organised armed groups, neither of which is the government of a state, which results in at least 25 battle-related deaths in a year.
[3]The deliberate use of armed force by the government of a state or by a formally organised group against civilians which results in at least 25 deaths in a year.

163. Campoy, A. et al., "Economic Warfare", *Quartz*, March 2022.

164. "What are sanctions, and are we in a new era of economic war?", radio interview with Mikael Wigell, Research Director, Finnish Institute of International Affairs, World Economic Forum, April 2022.

165. Harrison, M., Economic warfare and Mancur Olson: Insights for great power conflict", CEPR, March 2022.

166. "Cyber Warfare", Rand Corporation, 2022.

167. "History of Cyber Warfare and the Top 5 Most Notorious Attacks", Fortinet, 2022.

168. Cveticanin, N., "The largest battlefield in history – 30 Cyber warfare statistics", DataProt, November, 2022.

169. Cveticanin, N., "The largest battlefield in history – 30 Cyber warfare statistics", DataProt.

170. Testimony of PETER SINGER, STRATEGIST AND SENIOR FELLOW, NEW AMERICA FOUNDATION, before the COMMITTEE ON ARMED SERVICES HOUSE OF REPRESENTATIVES, March 1, 2017, page 3.

171. Carus, W., "A Short History of Biological Warfare: From Pre-History to the 21st Century", National Defense University Press, August 2017, page 44.

172. Carus, W., "A Short History of Biological Warfare: From Pre-History to the 21st Century", page 44.

173. Gisselsson, D., "Introduction Next-Generation Biowarfare: Small in Scale, Sensational in Nature?" Mary Ann Liebert, Inc. (publisher), April 2022.

174. Gisselsson, D., "Introduction Next-Generation Biowarfare: Small in Scale, Sensational in Nature?".

175. Gisselsson, D., "Introduction Next-Generation Biowarfare: Small in Scale, Sensational in Nature?".

176. Carus, W., "A Short History of Biological Warfare: From Pre-History to the 21st Century", page 45.

177. Gisselsson, D., "Introduction Next-Generation Biowarfare: Small in Scale, Sensational in Nature?".

178. Bohm-Bawerk, E., "That 70s show – episode 4", Bawerk.net, August 2015.

179. "Debt and (not much) deleveraging", McKinsey and Company, February 2015.

180. Mbaye, S., and Badia, M., "New Data on Global Debt", IMF Blog, January 2019.

181. April 7, 2020 Tweet – 1995 and 2007 data; Wilkes, T., "Emerging Markets Drive Global Debt to Record $303 Trillion – IIF", Reuters, February 2022.

182. Mbaye, S., and Badia, M., "New Data on Global Debt", IMF Blog.

183. Gaspar, V., Medas, P., and Perrelli, R., "Global Debt Reaches a Record $226 Trillion", IMF Blog, December 2021.

184. Gaspar, V., Medas, P., and Perrelli, R., "Global Debt Reaches a Record $226 Trillion", IMF Blog.

185. Gaspar, V., Medas, P., and Perrelli, R., "Global Debt Reaches a Record $226 Trillion", IMF Blog.

186. April 7, 2020 Tweet – 1995 and 2007 data; Wilkes, T., "Emerging Markets Drive Global Debt to Record $303 Trillion – IIF", Reuters.

187. Wilkes, T., "Emerging Markets Drive Global Debt to Record $303 Trillion – IIF", Reuters, February 2022.

188. Holodny, "The 5,000 year history of interest rates shows just how historically low US rates are right now", *Business Insider*, December 2016. (See Chart1: Still the lowest interest rates in 5000 years!)

189. Holodny, "The 5,000 year history of interest rates shows just how historically low US rates are right now". (See Chart1: Still the lowest interest rates in 5000 years!)

190. "Interest rates – Long-term interest rates", OECD Data, 2022.

191. "China Prime Lending Rate – August 22 Data – 1991-2021 Historical", tradingeconomics.com, 2022.

192. Randow, J., Kennedy, S., "Negative Interest Rates", *Bloomberg*, March 2017.

193. "Interest rates – Short-term interest rates, OECD Data, 2022.

194. Ferguson, N. et al., "Central Bank Balance Sheets: Expansion and Reduction Since 1900", ECB Forum on Central Banking, May 2014, page 7. (See Figure 1: Balance sheets relative to GDP on page 7)

195. Ferguson, N. et al., "Central Bank Balance Sheets: Expansion and Reduction Since 1900", page 7. (See Figure 1: Balance sheets relative to GDP on page 7)
196. Flasseur, V., "G4 Central Banks' Balance Sheets", Refinitiv Datastream via Thomson Reuters, 2022. Note that the PBOC's balance sheet, which has remained relatively stable between 2014 and 2022, actually decreased as a percent of China's GDP during the period, from 37% to 17%. "PBoC Balance Sheet as a Percentage of Chinese GDP", IMF, 2023.
197. Warburton, P., "The debasement of world currency: It's inflation but not as we know it", GATA, April 2001.
198. Global Broad Money was derived from "Broad Money (% of GDP)", International Monetary Fund, International Financial Statistics and data files, and World Bank and OECD GDP estimates, 2022; "GDP (Constant US $)", World Bank national accounts data, and OECD National Accounts data files, 2022.
199. "Broad Money (% of GDP)", International Monetary Fund, International Financial Statistics and data files; World Bank OECD GDP estimates, 2022.
200. Moy, E. "Understanding the Money Supply Increase in the U.S. and its Potential Consequences", Wheaton Center for Faith, Politics, and Economics, 2021.
201. "Relative Values" (CPI for US dollar and RPI for British pound), Measuring Worth – Relative Worth Comparators and Data Sets, 2022.
202. Engstrom, D., "The Next Global Debt Crisis – 5 Clues to When", Lear Capital, January 2015.
203. Samans, R., et al., "We'll Live to 100 – How Can We Afford It?", World Economic Forum, May 2017, page 7; Yik, H., "Closing the Global Retirement Savings Gap: A Tale of Two Numbers", Georgetown Center for Retirement Initiatives, Georgetown University, March 2018 [US $28 trillion gap].
204. "The U.S. Fiscal Imbalance: June 2022", Penn Wharton Budget Model, June 2022.
205. Tan, H., "The wealth of American households has declined for the first time since the pandemic began, due to a $3 trillion stock-market wipeout", Business Insider, January 2022.
206. "GDP (Constant US $)", World Bank national accounts data, and OECD National Accounts data files, 2022.
207. "Global Wealth Report 2022", Credit Suisse, 2022.
208. "Global Peace Index 2019", Institute for Economics and Peace, 2019, page 4.
209. Dylan, B., "Like a Rollin' Stone", 1964.
210. Dye, L., ABC News/Technology, abcnewsgo.com, story ID 158266.
211. "Stress: The different kinds of stress", American Psychological Association, 2019.
212. Ray, J., "World Unhappier, More Stressed Out Than Ever", Gallup, June 2022.
213. Ray, J., "World Unhappier, More Stressed Out Than Ever", Gallup.
214. Ray, J., "World Unhappier, More Stressed Out Than Ever", Gallup.
215. "World Mental Health Report: Transforming mental health for all" (Report is available for download), World Health Organization, June 2022, page xiii.
216. "World Mental Health Report: Transforming mental health for all" World Health Organization, page vi.
217. Dattani, S., Ritchie, H., and Roser, M., "Mental Health", Our World in Data, 2022; "Mental disorders as a share of total disease burden, 1990 to 2019" (graph), Our World in Data (from IHME), 2022.
218. "The Facts About Mental Illness"/"Mental Illness by the Numbers", About Mental Illness – Clubhouse International, 2022.
219. "UNDOC World Drug Report 2022" (Press Release), UN Office on Drugs and Crime (UNODC), June 2022.
220. "Addicts and consumers of illegal drugs worldwide 1990-2019", Statista, 2022.
221. "Deaths from Substance Use", Our World in Data (from IHME), 2022.
222. "Deaths from Substance Use", Our World in Data (from IHME), 2022.
223. "Deaths from Substance Use", Our World in Data (from IHME), 2022.
224. "Suicide Deaths Have Risen by 20,000 Over the Past 30 Years", British Medical Journal (BMJ) [Press Release], August 2021.

225. "Growing social fragmentation driven by rising single people and private renters" (Press Release), quote from Professor Evan Kontopantelis, University of Manchester, January 2019.

226. "Growing social fragmentation driven by rising single people and private renters", University of Manchester, January 2019, page 1036.

227. "Global Peace Index 2022", Institute for Economics and Peace, 2022, page 4.

228. Beieler, J., "Worldwide Protests 1979-2013", Vimeo, 2019 (article – Stuster, J., "Mapped: Every Protest on the Planet Since 1979", Foreign Policy, August 2013), 2013; data from the GDELT Project – gdeltproject.org.

229. "An Age of Mass Protests: Understanding an Escalating Global Trend" (Press Release), Center for Strategic and International Studies (CSIS), March 2020.

230. "Political protests have become more widespread and more frequent" (See "Street politics" graph), *Economist*, March 2020.

231. Taylor, A., "Why is the world protesting so much? A new study claims to have some answers" (See "The number of protests around the world has tripled in under 15 years" graph), *The Washington Post*, November, 2021.

232. Taylor, A., "Why is the world protesting so much? A new study claims to have some answers", *The Washington Post*, November, 2021.

233. Barrett, P., "Social Unrest is Rising, Adding to Risks for Global Economy", IMF, May 2022.

234. "An Age of Mass Protests: Understanding an Escalating Global Trend" (Press Release), Center for Strategic and International Studies (CSIS), March 2020.

235. "Trends in Civil Unrest: Global Protests and Riots Almost Double from 2011 to 2018" (Press Release), (See "Global trends in civil unrest, 2011-2018" graph), Institute for Economics and Peace, 2020.

236. Barrett, P., Appendino, M., Nguyen, K., and Miranda, J., "Measuring Social Unrest Using Media Reports", (See "Fraction of countries with social unrest events, 12 month moving average", page 10), IMF, August 2020, page 10.

237. Barrett, P., Appendino, M., Nguyen, K., and Miranda, J., "Measuring Social Unrest Using Media Reports", (See Figure 31: RSUI vs. ACLED, 27 countries, January 2000 - March 2020, simple average on page 57), IMF, August 2020, page 56.

238. Barrett, P., Appendino, M., Nguyen, K., and Miranda, J., "Measuring Social Unrest Using Media Reports", (See Figure 32: RSUI vs. CNTS, 117 countries, January 1995 - March 2020, simple average on page 57), IMF, August 2020, page 56.

239. "Trends in Civil Unrest: Global Protests and Riots Almost Double from 2011 to 2018" (Press Release), (See "Global trends in civil unrest, 2011-2018" graph), Institute for Economics and Peace, 2020.

240. "Trends in Civil Unrest: Global Protests and Riots Almost Double from 2011 to 2018" (Press Release), Institute for Economics and Peace, 2020.

241. Barrett, P., "Social Unrest is Rising, Adding to Risks for Global Economy", IMF, May 2022.

242. "World less peaceful as civil unrest and political instability increases due to COVID-19 pandemic, reveals IEP" (Press Release), Institute for Economics and Peace, June 2021.

243. "Homicides", Our World in Data, (from IHME), 2022.

244. "This is the state of stress in 2018", Global News, April 2018.

Chapter 8

1. "Global Material Flows and Resource Productivity", UNEP, page 24.

2. Blain, C., "Trends in discovery: Commodity and Ore-type Targets", North Atlantic Mineral Symposium, Dublin, Ireland, January 1999, page 189.

3. See Appendix B for details.

4. Beaty, "The Declining Discovery Trend: People, Science or Scarcity?" page 3.

5. "Syverson, C., "The Slowdown in Manufacturing Productivity Growth", Brookings, July 2016, page 1.

6. Humphreys, D., "Mining productivity and the fourth industrial revolution", page 116. (See Figure 1 on page 116)

7. Canart, G., Kowalik, L., Moyo, M., and Kumar, R., "Has global mining productivity reversed course?" (See Exhibit 1), McKinsey and Company, April 2020, Page 1.

8. Gordon, R., "Why Has Economic Growth Slowed When Innovation Appears to be Accelerating?", page 23.

9. "Global Productivity Slowdown and the Role of Technology Adoption in Emerging Markets", International Finance Corporation (World Bank Group), May 2016, page 1. (See Figure 1 on page 2)

10. Moss, E., Nunn, R., and Shambaugh, J. "The Slowdown in Productivity Growth and Policies That Can Restore It", The Hamilton Project (Brookings Institution), June 2020, page 6.

11. "Conference Board Global Labor Productivity 1995-2020", *Total Economy Database™ - Key Findings*, The Conference Board, April 2022.

12. Buttiglione, L., et al., "Deleveraging? What Deleveraging? Geneva Reports on the World Economy, International Center for Monetary and Banking Studies, September 2014, page 2.

13. "Uncertain Times, Unsettled Lives – Shaping our Future in a Transforming World" (Press Release), Human Development Report 2021/2022 (Overview), UNDP.

14. See Appendix B for details.

15. "Uncertain Times, Unsettled Lives – Shaping our Future in a Transforming World", Human Development Report 2021/2022 (Overview), UNDP, page 4.

16. "The Foundational Elements of Prosperity" (Home Page), The Legatum Prosperity Index 2021, 2021.

17. Repucci, S. and Slipowitz, A., "The Global Expansion of Authoritarian Rule" (Abridged Version), Freedom House, 2022, page 1.

18. "Global Findings – Trend Toward Authoritarian Governance Continues", BTI Transformation Index, 2022.

19. Repucci, S. and Slipowitz, A., "The Global Expansion of Authoritarian Rule" (Press Release), (See "Living in a Less Free World" graph), Freedom House, 2022

20. Repucci, S. and Slipowitz, A., "The Global Expansion of Authoritarian Rule" (Abridged Version), Freedom House, 2022, page 2.

21. Gallagher, K. and Kozul-Wright, R., "The global economic system is in dire need of an overhaul", UNCTAD.

22. "Chart Book: The Legacy of the Great Recession", Center on Budget and Policy Priorities, June 2019.

23. Duignan, B., "Great Recession: Causes, Effects, Statistics, and Facts", *Encyclopedia Britannica*, 2022.

24. "Economy Report", *BTI 2022*, BTI Transformation Index, 2022.

25. Georgieva, K. "Facing Crisis Upon Crisis: How the World Can Respond", IMF, April 2022.

26. Mims, C., "Why Social Media Is So Good at Polarizing Us" Wall Street Journal, October, 19, 2020.

27. "Global Peace Index 2020", Institute for Economics and Peace, 2020, page 4.

28. Devlin, K., Fagan, M., and Connaughton, A., "People in Advanced Economies Say Their Society Is More Divided Than Before Pandemic" (Press Release), Pew Research Center, June 2021.

29. "The Global Risks Report 2022", World Economic Forum, 2022, Page 7.

30. "Conflict in Ukraine", Global Conflict Tracker, Council on Foreign Relations, November 2022.

31. EY, "The fragmentation of everything", *MIT Technology Review*, December 2020.

32. "Pathways for Peace – Inclusive Approaches to Preventing Violent Conflict" (Executive Summary), World Bank Group, 2018, Page iv.

33. Uppsala Conflict Data Program, Department of Peace and Conflict Research, Uppsala Universitet, 2019. (See Number of Conflicts graph on the home page)

34. Repucci, S. and Slipowitz, A., "The Global Expansion of Authoritarian Rule" (Press Release), (See "Living in a Less Free World" graph), Freedom House, 2022

35. de Soyres, F., Santacreu, A., and Young, H., "Fiscal Policy and Excess Inflation During Covid-19: a cross-country view", *Fed Notes*, US Federal Reserve, July 2022.

36. "Debt and (not much) deleveraging", McKinsey and Company, February 2015.

37. Mbaye, S., and Badia, M., "New Data on Global Debt", IMF Blog, January 2019.

38. April 7, 2020 Tweet – 1995 and 2007 data; Wilkes, T., "Emerging Markets Drive Global Debt to Record $303 Trillion – IIF", Reuters, February 2022.

39. O'Byrne, M., "Global Debt Now $200 Trillion!", Gold-Eagle, May 2015.

40. Randow, J., Kennedy, S., "Negative Interest Rates", *Bloomberg*, March 2017.

41. Yardini, E., and Quintana, M., "Central Banks: Monthly Balance Sheets", Yardini Research, Inc., 2022, page 1. (See Figure 2); Marsh, C., "The Remarkable Expansion of Global Central Bank Balance Sheets During the Pandemic", *Money: Inside and Out*, June 2021.

42. "Broad Money (% of GDP)", International Monetary Fund, International Financial Statistics and data files; World Bank OECD GDP estimates, 2022.

43. Labott, E., "Get Ready for a Spike in Global Unrest", *Foreign Policy*, July, 2021.

44. Stress in America™ 2021: Stress and Decision-making during the Pandemic", American Psychological Association, October 2021, page 5.

45. Stress in America™ 2021: Stress and Decision-making during the Pandemic", American Psychological Association, page 5.

46. Ritchie, H., Roser, M., and Ortiz-Ospina, "Suicide", Our World in Data, (from IHME), 2022.

47. "World less peaceful as civil unrest and political instability increases due to COVID-19 pandemic, reveals IEP" (Press Release), Institute for Economics and Peace, June 2021.

48. "Global Peace Index 2022", Institute for Economics and Peace, 2022, page 4.

49. "World less peaceful as civil unrest and political instability increases due to COVID-19 pandemic, reveals IEP" (Press Release), Institute for Economics and Peace, June 2021.

50. Todorovic, S., "Allianz: Businesses need to prepare for a rise in social unrest incidents", Allianz Global Corporate and Specialty, June 2022.

Chapter 9

1. Youngquist, W., "*Geodestinies – The inevitable control of Earth resources over nations and individuals*", page 158.

2. Catton, W., "The Future Won't Be What It Used to Be", Conference on Michigan's Future: Energy, Economy & Environment", November 2013.

3. Catton, W., *Overshoot – The Ecological Basis of Revolutionary Change*, University of Illinois Press, 1982, page 96.

4. Skinner, B. J., *earth resources*, page 1.

5. "Strategic Metals: Will future supply be able to meet future demand?" Mission 2016: The Future of Strategic Natural Resources", MIT, 2016.

6. "Global Material Flows and Resource Productivity", UNEP, page 17.

7. "Global Material Flows and Resource Productivity", UNEP, page 16.

8. Wouters, H. and Bol, D., "Material Scarcity – An M2i Study", Materials Innovation Institute, November 2009, page 3.

9. "Global Material Flows and Resource Productivity", UNEP, page 16.

10. "Strategic Metals: Will future supply be able to meet future demand?" MIT.

11. Heap, A., "China – The Engine of a Commodities Super Cycle", Citigroup- Smith Barney, 2005, page 17.

12. Jacks, "From Boom to Bust: A Typology of Real Commodity Prices in the Long Run", page 23.

13. Dieppe, Alistair, ed. 2021. Global Productivity: Trends, Drivers, and Policies. Washington, DC: World Bank. doi:10.1596/978-1-4648-1608-6. License: Creative Commons Attribution CC BY 3.0 IGO, page 16.

14. Humphreys, D., "Mining productivity and the fourth industrial revolution", page 124.

15. Wladawsky-Berger, I., "Are Innovation and R&D Yielding Decreasing Returns?" irvingwb.com, July 2018; also appeared in the Wall Street Journal, "In an Era of Tech Innovation, Whispers of Declining Research Productivity, July 13, 2018.

16. Wladawsky-Berger, I., "Are Innovation and R&D Yielding Decreasing Returns?" irvingwb.com, July 2018; also appeared in the Wall Street Journal, "In an Era of Tech Innovation, Whispers of Declining Research Productivity, July 13, 2018.

17. Sprague, S., "The U.S. productivity slowdown: an economy-wide and industry-level analysis", *Monthly Labor Review*, US Bureau of Labor Statistics, April 2021.

18. Wladawsky-Berger, I., "Are Innovation and R&D Yielding Decreasing Returns?" irvingwb.com, July 2018; also appeared in the Wall Street Journal, "In an Era of Tech Innovation, Whispers of Declining Research Productivity, July 13, 2018.

19. Mann, C. "The Future of Productivity" (presentation by Catherine L. Mann, OECD Chief Economist), OECD, July 2015.

20. Humphreys, D., "Mining productivity and the fourth industrial revolution", page 122.

21. Laurent, H., and de Boer, E., "The Next Economic Growth Engine – Scaling Fourth Industrial Revolution Technologies in Production", World Economic Forum and McKinsey and Company, January 2018, page 4.

22. Geschwindt, T., "Mining's New Horizons: Risk and Reward and the Dawn of the Fourth Industrial Revolution", S-RM, February 2021.

23. "Mining technology and the culture change" (See table), Mining Magazine, September 2016; Humphreys, D., "Mining productivity and the fourth industrial revolution", pages 115-125.

24. "Overview of Technology and Mining (Chapter 2), *Evolutionary and Revolutionary Technologies for Mining*, National Research Council, The National Academies Press, Washington, DC, 2002, page 17.

25. Russman, M. et al., "Industry 4.0: The Future of Productivity and Growth in Manufacturing Industries", Boston Consulting Group, September 2015.

26. Gregolinska, E., Khanam, R., Lefort, F., and Parthasarathy, P., "Capturing the true value of Industry 4.0", McKinsey and company, April 2022.

27. Humphreys, D., "Mining productivity and the fourth industrial revolution", page 116.

28. Beaty, R., "The Declining Discovery Trend: People, Science or Scarcity?", page 2.

29. Humphreys, D., "Mining productivity and the fourth industrial revolution", page 124.

30. "Uncertain Times, Unsettled Lives – Shaping our Future in a Transforming World" (Press Release), Human Development Report 2021/2022 (Overview), UNDP.

31. See Appendix B for details.

32. See Appendix B for details.

33. Catton, W., *Overshoot – The Ecological Basis of Revolutionary Change*, page 175.

34. Expedients such as "social entitlements", "welfare" programs, subsidies, quotas, tariffs, wage controls, price controls, interest rate suppression, and bailouts – while benefitting targeted population segments – actually involve massive resource misallocations through waste, corruption, incompetence, and malinvestment. The illusion that these expedients "worked" was made possible by the extraordinarily favorable natural environment that existed during our Old Normal. The enormous surplus wealth and rapidly improving prosperity afforded by relative global NNR abundance both masked our enormous resource misallocations and inflated our collective self-perception as extraordinarily ingenious problem solvers.

35. Youngquist, W., "*Geodestinies – The inevitable control of Earth resources over nations and individuals*", page xiv.

36. See (among others) Tainter, J., *Collapse of Complex Societies*, Cambridge University Press, 1988; and Diamond, J., *Collapse: How Societies Choose to Fail or Succeed*, Penguin Books, 2005.

37. Catton, W., and Dunlap, R., "A New Ecological Paradigm for Post-Exuberant Sociology"; American Behavioral Scientist, Vol. 24 No. 1, September/October 1980, page 25.

38. Moyo, "The world will be drawn into a war for resources".

39. Smith, J., and Wille, D., "2020's sting in the tail: Political instability will rise in 88 countries (Political Risk Outlook 2021)", Verisk Maplecroft, March 2021.

40. Catton, W., *Overshoot – The Ecological Basis of Revolutionary Change*, page 213.

Appendixes

1. Clugston, C., "Blip – Humanity's 300 year self-terminating experiment with industrialism", pages 271-279, list on page 280.